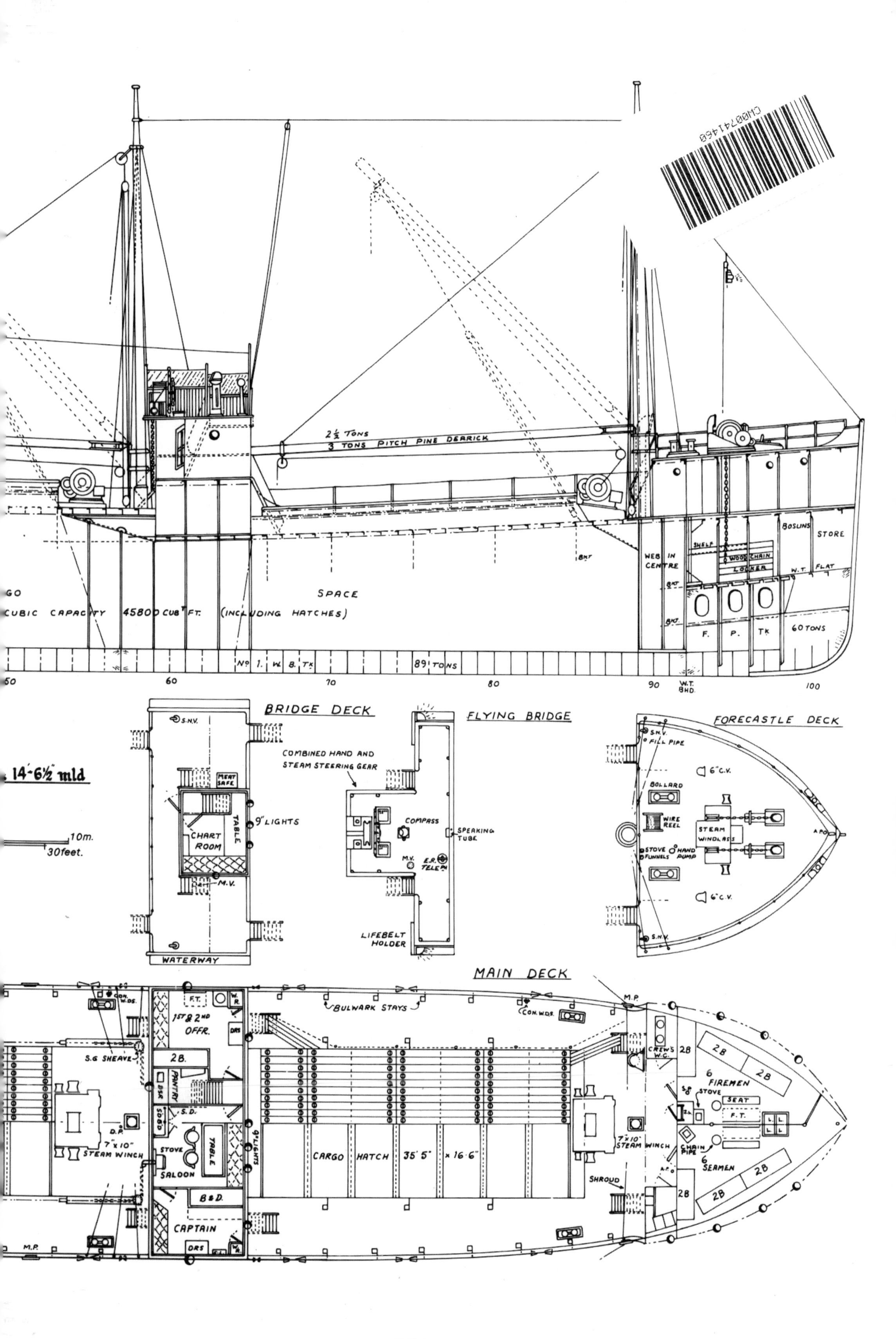

2½ TONS
3 TONS PITCH PINE DERRICK
BOSUNS STORE
SHELF
WOOD CHAIN LOCKER
W.T. FLAT
WEB IN CENTRE
BKT
GO
SPACE
CUBIC CAPACITY 45800 CUB FT. (INCLUDING HATCHES)
F. P. TK 60 TONS
No 1. W. B. TK 89 TONS
50
60
70
80
90
W.T. BHD.
100
14'-6½" mld
10m.
30feet.
BRIDGE DECK
S.N.V.
MEAT SAFE
CHART ROOM
TABLE
9" LIGHTS
M.V.
WATERWAY
FLYING BRIDGE
COMBINED HAND AND STEAM STEERING GEAR
COMPASS
SPEAKING TUBE
M.V.
E.R. TELE.PH
LIFEBELT HOLDER
FORECASTLE DECK
S.N.V.
FILL PIPE
6" C.V.
BOLLARD
WIRE REEL
STEAM WINDLASS
STOVE FUNNELS
HAND PUMP
A.P.O.
MAIN DECK
M.P.
CON. W.DS.
F.T.
W.R.
1ST & 2ND OFFR.
DRS
BULWARK STAYS
S.G SHEAVE
2B.
PANTRY
DSR
SDBD
S.D.
D.P.
7"x10" STEAM WINCH
STOVE
TABLE
SALOON
9" LIGHTS
B&D.
CAPTAIN
DRS
CARGO HATCH 35' 5" x 16' 6"
CREWS W.C.
2B
6 FIREMEN
S.P.
STOVE
SEAT
F.T.
CHAIN PIPE
6 SEAMEN
SHROUD
A.P.O.

WILLIAM ROBERTSON
and the
GEM LINE

Roy Fenton and Philip Robertson

Ships in Focus Publications

Published in the UK by Ships in Focus Publications
18 Franklands, Longton
Preston PR4 5PD

Printed in the UK by Amadeus Press Ltd., Cleckheaton, West Yorkshire
ISBN 978-1-901703-57-3

Front cover: *Olivine* (5) in the Manchester Ship Canal in May 1972 and *Sard* (1) off Whitehaven about 1891. *[Paul Boot; George Nelson/Philip Robertson collection]*
Back cover: *Emerald* (3) on the Nieuwe Waterweg in May 1974 and *Gem* (6) approaching Eastham in February 1976. *[Both Paul Boot]*
Title page: Robertson's longest-serving ship, the *Pearl* of 1896, in an industrial setting. *[Roy Fenton collection]*
Front endpapers: general arrangement drawings of *Sphene* (3) of 1920. *[C.V. Waine]*
Rear endpapers: *Citrine* (4) of 1939. *[C.V. Waine]*

The *Flucr* (1) of 1898 at 200 feet was one of Robertson's largest steamers. The photograph shows the walkway placed across her well deck, probably when she crossed the Atlantic. *[Glasgow University Archives]*

PREFACE AND ACKNOWLEDGEMENTS

When the co-authors of this book were put in touch during 2006, it felt close to achieving a long-cherished ambition of producing a history of William Robertson, the doyen of coaster owners. Roy Fenton had long ago inherited a Robertson fleet list that obviously had input from a number of researchers. With the help of others this list had been gradually developed and checked, and details added from closed registration documents in the National Archives. However, there was so little information available on the company itself that compilation of a publishable history seemed a lost cause without input from family members, contact with whom proved elusive. The answer came when Philip Robertson, great grandson of the founder and youngest son of Frank and Elizabeth Robertson, contacted Bill Harvey of the World Ship Society, who in turn very kindly put him in touch with Roy.

This book came from the resulting collaboration. Philip drafted his version of the history, including much that came from the memories of family members, some recent archives and the relatively few business documents surviving from the 19th century and beginning of the 20th. Using the fleet list as a skeleton, Roy then reworked the story, and the draft was developed jointly. Charles Waine generously offered information he had gathered at the company's offices over 20 years ago, and this was incorporated.

It will be clear from the genesis of this book as described above that the co-authors have many people to thank, including A.L. Bland, David Burrell, Colin Campbell, John Clarkson, Terry Conlan, Malcolm Cooper, Ron Evans, Ken Garrett, Roy Griffin, Rowan Hackman, Margaret Harrison, Bill Harvey, Reverend G. William Jones, Mike Macdonald, Edward Martin, Archie Munro, Peter Robertson, Bill Schell, Alan Smith, Graeme Somner, P.N. Thomas, Charles Waine, Captain Ian Walker, David Whiteside, Ian Wilson and Tom Wilson. Also gratefully acknowledged are the use of the facilities of Lloyd's Register, the National Archives of both England and Scotland, the Guildhall Library, the Mitchell Library, Strathclyde University Archives and the World Ship Society's Merchant Ship Library and Archive. Thanks also to Heather Fenton for editorial work, and to Marion Clarkson for accountancy services.

We are grateful to all who gave permission for their photographs to be used, and particularly to Paul Boot, Michael Charles, John Clarkson, Ian J. Farquhar, Nigel Farrell, Nigel Jones, Peter Newall, Dave Salisbury and Alan Smith; to David Whiteside, Jim McFaul and Tony Smith of the World Ship Photo Library; and to the Ballast Trust and Glasgow University Archives. In line with our policy we show the names of both the photographer (where known) and the collection from which it was obtained. Note that photographs credited to 'Robertson archives' are now held by Strathclyde University and not by the Robertson family.

Artwork for the house flag was kindly provided by J.L. Loughran, custodian of the Ships' Liveries section of the World Ship Society's Merchant Ship Library and Archive. Charles Waine expertly redrew the general arrangements on the endpapers. Particular thanks to Alan Smith who kindly checked photographs and advised on the geography of Llanddulas, and Bill Harvey for data used to check the fleet lists.

Roy Fenton, London Philip Robertson, Edinburgh

October 2009

CONTENTS

Amber (2) of 1956 running trials. *[Robertson archives]*

William Robertson and his successors

William Robertson was the founder of the largest and most respected fleet of ships engaged in the coastal bulk trades on the west coast of the British Isles. The 'Gem Line', as it was dubbed from its naming scheme, showed a remarkable ability to increase in good times. Even more importantly for a company in a business subject to such peaks and troughs as shipping, it managed to survive and even to grow during adverse conditions. The history of the Robertsons of Glasgow almost exactly reflects the rise and decline of the British steam coaster and its diesel-propelled successor. Beginning in the earliest days of the steam coaster and its gradual replacement of sail, Robertson's story spans more than 130 years, and the end of the company's independent existence came at a time when the coasting trade under the British flag was in seemingly terminal decline.

The company's founder, William Robertson.

Robertson and Glasgow

By the middle of the 19th century, Glasgow was well on its way to becoming the second city of the British Empire. Out of an early involvement in the North Atlantic trades it had developed a textile manufactory and alongside this had grown an industry producing dyes and other chemicals. The textile trade gradually declined as spinning and weaving moved elsewhere in the United Kingdom and abroad. The chemical industry was also eclipsed, but in this case because it had lagged behind in technological development. The St. Rollox chemical works of Charles Tennant manufactured sodium hydroxide (caustic soda or alkali) using the Leblanc process, but this was superseded in the 1860s by the Solvay process.

However, the loss of textiles and chemicals was more than compensated for by the massive growth of the iron and steel industry which used the coal and ore which were available locally. The output of steel in the neighbouring towns of Cambuslang, Coatbridge, Gartcosh, Motherwell, Mossend and Wishaw grew from 50,000 in 1879 to 1,250,000 in 1911 and doubled again by 1918, according to Checkland's history of Glasgow's industries.[1] The River Clyde ensured that the steel industry survived the depletion of local iron ore reserves, and – significantly for William Robertson's business – also allowed ready importation from Ireland and Wales of the limestone used as a flux in steel making.

Dependent on the steel industry for its material, but independent in the massive skills base which it commanded, was the heavy engineering which developed on Clydeside. Best known were shipbuilding and marine engineering. From 1870 to 1913, the output of Clyde yards grew from 200,000 tons to 757,000 tons, most of it steam tonnage. In terms of the innovations it produced and its extraordinarily varied output – from puffers to the largest warships – this industry was in advance of everything in the world, at least until the First World War. One third of all Britain's tonnage was constructed by these yards, and their output exceeded that of all German yards combined. But Glasgow also nurtured other types of heavy engineering, notably locomotive building. Three of Britain's four major builders were based in the city, and in 1903 they merged to form the massive North British Locomotive works. The heavy engineering quartet was completed by another major consumer of steel, bridge building, with Sir William Arrol responsible for such monuments to engineering skills as the Forth and (second) Tay railway bridges and Tower Bridge.

The engineering industries relied on a cadre of highly skilled craftsmen, who had often worked a long apprenticeship, plus – in shipbuilding – a less-skilled workforce of platers, riveters and others who might be hired and fired as the inevitable cycles of recession repeated themselves. Checkland suggests that the skills base and the intense pride manifested in the engineering industries of Glasgow resulted at least partly from the relatively high standards of education in Scotland, allied with the stern discipline and self-reliance inculcated by the country's Calvinistic religion.

From what we know or can imply about William Robertson's career, these same principles seem to have informed his business. Glasgow's industries offered considerable trading opportunities for coastal shipping, but there was probably another factor at work in the rise of a man like William Robertson. Glaswegians' horizons were never limited by the hills which surrounded their city, nor were they confined to Scotland. Indeed, as shown by the city's wisdom in refusing to back the doomed Jacobite cause in the eighteenth century, Glasgow had maintained its distance from the wild lands to the north and west. William Robertson and his successors could never have built up their impressive fleet by relying solely on local trades, and their achievement was in building on the mineral traffic of the west coast to embrace trade all around the coasts of Great Britain and Ireland and further afield.

A child of ordinary working folk[2], William Robertson turned out to be a remarkably gifted businessman. He was born in Paisley on 5th January 1832 and grew up in Renfrew, where he was educated at the Old Burgh and Blythswood Testimonial Schools. When made an Honorary Burgess of Renfrew in 1907 he recalled leaving school to start work for iron founders Henderson Brothers[3]:

> 'I well remember, as a boy, at the Blythswood Testimonial School, the late Mr David Henderson of the London Works, now the property of Messrs. William Simons and Co., looking for an office boy, came to the school, and from the collection of raw material … chose me.'

The 'counting house' of the iron foundry may have given William Robertson useful experience of office work, but he could not have remained there long as in May 1851, when he was still only 19, he had established a carrying business bringing coal and pig iron to Renfrew, with an office at Bowling on the Clyde. His notebook for May 1852 has the first reference to a vessel being owned, 'my first venture the scow *Ellen*', which cost 'ten pounds and repairs extra'. She had been bought from a Robert Marshall. According to a document believed to have been written by James Cassels Robertson, William's grandson, *Ellen* mostly carried coal during 1852 and 1853 and served Renfrew (where William Robertson later opened an office), Kirkintilloch, Dumbarton and Helensburgh. For some years, Robertson continued to describe himself as a coal merchant as well as a ship owner, so he was presumably involved in selling the coal which was the main cargo of his ships. *Ellen's* first freight was for J. and A. Frew but later many cargoes were consigned to J.W. Hoby, a Renfrew shipbuilder. *Ellen* cannot be found in contemporary ship registers, and nor can three successive acquisitions listed in Robertson's note book: the *Gem* (1) mentioned first in 1854, *Ruby* (1) in 1855, and the *Pearl* (1) in 1859. The term scow suggests that these early vessels might have been lighters for use on the Forth and Clyde Canal but *Pearl* (which is referred to as a smack) certainly carried sails, as there is a reference to her canvas needing replacement. Indeed, looking at their voyages down as far as the Island of Bute on the wide and often windy waters of the Firth of Clyde, these vessels could only have made such voyages with the help of sails. Given the common naming scheme involving precious stones, and which was to go on to give the fleet its familiar name, it would seem likely that at least the *Ruby* and *Pearl* were built for Robertson,[4] with the naming scheme possibly suggested by the secondhand *Gem.*

In addition to running his own ships, Robertson also acted as an agent. Surviving in his papers is a note addressed to him from the Monkland Iron and Steel Company requesting him to secure a vessel to take up to 200 tons of bar iron to Oporto. It notes that Bowling would do very well as a loading port because the company's scow could deliver the iron there direct from the works, saving cartage and time. For other vessels occasionally mentioned in Robertson's early account books he was almost certainly the agent or broker, as there is no evidence that he owned them: *Rover's Bride* (a record of freight paid to master in 1856), *Queen of Sheba* (1858), *Maid of Orleans* (1858 and 1864), *Helen* (1859), *Lone Star* (1861) and *Vixen* (1864).

Patterns of trade: early days

The operations of Robertson's first four vessels were confined to the Forth and Clyde Canal and the waters of the Firth of Clyde. Records of freights in 1859 show that *Pearl* traded as far afield as Rothesay and the Kyles of Bute,[5] including carrying 70 tons of stone from Erskine to Renfrew and 66 tons of stone from Govan to Greenock. A freight book kept from 1862 to 1866 confirms this pattern and Table 1 lists typical commodities carried and their destinations during this period. The most frequent cargo was coal, followed by stone, bricks and timber. Capacities of the three vessels involved appear similar, and tonnages of coal lifted are in the range 67 to 117 tons. *Pearl* and *Gem* could carry a total of 16,000 and 15,000 bricks, respectively. The freight book only rarely indicates where the cargo originated, and these few entries involve wood from Cloch Bay, Lochgoil, and Loch Ridden; turnips from Toward; and stones or bricks from Dumbarton (to Port Glasgow in the case of the bricks). The only identifiable origins given for the coal which preponderates amongst the cargoes are Banknock and Kirkintilloch, both on the Forth and Clyde Canal. From the almost invariable reference to both towage and trackage (the latter presumably haulage by horse, or possibly even by man) in the returns it is concluded that most of the coal and probably the bricks originated on this waterway, and that the vessels usually returned to the canal. Voyages in light condition are not listed, but it seems likely that inbound cargoes were not always available, although when possible timber, stone, or even manure or turnips would be carried. The only other employment recorded is that, in November 1864, *Gem* earned £3 10s 0d for two days work helping to lift the tug *Splendid.*

A typical voyage account for the *Ruby* in May 1866 has her carrying a relatively modest 67 tons of coal to the Holy Loch at 2/3d per ton, earning £7 10s 9p gross. From this was deducted £1 8s 0p for expenses including towage and dues. Over a half of the profit, £3 4s 4d, went to the master. This voyage yielded Robertson £2 18s 5d, from which he would have to pay for replacing equipment and, eventually, the vessel itself. From 1864 the 'master's half' progressively disappears from the accounts and instead there are regular entries for masters' wages, indicating that these gentlemen were no longer sharing in the profitability of the voyage. An interesting item on the voyage to the Holy Loch and on several others is the three shillings spent on whisky: clearly regarded as an unavoidable expense of seafaring which the owner met.

In 1862 the wooden smack *Topaz* (1) was built for William Robertson at Maryhill. She was the first of his vessels which has been found in registration documents and probably the first to operate outside the Firth of Clyde. For instance, in December 1863 she loaded coal in Renfrew and sailed for Oban via the Crinan Canal. At around 100 tons, her cargoes are no larger than those of earlier craft, but entries in the accounts for ballast and a mate's wages indicate that she was a more substantial vessel. Robertson was already setting his sights further afield.

By 1864 Robertson was operating both from an office at 75 Jamaica Street, Glasgow and from one at Port Dundas on the Forth and Clyde Canal. He listed his fleet as comprising five ships, omitting *Ellen* but adding *Garnet* (1), similar in size to *Topaz* and also trading outside the Clyde: wrecked on the Isle of Man in 1868, she was Robertson's first known loss. Despite iron-hulled steam vessels entering the fleet as early as 1865, Robertson continued to order wooden sailing vessels, and from 1874 to 1877 five entered the fleet, plus the iron schooner *Cameo* (1). The *Jacinth* (1) of 1877 was the last sailing ship built for Robertson, and he was soon disposing of his sail tonnage, with *Topaz* (1) going in 1879 and the fleet further decreased in that year with the loss of *Chrysolite* whilst returning in ballast from Sligo. This, only Robertson's second loss, was creditable given that all of Robertson's wooden sailing ships became casualties after sale to other owners, the resurrection and survival of the former *Jacinth* (1) recorded in the fleet list being exceptional. Sail was retained in the fleet until 1888 when *Cameo* (1) and *Gem* (2) were sold.

Table 1: Cargoes of *Ruby*, *Pearl* and *Gem* from 1862[6]	
Destination	**Cargoes**
Ardentinny	coal; stones
Arrochar	coal
Banknock	coal
Benmore	stones and coal
Blairvaddoch	coal
Blythswood	coal
Bowling	coal
Cloch	bricks
Cove	coal; stones
Drumognil	coal
Dumbarton	coal; lime and sand
Dunoon	coal
Erskine Ferry	bricks
Forge	coal
Gareloch	coal; drain pipes
Gourock	coal; stones; turnips
Greenock	coal; stones
Helensburgh	bricks; wood
Holy Loch	coal; stones
Hunters Quay	stones
Hyndburn	coal
Inellan	stones
Inverkip	bricks
Kames	coal
Kilcreggan	stones
Kilmun	stones
Langbank	bricks
Lochgoil	stones
Paisley	bark; stones
Port Bannatyne	coal
Port Dundas	manure
Port Glasgow	coal; sleepers
Renfrew	stones
Rocksoles	coal
Rothesay	drain pipes; stones; stones and bricks
Shandon	coke; manure
Skelmorlie	coal
Tignabruich	stones
Wemyss Bay	coal

Steam and expansion

With his obvious ambition to expand his ship owning business, Robertson could not resist a move into steam. His cheapest option for a new building was a small craft capable of using the Forth and Clyde Canal, the locks of which limited vessels to a length of 66 feet. Reputedly costing just £906, *Jasper* (1) of 1865 was formally described as an iron steam lighter, and was essentially a Clyde puffer, with a simple non-condensing engine, and without the capacity for water ballast which distinguished the more substantial and larger steam coaster. As well as trading on the Forth and Clyde Canal, *Jasper* is known to have carried stone from Arran for building Troon harbour.

One of Robertson's sailing ship masters was appointed to the *Jasper*, Alex Munro who had previously been in the *Ruby*. In turn, J. McNeillage was transferred from *Pearl* to *Ruby*. *Ruby* was clearly either a larger or a newer vessel than *Pearl*, and this is borne out by 1864 figures which value *Ruby* at £120, *Pearl* at £100 and *Gem* at just £80. In the same list the 1862-built *Topaz* was valued at £500 and the newly-built *Garnet* at £630.

The next 12 years saw Robertson expand his steam fleet, with new buildings that were little different in dimensions from his earlier steamers. *Diamond* (1) of 1867 was very similar to *Jasper*, but the 100-foot *Amethyst* (1) from the same Maryhill yard in 1870 was too large for Forth and Clyde Canal trading. *Diamond* (1) and *Amethyst* (1) and probably other Robertson steamers operated a regular service from Glasgow to Irvine, Ayr and Girvan.

Duckworth and Langmuir claim that in 1871 Robertsons began a service to the West Highlands with the screw steamer *Marchioness of Lorne*, which sailed from Glasgow on Wednesdays for Ardrishaig, Lochgilphead, Oban, Tobermory, Tiree and Coll, on alternate weeks calling at Salen or Strontian.[7] However, no ship with this name can be identified at around this date.[8] From 1872 the paddle steamer *Celt* (215/1848) ran from Glasgow to Islay, again reportedly for Robertson. This ship can be identified as a Denny-built former unit of the Campbeltown and Glasgow Steam Packet Joint Stock Company, Campbeltown, but her owner in 1872 was Daniel McCrae of Greenock. At this time Robertson had an office on the Broomielaw, a Glasgow quay from which many local steamer services departed, and it is possible that he was acting as agent for these services, probably selling tickets and booking freight. Two other paddle steamers are noted as being associated with Robertson, both from the yard of T.B. Seath at Rutherglen, which also built for Robertson. The iron *Vale of Clwyd*[9] (155/1865) and the *Bonnie Doon* (213/1870) were owned by a David Hunter of Ayr with the builder having a residual interest, and again Robertson may have been employed as agent for the sailings of these vessels. The *Vale of Clwyd* – built and named for service along the North Wales coast – was running between Glasgow and Ayr by the late 1860s. These ships are not included in the fleet list as there is no evidence for Robertson having any financial interest. He concentrated on owning coastal cargo ships rather than those carrying passengers.

The 120-foot *Agate* (1) of 1878 was the true forerunner of Robertson's massive steam coaster fleet, and it has been suggested that she played a part in developing this breed of ship which was to become so numerous in British and other waters. It was not just her size that enabled *Agate* to trade more widely than Robertson's earlier steamers. She undoubtedly had heavier scantlings, so that frames and stringers were stronger, as reflected in her being classed by Lloyd's Register of British and Foreign Shipping. An important feature was her two-cylinder compound engine which, with an enhanced boiler pressure, considerably improved her economy compared with *Amethyst* (1) and the puffers propelled by simple engines. A modest capacity for water ballast helped *Agate* to make coastal and short sea passages between cargoes. Ballast tanks required pumps to empty them, and *Agate's* engine room would be better equipped with this sort of machinery than his smaller steamers.

With the collapse of the City of Glasgow Bank in 1878, and in its wake a dearth of funds for loans and mortgages, this was not a propitious time to invest the relatively large sums needed to build steamers. Nevertheless, from 1880 until the First World War, the Robertson story was one of almost continuous expansion. The years 1889 and 1890 were particularly notable for growth, with no fewer than six steamers joining in the former year (two being secondhand) and five in the latter (all new). Pace of expansion then slowed slightly, but five new steamers were delivered in 1894 and in 1898, and six in 1904 gave an owned fleet of 50 ships, making William Robertson the largest operator in the British coasting trade. Depressed trading conditions meant that there were few further orders over the next decade, but the size of the fleet was maintained and in 1914 it still comprised 49 steamers.

Robertson's rapid expansion demanded a ready access to capital, but it is not clear from where this came. As he does not appear to have had sufficient inherited wealth, and his coal merchant and agency businesses would not have made him wealthy enough to pay for these ships outright, it is intriguing to speculate on how William Robertson financed the fleet. When he began buying steamers a new one would vary in price from the £6,650 of the 120-foot *Agate* (1) of 1878 to the £12,000 for the 185-foot *Amethyst* (2) of 1883. For a few ships there are additional shareholders who would have helped finance them, for instance the schooner *Nugget* (1) of 1876 had four individuals with eight shares each, with Robertson holding the controlling interest. *Jacinth* (2) of 1888 was unusual in that William Robertson and James Reston each held 32 shares, and the latter also held ten shares in *Nugget* (2) from September 1889 to January 1896. Mortgages were obtained on some vessels, for instance the *Agate* (1) was mortgaged on completion in May 1878 to James Fyfe (described as a 'pavement merchant', presumably because he supplied stone for *making* pavements rather than selling goods *on* a pavement) and some form of mortgage was held on her until 1887.[10] *Ruby* (2) was mortgaged to the British Linen Co. Ltd. and *Jacinth* (2) to Fullertons, her Paisley builders. However, it is clear from registration documents that William Robertson bought many of his steamers outright and, with no mortgages from shipbuilders or financiers being recorded on the registration documents of individual ships, trading profits were clearly ploughed back into new ships. With careful management of vessels and finances, Robertson was to get into a position where he was loaning money on vessels, rather than borrowing. For instance, in November 1912 he advanced £8,000 to shipbuilder William Beardmore, the security being packets of shares which Beardmore held in vessels of the John Hay fleet.[11]

Despite running a substantial fleet of his own, in 1885 Robertson began managing ships for others: the shipbroker James Reston, the Paisley businessman Hugh Smiley and the engine builder William King, also of Paisley. In May 1888 Glasgow ship owner Alexander Hay was declared bankrupt, and as a consequence in September 1888 Rudolph Feldtmann who held a mortgage on *Strathavon* and John Anderson who was part owner of *Strathgarry* appointed William Robertson as the manager of these ships. On Hay's bankruptcy Robertson bought four of his ships: *Strathesk*, *Strathadder* (which became *Cameo* (2)), *Strathnairn* (renamed *Cairngorm* (1)) and *Strathness* (renamed *Onyx* (1)). Previous to this, the only second hand steamer purchased had been the Belfast-owned *Larry Bane* which joined the fleet in January 1888, so Robertson reversed the usual pattern of acquisitions, by moving from exclusively new ships to a mixture of new and secondhand.

The rapidly expanding business clearly demanded an increase in office staff and accommodation, and Robertson's business moved several times in this period: his various addresses and dates are listed in Table 2. The move to 45 West Nile Street came when the fleet was approaching its peak in terms of numbers of ships, and no further moves were necessary over its remaining 75 years.

Table 2: Office addresses

1852-1861	Renfrew
1861-1866	75 Jamaica Street, Glasgow
1866-1869	79 Jamaica Street, Glasgow
1869-1875	74 Broomielaw, Glasgow
1875-1882	118 Broomielaw, Glasgow
1882-1889	88 Great Clyde Street, Glasgow
1889-1907	15 Gordon Street, Glasgow
1907-1982	Gresham Chambers, 45 West Nile Street, Glasgow

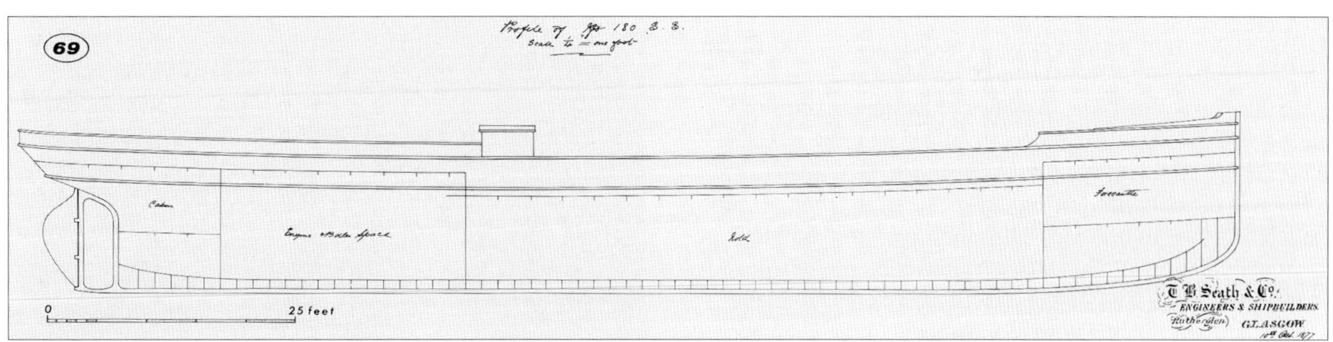

Shipbuilder T.B. Seath's profile drawing of *Agate* (1), dated 10th October 1877. The low forecastle was typical of early steam coasters, full height ones being adopted as a safety measure by 1890.

On 4th October 1889, *Agate* was off Brodick Bay, Arran inward bound for Glasgow with a cargo of iron ore when she collided port bow to port bow with the State Line steamer *State of Georgia* (1,507/1873), outward bound for New York with 100 passengers and general cargo. Both ships were considerably damaged, with plates knocked in and frames bent, and only her collision bulkhead prevented *Agate* from foundering. Damage to the *State of Georgia* was entirely above the waterline, but a trimmer was killed in the forecastle by a falling plate. At the subsequent enquiry, *Agate* was held to have behaved correctly, and the master of *State of Georgia* was blamed for not taking avoiding action until too late, and had his certificate suspended for three months. *Agate* was repaired at Bowling and gave another 22 years of service. *[Courtesy of Charles Waine]*

The steam fleet, 1878-1917

Following the delivery of *Agate* (1) in May 1878, expansion of the steam fleet was initially slow, but it appears to have been well planned, and suggests that William Robertson was building steamers of various sizes to suit different trades. At 120 feet, *Agate* was at the very bottom of the size range; indeed over the next four decades Robertson built or bought only six steamers shorter than 139 feet. Following *Agate*'s arrival, over two years elapsed before the *Jasper* (2) was delivered in August 1880, representing a jump to 145 feet with a corresponding increase in cost. After a further 16 months, *Sapphire* (2) was delivered in December 1881, showing another increase, this time to 160 feet. Length peaked, at least temporarily, in April 1883 with the *Amethyst* (2) which measured 185 feet. In terms of tonnage, *Amethyst* was three times the size of *Agate*, and was a very different ship in terms of carrying capacity. Subsequent deliveries were slightly smaller than *Amethyst*: the *Topaz* (2) of 1883 at 160 feet, *Pearl* (3) of 1885 at 170 feet and *Diamond* (2) of 1886 at 175 feet. Analysis of the fleet by length must be done cautiously, as there was a trend for the size of coasters and other ships to increase over time, but Robertson clearly favoured ships between 160 and 179 feet, with 27 of this size out of a total of 73 built or bought up to 1917. The tendency of size to increase over time meant that the next most popular length was the 180 to 199 feet band, with 22 steamers built. As a prudent investor, Robertson would have judged these relatively large coasters to give the best combination of earning power and flexibility for the many trades in which he engaged.

Agate may have been a pioneer but T.B. Seath and Co., the Rutherglen builder responsible, received only two more orders from the company, for *Jasper* (2) of 1880 and *Topaz* (2) of 1883. Instead orders went initially to the Paisley yard of John Fullerton and Company, beginning with *Sapphire* (2) of 1881. Appendix 1 lists the steamers ordered from each builder. It shows that Fullerton's yard, with seven new buildings, was itself overtaken by Scott of Bowling which contributed no fewer than 39 new ships to the fleet, beginning with *Diamond* (2) of 1886. From the *Coral* (1) of 1892 John Shearer and Son of Kelvinhaugh began to make an appreciable contribution, eventually adding ten steamers. Shearer also built some larger ships, but for these Robertson turned mainly to A. Rodger and Co. of Port Glasgow, the yard which delivered and engined seven large ships beginning with the *Axinite* (1) of 1899 and ending with the *Felspar* of 1908. Amongst the smallest ships of the fleet at 135 feet were the sisters *Prase* (1) and *Plasma* from Carmichael, McLean and Co. of Greenock. The *Sard* (2) of 1909 was the only pre-war product of Ailsa at Troon, a yard which was later to become Robertson's preferred builder, eventually delivering four steamers and eight motor ships. The *Sard* was the first ship built for Robertson beyond the Clyde, and it is notable how few members of the fleet were ever ordered outside Scotland: one steamer and six motor ships from the Netherlands and a motor ship from Germany. It was natural for owners to favour local builders, whom they would get to know, and this would make it simpler to agree designs and supervise progress. In any case, with the Clyde becoming pre-eminent in building steam coasters (and much else), there was little need to look elsewhere.

The smallest Robertson ships tended to have engine and bridge (such as it was) right aft, with those between 140 and 219 feet being of the engines-aft, bridge-amidships, and raised-quarterdeck design. In the earlier and smaller vessels such as the *Nugget* (2) the hatch between bridge and engine room was noticeably shorter than that forward of the bridge. The five steamers of 220 feet and over had their engines and bridge amidships, with long raised quarter decks, and were clearly intended for working outside the British coasting trade.

Evolution in the design of Robertson ships – indeed of all steam coasters – was steady up until the early 1890s, after which design tended to fossilise. The early compound-engined steamers had boiler pressures of around 60 lbs per square inch, and this rose to 130 lbs per square inch. *Gem* (3) of 1887 was the first Robertson vessel in which a triple-expansion engine was installed, permitting the steam from a boiler pressurised to at least 160 lbs per square inch to be used more economically than was possible in a two-cylinder compound engine. The triple-expansion engine was to become standard, with boiler pressures rising to 200 lbs per square inch, although the more compact two-cylinder engine continued to be fitted in some smaller ships in which space was at a premium, such as *Peridot* of 1890.

One of the few changes to affect hull form concerned the height of the forecastle. Originally, the seamen and firemen were accommodated below main deck level and under the low-height forecastle. It was usually impossible to open a porthole whilst the vessel was at sea, so this space was difficult to ventilate and lighting required oil lamps. For steamers built from around 1890 the crew accommodation tended to be moved into the forecastle itself, which improved accessibility, lighting and ventilation. The forecastle was increased in height, as can be seen from a comparison of the *Cameo* (2) of 1883 (opposite page top) with later vessels such as *Cornelian* of 1890 (at the foot of the opposite page). However, the crew's accommodation was scarcely palatial, still vulnerable in the event of a collision, and all but inaccessible when at sea in really rough weather. Not until the end of regular steam coaster building in the late 1930s was accommodation for these crew members moved aft.

The builder's plaque on the bridge front informs us that this vessel, crammed with local worthies, was built by John Shearer and Son of Kelvinhaugh, but unfortunately it carries no yard number. The vessel appears small, and may well be the *Morion* (1) of 1894, Shearer's yard number 16. *[Robertson archives]*

steam coaster, was largely a product of builders and owners on this coast. The trades these coasters entered, and helped capture from sailing vessels, were numerous. Coal was a staple cargo, loaded particularly at ports in western Scotland, Cumbria, Lancashire and South Wales and carried to Irish ports and as far south as the French channel ports. The Irish ports served included not only the bigger ones on the east coast, including Belfast, but also smaller ports on the much more exposed Atlantic coast, including Galway, Limerick and Kenmare. The length of his ships meant that Robertson did not participate greatly in the coal trade to Dublin and Newry. These two ports generally required ships of less than 145 feet which could dock in Ringsend Basin or enter the Newry Ship Canal and of these there were only half a dozen in the Robertson fleet. Shipping coal to Dublin and Newry was largely left to others, although *Onyx* (2) was lost on a voyage to Dublin with coal. Coke was also carried, and being lighter than coal would also be loaded as a deck cargo, at least in spring and summer months; *Amber* (1) loading just 290 tons in her hold and on deck for a voyage from Liverpool to Dublin in April 1910.

Shipment of limestone was second only to coal in importance to the Robertson fleet. Indeed, from the 1880s local directories cease to list William Robertson as a coal merchant and shipping agent, and begin to refer to him as a steam ship owner and agent for Irish and Welsh limestone. Limestone was brought to Clydeside and other areas for use as a flux in iron and steel making. In Ulster, Carnlough Limestone Co. Ltd. was a major supplier; indeed, Robertson managed their steamer *Olderfleet*. Quarries in North Wales, and particularly at Llanddulas, were also important sources of limestone, and as early as 1880 *Agate* (1) was chartered to the owners of the Llanddulas quarries, Kneeshaw. Lupton and Co. So important did the limestone trade become that in

An important development not apparent externally was the removal of pillars in the hold and their replacement by cantilever brackets. Taking place around 1900, this not only meant that bulk cargoes could be discharged more readily, but also enabled large pieces of machinery and steel plates to be carried. This development led to a desire to increase the size of hatches, and where two hatches had served a hold these were often reduced to one. Increasing the hatch size both expedited unloading and reduced the need for trimmers to work on a bulk cargo after loading. However, the conventional method of closing a hatch limited the extent to which the opening could be enlarged. This involved steel beams between which were laid wooden hatch boards which were covered with tarpaulins, and was the weakest part of the ship: there were regular losses through the hatches being stove in during foul weather. A solution was only arrived at when folding steel hatch covers were perfected, well after the demise of the steam coaster.

Patterns of trade: pre-First World War

William Robertson was firmly based on the west coast of Britain, and the type of vessel he helped pioneer, the

The half-height forecastle of the 1883-built *Cameo* (2) (top) contrasts with the full-height version of the 1890-built *Cornelian* (above). *[J. and M. Clarkson (2)]*

1922 Robertsons bought a quarrying operation at Llanddulas. Trading to quarry jetties, close inshore, was not without risk, but it is to the credit of Robertson's crews that no serious casualties were recorded, although as the photographs show there were several lesser incidents, including those in 1907 involving *Onyx* (3) (see page 62-3) and *Cameo* (2) (this page).

Other minerals were also carried, including iron ore from Duddon and other ports to the Clyde and pebbles from Fecamp to Harrington. Less usual cargoes included soda ash from Mostyn on the River Dee to the Tyne, and phosphate from Ghent. When lost in March 1906, *Sard* (1) was carrying a smelly consignment from London to Coleraine consisting of manure, presumably generated by horses. Similarly odoriferous would have been the barrels of oil, glue and bone collected by *Cameo* (2) from the whaling station on the Isle of Harris, to which she had taken coal, coke and empty barrels. In 1907 *Diamond* (2) delivered herrings in barrels from Lerwick to Hamburg. Salt was needed in the herring curing ports, and in August 1908 *Opal* (1) loaded Cheshire salt at Weston Point for Wick. A cargo of hay from Limerick to Newport carried by *Coral* (1) in July 1907 represented a rare return cargo from the west of Ireland to a coal port. Heavy manufactured items were also carried, including rails from Workington to the Clyde or Ireland, steel plate from South Wales to Ireland, railway sleepers from Ardrossan to Barrow, and cable from Greenock to Plymouth. Grain was also loaded, the large *Achroite* being a somewhat unusual choice to lift South African maize from Southampton to Glasgow. In April 1896 *Jacinth* (2) took malt from Grimsby to Cork. As the last-named voyage indicates, Robertson's ships were by no

On 15th October 1907, *Cameo* (2) was partly loaded at Llanddulas when a gale suddenly sprang up from the north west. Attempting to put out to sea, she backed off the berth, but her rudder struck ground and jammed. Unable to steer, the wind and sea forced her broadside on to the end of the loading stage, the piles of which penetrated her starboard bulwarks and her engine room, breaking off the steam pipe to the engine. Without power, *Cameo* drifted on to the beach broadside on about 30 yards east of the stage, listing to seaward, with her funnel gone and her holds tidal. The upper photograph shows her damaged rudder, and work in progress to unload her cargo of limestone. Once this had been done and her hull patched up, she was refloated on the night of 23/24th October and put alongside the loading stage, ready to be towed to Liverpool the next day. *[Robertson archives]*

means confined to the west of Britain, and visited east coast coal ports, often to load for southern ports.

Robertson also tried some longer distance trades, including a liner service, that between Preston and Hamburg, which continued from 1892 when the Albert Edward Dock opened until 1914. The larger ships were used on the Hamburg service, including *Achroite*, *Amethyst* (2), *Obsidian* (2) and *Tourmaline* (1), their cargoes mainly comprised generals and sugar. Records at Preston show that between 1882 and 1914 an extraordinary total of 68 different Robertson ships came up the Ribble, doing so even before the Dock was built in 1892, and with a wide variety of cargoes. The visitors included ships of all the sizes in the fleet, the smaller vessels including the *Agate* (1) of 1878 naturally tending to be confined to voyages to and from UK ports, and usually loading coal.

Felspar of 1908 alongside a Llanddulas jetty. *[Robertson archives]*

Hamburg was just inside home trade limits, defined as ports in the range Brest to the Elbe, within which officers did not need to hold full certificates. Definitely outside these limits was the voyage of *Jacinth* (2) in September 1896 when she loaded wood pulp in Gothenburg, arriving at Preston on the 20th. This was one of her four visits to Preston that year, and in May she came from Hamburg with general cargo, in October with pig iron from Middlesbrough and in November from London with cement.

Ever ambitious, Robertson was to send some of his larger ships to trade on the east coast of North America. On 21st August 1888, his new, 175-foot *Ruby* (2) sailed from the Clyde to Labrador, from where she loaded a cargo for Livorno in Italy, returning to the Clyde on 21st October. In 1890 the managed *Latharna* was lost on a ballast voyage from Philadelphia to Labrador. During the 1890s five larger vessels were built for the longer distance trades, including *Axinite* (1) and *Citrine* (2), the largest steamers Robertson ever owned at 260 feet.

That the biggest ships were sold off, in some cases within months of completion, suggests that the company had decided to concentrate on coastal and near-continental trades. In January 1900, for instance, only two members of the fleet were working beyond the home trade limits of the Elbe and Brest. *Fluor* (1) was in the Mediterranean, calling at Gibraltar, Malta and Candia, and *Axinite* (1) made a voyage from Ardrossan to Savona, probably with coal. *Achroite* is recorded as bringing a cargo of cork waste from Seville to Heysham, probably a low-value return cargo after she had delivered coal.

Clerks and captains

With a fleet expanding to almost 50 ships, William Robertson could not himself have carried out the necessary administrative work, especially finding cargoes for all of them. This work would be delegated to a chartering clerk, a figure who became of paramount importance to the organisation. A gentlemen named Cooper occupied this position at one time, but the doyen was to be Charles E. Bell. In January 1913 he agreed with Robertsons to remain in their employment for five years and to respect their confidentiality. In return Bell was to be paid £600 per annum and acquired shares worth £5,000 in 45 steamers (an average of one per ship, although he was to have four in *Agate* (2) of 1917). The agreement was described as co-partnery, but it was an unequal partnership, with Robertsons being at liberty to sell the ships in which Bell had an interest without consulting him, and Bell prohibited from holding any other shipping property. The original agreement was renewed after five years and, with various adjustments, at intervals until 1939. It gave Bell a substantial income - in 1936 he was making £1,284 - although the founder's sons were drawing substantially more.

The elevation of Bell to the position of shareholder in 1913 may have reflected William Robertson's conclusion that members of his family were not going to fulfil the same key role in the business that he had done. There were no children to his first marriage to Agnes Bryce in 1857 but to Isabella McKellar, whom the widower married in 1878, were born William Francis Robertson in May 1882 and John McKellar Robertson in May 1883. Both received excellent educations, culminating in degrees at Glasgow University, from where William graduated with a BSc in engineering

Sagenite of 1904, and probably other large Robertson steamers, occasionally took heavy lifts. *[Robertson archives]*

and naval architecture. However, neither son seems to have thrown himself completely into the business of running a coastal shipping company, an activity which required a high degree of micro-management to ensure its continuing, day-to-day success. With ships mostly making voyages of no more than a week's duration, it was a complex operation, which required cargoes to be found, and ships matched with cargoes in terms of their availability, their geographical position, their size and the certificates held by their officers. Freight rates had to be finely calculated, and decisions taken on whether a given voyage would put a ship in a good position for a further cargo. Dry dockings, regular surveys and repairs had to be scheduled, and crews and masters found, and allowed occasional leave. Bunkers had to be taken at coal ports, and the ships stored. Anecdotal evidence suggests both sons William and, to a lesser extent, John, were somewhat remote from the daily tasks that kept a large fleet gainfully employed. When William F. Robertson paid his occasional courtesy visits to the London broker who fixed many of Robertson's cargoes, he disdained discussion of business, claiming 'that's Bell's worry', and instead chatted with one of the broker's principals about his great passion, yachting. However, he continued his father's interest in the design of coastal ships. It seems that his brother 'Mr. John' concerned himself particularly with problems of damage to the ships. With founder William Robertson being 82 years old in 1913, he needed to tie Bell, his key employee, into the business, and used the time-honoured method of offering him a share in the profits that his work helped generate.

Fred Donaldson, a London shipping agent with an office in Fenchurch Street, recorded some reminiscences concerning masters of Robertson ships.[12] Donaldson's firm, which was previously run by his father Samuel, dealt with most Robertson vessels loading or unloading locally, and their masters were frequent visitors to its offices.

A story also told elsewhere concerns Peter MacGlashan, master of the *Sphene* (3), who was in Rotterdam or Antwerp when he received a telegram which told him to 'sail for Bonawe', a quarry in the west of Scotland. He set off, but his acknowledgement caused consternation in the Glasgow office as the instructions sent to him had actually been to 'sail for Boulogne'. Telegrams were dictated over the phone, and the Scottish clerk had interpreted Boulogne as Bonawe. Charles Bell in the Glasgow office immediately tried to get a message to *Sphene*, but neither the signal stations at Dover nor at St. Catherines could contact her. The station at the Lizard finally managed to turn the vessel back for Boulogne.

Dan MacCormack was remembered as a fine player of the bagpipes, writing his own pipe tunes and playing them aboard his command. Another talented skipper was Neil Maclean who had a 'fantastic knowledge of astronomy, history and geography', noted Donaldson, adding slightly acerbically that he could have been an academic 'if he left the bottle alone'. Some masters were indeed serious drinkers, but Wee Willie Walker, master of *Bronzite*, was an ardent teetotaller and bible reader, although a heavy smoker. His morning routine was to stand behind the bridge and strip off whilst crew members threw buckets of cold seawater over him. Washed, he could enjoy his breakfast, his pipe and his bible, in that order. Dan Mackinnon, master of one of Robertson's larger ships, was recalled as being particularly taciturn, just giving the occasionally nod when spoken to.

Coastal seamen knew each other well, but sometimes their camaraderie broke down. The *Iolite* under Captain Alex Johnson once lost her propellor off Dungeness in a south west gale. She was picked up by Jack Hewitt in the coaster *Test* (466/1890), then owned by Bain and Sons of Portreath, and towed into Dover. Johnson thought that the end of the matter, but Hewitt approached Robertsons with a claim for fully salvaging the *Iolite*. Johnson never spoke to Hewitt again.

The First World War

The Robertson fleet comprised 49 steam coasters at the outbreak of the First World War. Of these, 16 were lost during the conflict: nine sunk by submarines, two by mines, three in collisions, and two after being trapped in the Baltic. In addition, three of the six managed ships were torpedoed (see Appendix 2 for a chronological table of losses). During the war the most dangerous place for Robertson steamers was in the English Channel where there were six losses, followed by the Irish Sea with four including one in the North Channel. *Malachite* (2), sunk off Le Havre in November 1914, was only the second British vessel to fall victim to a German submarine, and according to Robertson's records she was uninsured. The losses tended to cluster distressingly. On 31st July 1915 *Turquoise* (1) and *Nugget* (2) were both sunk by *U 21* when on their way, unescorted, to make their modest contributions to the Dardanelles fiasco as Commissioned Fleet Messengers. There is evidence that the submarine fired on the crew in the boats, killing one and wounding eight others from the *Turquoise*.[13] The managed *Huntsland* and *Hunsgrove* were torpedoed just two days apart in June 1918.

Unlike the unfortunate *Turquoise* (1) and *Nugget* (2), *Asteria* (1) did reach the Dardanelles and spent time there as a Commissioned Fleet Messenger under

Bronzite at Preston. Like many of Robertson's masters and despite his name, *Bronzite's* Wee Willie Walker was a larger-than-life character *[Ships in Focus]*

the command of Captain D. Lamont, who was awarded a DSC. *Pebble* (1) was requisitioned as a messenger within days of the other three, and it is likely she too was at the Dardanelles. Seriously damaged, she remained in the Eastern Mediterranean at the end of the war, when the Admiralty acquired her, later selling her on to a Greek owner. After service as a collier, *Spinel* (1) also became a Fleet Messenger.

The Baltic adventures of *Fluor* (1) and *Obsidian* (2) are intriguing, but details are sparse. The ships were trading to the Baltic and were trapped at Riga on the outbreak of war in August 1914: *Obsidian* had been loading sleepers for Goole. The British Government assumed responsibility and loaned them to Russia, presumably with their crews repatriated via neutral Sweden and Norway. In April 1918 *Obsidian* was in Helsinki (then under Russian sovereignty) and was caught up in the civil war between Bolsheviks and 'White' Finnish forces, with German troops also approaching the port. A British naval officer named Cromie was determined that *Obsidian* and two other British ships should not fall into German hands. With a combination of threats and persuasion, he managed to establish that the ships were British and took them over. Armed Bolshevik guards were put on board, but Cromie managed to bribe them with pairs of trousers from the cargo, which consisted of a bizarre mix of clothing and torpedoes. With a scratch crew of five Russian army officers on *Obsidian*, and despite obstructions from both local authorities and threats from the Germans, he took the three ships out of the ice-filled harbour and sank them in Sveaborg Roads on 9th and 10th April. Less is known about *Fluor's* fate. She is reported both as being scuttled at Leningrad and as being taken in prize by German forces at Riga, both events allegedly taking place in March 1918. The latter explanation is the more likely, as she later came into the ownership of the Board of Trade, presumably being taken over at the end of the war, and was eventually broken up at Bremen. The *Gem* (3) under Captain Jimmy Mackeegan from Islandmagee almost shared the fate of *Fluor* and *Obsidian*, and is reputed to have been the last British ship to get away from Hamburg just before the declaration of war in August 1914. The reprieve was temporary, however, as she was sunk by a German mine in December 1914.

The only ship delivered new to the fleet during the First World War, *Agate* (2) may have been ordered prior to the outbreak but delayed because of the government giving priority to naval shipbuilding until merchant ship losses became acute. Wisely Robertson did not pay inflated wartime prices for secondhand additions, and indeed actually sold a considerable number of ships during the conflict. With losses and a proportion of his fleet requisitioned, the number of ships Robertsons actually controlled by 1918 was relatively small. *[J. and M. Clarkson]*

Despite her 22 years, *Spinel* (1) was requisitioned as a Fleet Messenger in 1915. Returning to Robertson's fleet in 1920, she worked until 1933, and probably never received a closed wheelhouse. *[J. and M. Clarkson]*

Robertson was asked by the Shipping Controller to manage six ships taken in prize and previously owned by, or working for, Germany or Austria-Hungary, two of which themselves became war losses. All were well beyond the maximum size of Robertson's own vessels, and it is puzzling why an owner specialising in coasters was asked to manage large, ocean-going ships of which the company and most of its crews would have little or no experience.

Hematite spent four and a half years on requisition during the First World War, designated mainly as an ammunition carrier. She was photographed off Gravesend on 3rd November 1930. *[Ships in Focus]*

Of the 49 ships in the fleet in 1914, 18 were at some point on British Government service, including the two trapped in the Baltic and the four Commissioned Fleet Messengers mentioned above (see Table 3). Of the remaining 12, all but *Olivine* (2) were employed at some point as colliers. This drudgery was occasionally punctuated by voyages to French ports, usually carrying ammunition, during which they were temporarily reclassified as Expeditionary Force Transports. Five including *Hematite* began service as ammunition carriers (and judging by the low numbers allocated, were amongst the first on this work) and later became colliers. As with other companies, the number of ships requisitioned increased as the conflict dragged on, and it is notable that six ships served from virtually the outbreak of war until, in several cases, well after the Armistice. Of these the longest and also the most intriguing service was that of *Spinel* (1), which from August 1919 to June 1920 was in the Eastern Mediterranean for what is officially described as temporary duty with the Principal Naval Transport Officer. The six managed ships were working for the government for the entire period they were under Robertson's supervision.

William Robertson (centre) on a sea excursion. *[Robertson archives]*

Post-war changes

William Robertson died of cerebral thrombosis at the age of 87 on 19th March 1919. Unlike some ship owners, he did not pursue a prominent career in public life, but did hold a number of offices. From 1892 to 1917 he was a member, and at one time Chairman, of the Clyde Navigation Trust. In 1900 Robertson took his turn to become for one year the Deacon of the wonderfully-named Incorporation of Hammermen of Glasgow. The Incorporation was originally a craft guild, and considers itself the foremost one in Glasgow, tracing its name to the achievements of warriors at the battle of Langside in 1568. Like the guilds in other cities, it was originally formed to reserve given trades to men who had served their time, but by 1900 was essentially a social and business networking organisation with charitable aims. Each deacon chose his own insignia, in Robertson's case a life buoy and steam ship. His sons, grandsons and great grandsons were to continue the family association with the Hammermen.

In October 1907 Robertson had been made an Honorary Burgess of the Royal Burgh of Renfrew. In return, he had presented his home town with 30 acres of land for recreational purposes which opened as Robertson Park in 1912, Robertson and his wife Isabella having ceremonially cut the first sod with a silver spade.[14] Robertson also gave various gifts to local hospitals: an operating theatre to the Western Infirmary and a clinical research laboratory to Victoria Infirmary.

William Robertson's rise from relatively humble origins to become the doyen of coaster owners was attributable largely to hard work and good judgement. He was not content to keep his ships in familiar trades out of the Clyde, but sought employment for them right round - and at times well beyond - the British coast, and to suit these trades he built ships of widely varying sizes. The bankruptcy of at least two contemporary Glasgow coaster owners (James Macfarlane in 1886 and Alexander Hay in 1888) may have given Robertson pause, but a wave of expansion followed these failures, with him buying several of the bankrupt owners' ships. What evidence there is of how Robertson financed his fleet suggests that

Table 3: Government service of Robertson owned and managed ships during the First World War

Robertson-owned ships are listed in order of date of requisition, followed by the managed ships (which were not under Robertson's management for the entire period). *Indicates lost whilst on government service.

Ship	Type of service	From	To
Spinel (1)	Collier No. 257	26.8.1914	5.10.1915
	Commissioned Fleet Messenger No. 55	6.10.1915	29.6.1920
Felspar	Ammunition Carrier No. 3	1.9.1914	30.7.1918
	Collier	31.7.1918	6.2.1920
Sagenite	Ammunition Carrier No. 6	7.9.1914	15.7.1916
	Collier No. 1,218	16.7.1916	31.3.1919
Emerald (2)	Ammunition Carrier No. 9	17.9.1914	29.4.1915
	Collier No. 653	30.4.1915	13.11.1916
	Store Carrier No. 72	14.11.1916	4.4.1919
Achroite	Ammunition Carrier No. 10	28.9.1914	26.5.1918
	Collier No. 2,218	27.5.1918	1.11.1919
Hematite	Ammunition Carrier No. 13	9.10.1914	23.4.1918
	Collier No. 2,237	24.4.1918	29.4.1919
Pearl (4)	Expeditionary Force Transport	30.3.1915	8.5.1915
	Collier	22.3.1918	12.9.1918
Olivine (2)	Expeditionary Force Transport	1.4.1915	4.4.1915*
Brilliant (1)	Ammunition Carrier No. 38	17.1.1915	15.5.1916
	Collier No. 1,162	16.5.1916	26.2.1919
	Collier No. 1,162	6.8.1919	25.8.1919
	In 1917 made three voyages carrying ammunition		
Asteria (1)	Commissioned Fleet Messenger No. 29	20.7.1915	22.1.1921
Turquoise (1)	Commissioned Fleet Messenger No. 30	22.7.1915	31.7.1915*
Nugget (2)	Commissioned Fleet Messenger No. 38	23.7.1915	31.7.1915*
Pebble (1)	Commissioned Fleet Messenger No. 31	24.7.1915	23.5.1919
Obsidian (2)	Russian Government Service	1.5.1916	19.4.1918*
Fluor (1)	Russian Government Service	1.5.1916	31.3.1919*
Tourmaline (1)	Collier No. 1,703	26.6.1917	4.5.1918
	In 1917 made two voyages carrying ammunition from Dagenham to Dunkirk		
Girasol (1)	Collier No. 2,100	17.3.1918	21.12.1918
	In September and October 1918 worked out of Newhaven as Expeditionary Force Transport		
Nephrite (1)	Collier No. 2,151	20.3.1918	10.3.1919
	In February 1919 made one voyage from Havre to Newport with defective ammunition		
Hunsgrove	Collier No. 396	-	3.11.1915
	Expeditionary Force Transport G 268. Avonmouth, Portsmouth and Southampton to France	4.11.1915	10.6.1917
	Collier No. 396	11.6.1917	13.7.1917
	Expeditionary Force Transport G 268. Cross-channel	14.7.1917	7.9.1917
	Expeditionary Force Transport G 268. UK to Egypt	8.9.1917	7.1.1918
	Collier No. 396	8.1.1918	8.6.1918*
Hunsgate	Expeditionary Force Transport C 6082. West Coast UK to France	21.6.1915	9.2.1919
	Collier No. 2442	10.2.1919	6.4.1919
	Sugar from Cuba	7.4.1919	7.7.1919
	Expeditionary Force Transport C 6082. UK to Baltic	8.7.1919	17.2.1920
Huntsland	Expeditionary Force Transport G 610	18.11.1915	6.6.1918*
Huntscape	Expeditionary Force Transport G 820. Stores to France	5.2.1916	10.1.1919
	Collier No. 2443	11.1.1919	13.2.1919
	Expeditionary Force Transport G 820. To Egypt and Syria	14.2.1919	7.4.1919
	Collier No. 2443	23.6.1919	17.2.1920
Huntsholm	Commercial Branch	5.1916	7.11.1916
	Expeditionary Force Transport G 1826. Cross Channel	8.11.1916	11.6.1917*
Clutha	Expeditionary Force Transport E 128. Cross Channel	-	8.10.1918
	Collier No. 2066	9.10.1918	6.12.1918
	Wheat from USA	7.2.1918	4.4.1919
	Expeditionary Force Transport E 128. Cross Channel	5.4.1919	22.9.1919

William Robertson's executors: his widow Isabella, William Francis Robertson and John McKellar Robertson. *[Robertson archives]*

much of his earnings were ploughed back into new ships, with relatively little resort to outside shareholders or to mortgaging his ships, which could have left him vulnerable to a downturn in the market. Although evidently prudent, he was far from cautious, as evidenced by his fleet's rapid expansion of the late 1880s and early 1890s, with up to six ships acquired in a single year, to maximise opportunities he clearly saw. The fleet grew too large for one man to manage, and Robertson seems to have chosen well those such as Charles Bell to whom he deputed the work. Save for a brief flirtation with larger ships around 1898 (two out of three of which were quickly sold), it is hard to fault William Robertson's performance as a ship owner, building up from nothing a fleet that was valued at almost £357,000 at its peak just before the First World War.

William Robertson's executors included his widow Isabella and sons William Francis Robertson and John McKellar Robertson. In August 1919 the ships, which had all been formally registered in the name of William Robertson, were transferred to the joint ownership of his sons.

It is tempting to attribute the shifts in how the company was run in post-war years to the change of ownership following William Robertson's death. However, the war and its economic aftermath altered conditions for coastal ship owners, and brought to a close something of a golden age – although that is hardly how those who served in the ships would have described it. War losses and diversion of ships to government service resulted in some purely coastal shipping trades being lost to the railways. The depleted steamer fleets of coastal ship owners also faced increasing competition from the Netherlands. Healthy wartime profits earned as neutrals serving both sides enabled Dutch owners to invest in new and efficient oil-engined auxiliaries and, increasingly, pure motor ships, and these made major inroads into the United Kingdom coasting trade.

There were a couple of years of heady profits for British owners in the years immediately following the Armistice, a period characterised by reckless investment in ships and particularly coasters, which had not been built in sufficient numbers during wartime to replace losses. Prices of new buildings escalated, and when the inevitable fall in freight rates came in mid-1921 and with it the collapse of ship prices, many owners who had bought or built expensively were embarrassed, in many cases to the point of bankruptcy.

During the First World War the number of ships in Robertson's ownership fell from 49 in 1914 to 27 in 1919, and with several including *Asteria* (1) and *Spinel* (1) still away on government service the tonnage available to the company had been halved. Given their depleted fleet, the Robertsons might have been expected to order heavily, but the temptation was largely resisted. *Malachite* (3) came from Dutch builders in 1920 – the four month delay between launch and delivery to Robertsons suggests she was one of many coasters commenced speculatively in the Netherlands and was bought after completion. The two British new buildings, *Essonite* (2) and *Kyanite* (3), were from a yard better known for warship construction, Yarrow and Co. Ltd. of Scotstoun, and were ordered by a Dublin company which had difficulty paying for them, and they were sold to Robertsons for £47,500 each. Nothing else was ordered until the shipbuilding boom was over, when four steamers came from Ailsa and Scotts in 1924 at prices ranging between £16,350 for *Turquoise* (2) and £22,500 for

The last steamer built for the company, *Pyrope* (2) of 1936. Her cruiser stern is just visible. *[Nigel Farrell collection]*

An exception to the relatively new ships bought in the years between the wars was *Nugget* (4), built in 1913 and added to the fleet in 1934. Despite her age she lasted well, and is seen here at Preston in June 1952. *[J. and M. Clarkson]*

Fluor (2) – under half the price paid for the *Essonite* (2) and *Kyanite* (3). Ailsa were determined to get the orders, and made every effort to quote an attractive price. There were to be only two further steamers built for Robertsons: *Diamond* (3) from Burntisland (the first time Robertsons are known to have placed an order outside the west of Scotland) in 1927 and, as a last gasp of steam, the *Pyrope* (2) from Bowling all of nine years later.[15] As a small concession to modernity, *Pyrope* had a cruiser stern.

The most apparent change since pre-war years was the number of secondhand steamers now entering the fleet, 19 compared with just nine newly built. All but one of the acquisitions were comparatively new post-war vessels, largely coming from owners who had overstretched themselves financially. In the case of *Morion* (2) and *Nugget* (3) the previous owners had gone bankrupt or were unable to keep up mortgage payments. Notable acquisitions were four from D.R. Llewellyn, Merrett and Price Ltd. of Cardiff in 1925 and no fewer than eight steamers from H. Harrison (Shipping) Ltd. of London and the associated Edward T. Lindley in 1929 and 1930. Interestingly, but undoubtedly no coincidence, the new buildings and acquisitions gave a broadly similar mix of sizes to the pre-war fleet with the majority falling into the 165 to 190-feet band. The smallest was the Dublin-sized *Morion* (2) at 142 feet, the largest the *Corundum* (2) and *Olivine* (3) of around 190 feet in length and the 207-foot *Flour* (2). Robertsons thus succeeded in obtaining a relatively modern fleet of steamers without excessive expenditure, greatly assisting the company's survival in the shipping depression that began in the early 1920s and persisted until the outbreak of the Second World War. Family tradition has it that few if any of the ships were laid up during the inter-war years, although they did not always trade at a profit. As with all ship owners in the period, Robertsons practised economies and cut costs, including wages. The financial figures in Appendix 3 tell their own story, with losses being recorded for all but one year from 1921 to 1934.

An acquisition in 1922 was to prove of lasting benefit to Robertsons: a large quarrying operation at Llanddulas on the North Wales coast which was a major supplier of limestone to the Clydeside steel industry. It had been operating since at least the early part of the nineteenth century, and had been developed to its present size and importance by members of the Kneeshaw, Lupton and Raynes families.[16] Robertsons registered the quarrying operations under the name Kneeshaw, Lupton and Co. Ltd. The quarries depended almost totally on ships to carry away its limestone, and the previous owners operated a small fleet of steamers until the last was sold in 1916. It was to become increasingly important to Robertsons as a way of employing their ships, and by 1952 was providing 25% of the fleet's work, as well as being a significant money earner in its own right. Indeed, in poor trading years it proved more profitable than shipping.

Patterns of trade: between the wars

As well as reminiscences about masters, Fred Donaldson also gave details of cargoes carried to and from the Thames by Robertson's steamers. Rails from Workington were a regular cargo, sometimes for the railways south of the Thames and unloaded at Angerstein's Wharf, but also for the underground lines being constructed in central London and unloaded at Church Hole Tier. Iron segments to line tube tunnels were also carried to this wharf. Rails made at Workington and destined for South Africa were delivered to London docks for transhipping to a Union-Castle ship. The long rails were often a problem to unload from a coaster with a bridge amidships. Other inward cargoes were stone from Newlyn, Penlee Quarry or Guernsey, soda ash from Burn Naze near Fleetwood to Clyde Wharf, and bitumen in drums

An important part of the Robertson story was the ownership from 1922 of the two Kneeshaw, Lupton limestone quarries near Llanddulas, North Wales. The photographs opposite show the smaller Penmaenhead Quarry. In the upper shot Robertson's *Sapphire* (4) is alongside the loading jetty prior to 1956. The lower photograph was taken in the early 1960s.

Penmaenhead Quarry closed in 1962, as its working face grew too close to the tunnel of the North Wales coast railway line, which can be seen curving behind the quarry in the upper photograph opposite. At one time, trains had to be stopped when there were blasting operations. The floor of the quarry was used for the A55 North Wales Expressway.

The photographs on this page show Kneeshaw, Lupton's other quarry and its jetty at Llanddulas. It was taken over with the fleet by Powell Duffryn and after a July 1984 merger with the Amey Roadstone Corporation became ARCPD North Western Division. The quarry was mothballed in 1997, its last ship being Stephenson Clarke's *Dunany* (1,785/1983) on 22nd March. The photograph above shows a steamer loading at the quarry prior to 1947. Note the signal arms on the jetty.

Other limestone quarries in the vicinity included Raynes Quarry, which has also been served by Robertson's and Stephenson Clarke's ships. *[Robertson archives]*

from Stanlow to Shellhaven on behalf of Shell. Following the First World War, *Tourmaline* (1) and *Felspar* were chartered at monthly rates of £5,000 and £4,500 respectively to bring former War Department lorries back from France for the company that owned Slough Trading Estate, and was selling the vehicles for commercial use.

Outward cargoes from the Thames and Medway to Scotland were commonly cement, scrap or on occasion in 1923 spent oxide from Beckton Gas Works to Irvine. The East Coast cement trade was lost to John Kelly of Belfast who were desperate to win it. Charles Bell was blamed for losing this business which could have been retained if he had not dug his heels in and refused to accept a small reduction in rates. However, Bell was responsible for Robertsons winning business from scrap metal dealer Michael Cohen. There were some pointed remarks about 'the Scot trading with the Jew' but the relationship was a cordial one, often transacted with no written contract. Cargoes of one thousand tons of scrap from the battleships HMS *Erin* and *Orion* being broken up by Cohen were carried from Queenborough to the Clyde for use by steel makers Colvilles Ltd.

Donaldson's testament provides evidence that Robertsons did not just fix their own steamers. He notes that Bell could usually pull 'something out of the bag' when extra tonnage was needed, and steamers he fixed over the years included the *Arclight* (650/1921) and *Raylight* (723/1921) of Ross and Marshall and *Calchfaen* (421/1893) of Kneeshaw, Lupton. *Lady Dorothy* (578/1916), *Lady Gertrude Cochrane* (530/1904) and *Lady Anstruther* (527/1922) of Nobel's Explosives were also employed, their owners probably welcoming back cargoes for the north after they had delivered gelignite from Irvine to the Thames.[17]

The motor ship era begins

It was apparent from the success of the Dutch coasting fleet that the future lay with motor vessels, yet British coaster owners seemed reluctant to follow the Dutch in investing in such ships. This has been excused on the grounds that the colliery owners who provided so many coal cargoes would have been distressed to find their suppliers running ships which did not burn coal. Another reason cited has been that Glasgow coaster owner John Paton had his fingers badly burned in a venture known as Coasting Motor Shipping Co. Ltd. Between 1912 and 1914 this company took delivery of 18 small motor coasters of several different designs, powered by a variety of oil engines. Unreliability of certain types of engine, but more so of the steam-trained engineers employed to tend them, doomed the little company. It was fortunate in being able to sell off several of its worst mistakes to the British and Russian governments, although not before some were lost as a direct result of failures of engine or engineer.[18] The lesson would not be lost on other owners, especially those in Glasgow who would have watched Paton's venture with interest. However, a factor in the reluctance of Robertsons to go into motor ships was the unavailability of diesel engines of the requisite power for ships of about 200 feet – considerably larger than the typical Dutch coaster of the time.

Amongst British owners the lead into motor coasters was eventually taken by Coast Lines Ltd. with the small *Fife Coast* (367/1933). Robertsons followed cautiously, although family recollections suggest John Robertson took a particular interest in the applications of diesel power to ships. The Robertsons' first motor ship was *Sapphire* (3), built by Ailsa in 1935 with a Swedish diesel and the then-innovative electric winches. The bridge was placed right aft – unusual for a coaster of her size – so that 90-foot rails could be loaded in her hold. After a period of evaluation, during which another steamer was built, in early 1937 came *Cameo* (3) from Harland and Wolff with one of their licence-built Burmeister & Wain-type oil engines. *Cameo* seems to have settled the matter of choice of machinery as after her no more steamers were ordered. In line with their company's tradition, Robertsons' orders for motor vessel were initially placed with more than one builder and for vessels of several sizes. *Spinel* (2) and her sister *Jacinth* (3) came from Henry Robb Ltd., Leith. Built in the Netherlands, before the Second World War put a stop to fleet replacement, were the sisters *Prase* (2) and *Cairngorm* (3) plus the larger *Jade* (1) and *Citrine* (4). The Dutch ships had diesel engines made by Koln-Deutz of Germany, and so successful was this manufacturer's machinery that it continued to be fitted to many new Robertson ships throughout the company's independent existence.

Peter Robertson, John's son, recalled the excitement of seeing the *Sapphire* (3) built:

'He [my father] would take my brother Ian and myself to the yard at weekends to see progress and we caught the sense of history in the making. When it was suggested that we might go to sea in her during the next summer holidays, we jumped at the chance. It proved a great learning experience for us teenagers as well as some of the crew, especially the engineers. The advantage of having a steady shaft speed over 24 hours became apparent as we overtook one steam coaster after another. I later had the pleasure of a visit to Rotterdam when the *Jade* was handed over and another trip around the British coast in her. I remember dear old Captain Campbell being very worried at being asked to skipper a motor ship

Spinel (2), Robertson's third motor ship, just after her launch by Henry Robb Ltd. at Leith. Note that the white line on her hull extends the entire length of the accommodation, which was not Robertson's practice. It was later shortened. *[Robertson archives]*

Jade (1) at the Ford jetty at Dagenham to discharge limestone for the only blast furnace in southern England. *[Robertson archives]*

built in Holland (was it going to be a Dutch barge?) but, after a few months, he was more than happy and that pleased my father.'

Despite a higher initial cost, the motor coaster had definite advantages over a steamer. The major one was increased cargo capacity for a given hull size, as the need for boilers was eliminated. Absence of coal bunkers also gave more cargo space as oil could be stored in any compartment from where it could be pumped. In a 1953 paper to the Institution of Engineers, James Cassels Robertson (known as Jim) compared figures for cargo capacity for a 1906-built steamer of 185 feet and a 1953-built motor coaster of 199 feet – the best size comparison he could find.[19] The steamer had a capacity of 32,400 cubic feet and the admittedly bigger motor ship, 68,190 cubic feet. The greater capacity was largely due to an increased proportion of the hull being available for cargo, and also to deeper hatches and a longer raised quarter deck.

The oil engine was also considerably more economical although the exact figures depended on the costs of oil and of coal, which fluctuated over time. Jim Robertson presented figures showing a steamer burning about 3,700 tons of coal over the two years 1951 and 1952 at a cost of coal and lubricants amounting to £12,600. A similar-sized motor coaster doing the same work burned just over 600 tons of oil at a cost, including lubricants, of £8,230. The lower consumption of the diesel engine gave it a larger operating range, a bunker capacity of 75 tons of oil offering an endurance of 12.5 days compared with just 4.83 days with the 70 tons of bunker coal carried by the steamer, a factor which Robertsons were to exploit in post-war years. The motor ship was also about 1.5 knots faster than the steamer. The diesel engine gave the possibility of reducing engine room personnel but oddly both the 1906 and 1953 vessels are quoted as requiring a crew of 17. The actual weights of the two ships were not significantly different, 585 tons for the steamer and 642 tons for the motor vessel. Given the larger size of the motor ship, the paper's authors reckon that it represented a saving of about 10% of steelwork due to some use of welding and more efficient use of steel.

New managers and a new war, 1939-1945

The two Robertson brothers running the company died within six months of each other in 1939, John McKellar Robertson on 17th March and William Francis Robertson on 6th October, at the comparatively early ages of 55 and 57, respectively. William F. Robertson had followed his father on to the Clyde Navigation Trust and was a member for 26 years and a one time chairman. He was also a member of the Clyde Pilotage Authority and held the chair at the time of his death. Other important committees included that of the Clyde Steamship Owners Association, the Glasgow Committee of Lloyd's Register, and Lloyd's Register's governing body, the General Committee. A rather fawning obituary maintained that he was 'as unassuming as he was brave' and that he was 'loved for qualities of friendship and fellowship'. John Robertson became a member of the Royal Naval Voluntary Reserve in 1910, had served in this body throughout the First World War being promoted to captain in 1918, and became Commanding Officer of its East Scotland Division in 1928. He served as aide-de-camp to King George V from 1930 to 1933 and probably because of this he was awarded an OBE in 1932. As well as the family shipping business he had interests in companies drilling for oil in Lake Maracaibo, Venezuela. Both the brothers had been enthusiastic yachtsmen, and had sufficient money to indulge their tastes in both sail and steam yachts.[20] William had continued his father's interest in the design of coastal ships, and in 1927 had worked with Sir Amos Ayre, of Burntisland Shipbuilding fame, on losses of vessels in the coal trade which resulted in publication by the Board of Trade of 'Instructions to surveyors for coal-carrying vessels.'

John Robertson's financial interest in the ships passed to the William Robertson side of the family in the early 1940s. On the outbreak of war William and Harriet's eldest son, William Francis Robertson (known as Frank), had left Trinity College, Cambridge where he was reading economics, to join the Royal Naval Volunteer Reserve. However, he was released from the Navy following the death of his father in October 1939 so that he could join the family business, now considered of national importance. Charles Bell was named in William F. Robertson's will as steamship manager, and following Robertson's death Bell's contribution and value was recognised by his being made a partner in May 1940. Although something of an oxymoron, William F. Robertson was the 'sole partner' when he died in 1939, so Bell was now nominally in control, despite having a financial share which was equivalent to only one sixteenth of the fleet's value, the rest being held in a trust fund for Robertson family members. Frank Robertson became a partner in November 1940.

An unfortunate result of the continuing ownership of the ships in the names of William Robertson's descendants rather than a limited company was that they were part of an estate and hence death duties were payable on the fleet, which was valued at £344,000. In late 1939 and early 1940 seven ships had to be sold to pay these duties. Sales began with *Kyanite* (3) at the end of October, with *Diamond* (3) and *Morion* (2) going in November, and *Malachite* (3), *Essonite* (2) and *Sagenite* in December, and concluding with the *Nephrite* (2) to Stephenson Clarke in 1940.

At one time or another during the Second World War almost all of the Robertson fleet was under government direction and, apart from those sold or lost in 1939 and 1940, the only vessels to escape requisition were the steamers *Beryl* (2), *Olivine* (4) which was lost in 1941, *Pearl* (4), *Pyrope* (2), *Sard* (2) and *Turquoise* (2). Indeed, the Ministry of War Transport also employed one of Robertson's principals: Frank Robertson worked for the Coasting and Short Sea Division. As in the First World War, some Robertson ships were allocated to duties such as store and ammunition carriers whilst others - although under the control of the Ministry of War Transport - continued carrying their usual commercial cargoes around the coasts of Britain under perhaps the most continuously hazardous conditions then existing anywhere in the world. Requisitions are listed in Table 4. It is notable that the most common employment of Robertson's ships in the First World War, as naval colliers, had declined dramatically, and only *Bronzite* and *Felspar* were so employed during the Second World War. Several of the motor vessels were employed as cased petrol carriers to serve the needs of Army motor transport. During her requisition by the government between August 1940 and August 1942, *Emerald* (2) was converted into a dummy corvette. She then reverted to cargo carrying, but became Robertson's last casualty of the war in January 1944.

The Norwegian campaign and the evacuation of the Allied forces from Dunkirk in 1940 involved several Robertson ships. The *Cameo* (3) played a part in rescuing some men of the encircled Highland Division at St Valery-en-Caux, for which operation her master, Captain Stephen Masson, and his chief officer each received the Distinguished Service Cross. The *Spinel* (2) was trapped in dock in Dunkirk during the same campaign, and on orders from the military authorities was abandoned by her crew. She turned up in Jersey in May 1945 having been repaired by the Germans and operated to the Channel Isles by them (and for a short period by a local crew) throughout hostilities with little damage except for a few small holes caused by bullets from a British aircraft.[21] Initially laid up, for over a year from August 1945 she was managed as *Empire Spinel* for the British government, who had paid war loss insurance on her. In September 1946 she was bought back by Robertsons. Other ships involved in evacuations in the summer of 1940 included *Coral* (2) at Jersey, *Emerald* (2) at Le Havre, *Felspar* at both Cherbourg and Jersey, *Jade* (1) at St. Valery, and *Obsidian* (3) at Brest.

As during the First World War, the British government gave Robertsons a number of ships to manage, although this time they were a mixture of steam and motor vessels more typical of the company's own fleet. They included ships built for the government and one Danish

Emerald (2) had an eventful but ultimately tragic war. *[Robertson archives]*

and one Dutch vessel which came under British control when their owners' countries were invaded. At the end of the war two German ships which had been ceded to the United Kingdom were allocated to the company to manage. *Empire Conclyde* ran between Leith and London for the London and Edinburgh Shipping Company but was claimed by the USSR in February 1946. From January 1946 *Empire Congham* was laid up in the Gareloch until 7th August when she sailed from Greenock to be returned to Germany.

During the first four years of the war, and in spite of its many hazards, the only total loss which could definitely be attributed to hostilities was the managed Danish coaster *Dagmar*, bombed and sunk off Bournemouth in June 1941 with the loss of three lives. However, the company's owned fleet was not immune from losses as in April 1940 the *Girasol* (2) sank after a collision with a Harrison Line ship off the North Foreland, in June 1940 *Olivine* (4) disappeared with all hands in the Irish Sea and in December 1940 the *Agate* (2) ran aground in fog at Cairns Point, Islay. Wartime conditions may have contributed to all three casualties, as mines, enemy aircraft and the extinguishing of many lighthouses all added to the dangers of navigating round the coast. Later, in January 1944, *Emerald* (2) was torpedoed and sunk by a German motor torpedo boat south east of Beachy Head with heavy loss of life.

No fewer than 17 of the company's ships were involved in Operation Neptune and ran between British ports and the beachheads from D-day onwards: *Asteria* (2), *Cairngorm* (3), *Cameo* (3), *Coral* (2), *Corundum* (2), *Citrine* (4), *Felspar*, *Fluor* (2), *Gem* (4), *Jade* (1), *Jargoon* (2), *Nugget* (4), *Obsidian* (3), *Pebble* (2), *Prase* (2), *Sphene* (3) and *Topaz* (6). Taking part in these operations *Coral* (2) was torpedoed off the Isle of Wight in August 1944 with the loss of eight lives. Apart from this admittedly tragic loss, damage to the Robertson ships in Operation Neptune was relatively light. However, there were some extraordinary escapes, as when the *Citrine* (4) sat on a mine on a Normandy beach. At low water her master Captain William McKenzie inspected the damage and discovered

Table 4: Government service of Robertson owned and managed ships during the Second World War

Robertson-owned ships are listed by date of first requisition, followed by the managed ships for which details are given only for their period under Robertson's management. *Indicates lost whilst on government service.

Ship	Type of service	From	To
Axinite (2)	Armament Stores Carrier	27.8.1939	23.11.1945
	Coasting and Short Sea Service	24.11.1945	28.2.1946
Corundum (2)	Armament Stores Carrier	29.8.1939	8.11.1939
	Coasting and Short Sea Service	12.6.1941	18.4.1944
	Store Ship (Military)	19.4.1944	6.6.1945
	Coasting and Short Sea Service	7.6.1945	22.10.1945
Jade (1)	Cased Petrol Ship	4.9.1939	26.6.1940
	Store Ship (Military)	27.6.1940	18.8.1940
	Cased Petrol Ship	19.8.1940	5.10.1942
	Cased Petrol Ship	6.10.1942	3.1944
	Commercial	3.1944	25.4.1944
	Cased Petrol Ship	26.4.1944	3.6.1945
	Coasting and Short Sea Service	4.6.1945	23.11.1945
Spinel (2)	Cased Petrol Ship	6.9.1939	27.5.1940*
Jacinth (3)	Armament Stores Issuing Ship	6.9.1939	12.9.1939
	Armament Stores Issuing Ship	24.4.1940	15.8.1944
Cameo (3)	Cased Petrol Ship	7.9.1939	18.2.1940
	Naval Store Carrier	19.2.1940	13.3.1940
	Cased Petrol Ship and Store Ship (Military)	14.3.1940	8.8.1940
	Cased Petrol Ship	22.4.1944	19.8.1945
	Coasting and Short Sea Service	20.8.1945	7.2.1946
Jargoon (2)	Armament Stores Carrier	27.9.1939	13.11.1939
	Store Ship (Military)	21.4.1944	25.6.1945
	Coasting and Short Sea Service	26.6.1945	31.8.1945
Cairngorm (3)	Cased Petrol Ship	11.9.1939	16.10.1939
	Cased Petrol Ship	22.4.1944	28.4.1945
	Coasting and Short Sea Service	29.4.1945	19.7.1945
Felspar	Ammunition Ship	21.5.1940	4.7.1940
	Collier (Military)	5.7.1940	26.5.1940
	Collier (Military)	27.5.1944	3.10.1945
	Coasting and Short Sea Service	4.10.1945	22.5.1946
Obsidian (3)	Store Ship (Military)	11.6.1940	24.6.1940
	Store Ship (Military)	21.4.1944	26.6.1945
	Coasting and Short Sea Service	27.6.1945	5.11.1945
Emerald (2)	Miscellaneous Naval Service	9.8.1940	7.8.1942
	Coasting and Short Sea Service	28.12.1943	31.1.1944*
Bronzite	Collier (Military)	19.12.1941	5.5.1942
	Naval Store Carrier	24.3.1943	16.5.1943
	Store Ship (Military)	17.5.1943	31.5.1943
Fluor (2)	Coasting and Short Sea Service	29.11.1943	28.12.1943
	Store Ship (Military)	23.4.1944	2.8.1945
	Coasting and Short Sea Service	3.8.1945	9.1945
	Coasting and Short Sea Service	9.1945	1.11.1945
Citrine (4)	Miscellaneous Naval Service	28.3.1944	10.4.1944
	Coasting and Short Sea Service	11.4.1944	18.4.1944
	Cased Petrol Ship	19.4.1944	12.10.1944
Gem (4)	Store Ship (Military)	19.4.1944	1.5.1945
	Coasting and Short Sea Service	2.5.1945	26.7.1945
Topaz (6)	Store Ship (Military)	19.4.1944	15.1.1945
	Coasting and Short Sea Service	16.1.1945	22.2.1945
Asteria (2)	Store Ship (Military)	21.4.1944	8.5.1945
	Coasting and Short Sea Service	9.5.1945	18.8.1945

Sphene (3)	Store Ship (Military)	22.4.1944	6.8.1945
	Coasting and Short Sea Service	7.8.1945	19.11.1945
Coral (2)	Store Ship (Military)	23.4.1944	20.8.1944*
Pebble (2)	Store Ship (Military)	23.4.1944	17.5.1945
	Coasting and Short Sea Service	18.5.1945	17.8.1945
Prase (2)	Cased Petrol Ship	26.4.1944	5.1.1945
	Coasting and Short Sea Service	6.1.1945	9.2.1945
Nugget (4)	Store Ship (Military)	27.4.1944	9.1.1945
	Coasting and Short Sea Service	10.1.1945	4.4.1945
Dagmar	Coasting and Short Sea Service	4.5.1940	9.6.1940
	Store Ship (Military)	10.6.1940	19.6.1940
	Coasting and Short Sea Service	220.6.1940	9.6.1941*
Alcyone	Time chartered	29.5.1940	21.7.1944
	Time chartered on net basis (special)	22.7.1944	2.3.1945
	Time chartered and Coasting and Short Sea Service	2.3.1945	15.7.1945
Empire Cape	Coasting and Short Sea Service	10.7.1941	4.1944
Cataraqui Park	Coasting and Short Sea Service	30.6.1944	2.1.1946
Empire Fanal	Store Ship (Military)	17.11.1944	17.12.1944
Empire Dorrit	Coasting and Short Sea Service	6.12.1944	22.4.1945
	Store Ship (Military)	23.4.1945	14.8.1945
	Coasting and Short Sea Service	15.8.1945	27.9.1945
Empire Fang	Coasting and Short Sea Service	4.1.1945	24.7.1946
Empire Congham	Coasting and Short Sea Service	23.7.1945	21.8.1946
	Coasting and Short Sea Service	18.12.1944	1.8.1946
Empire Spinel	Coasting and Short Sea Service	3.8.1945	27.9.1946
Empire Conclyde	Coasting and Short Sea Service	19.11.1945	15.2.1946

that the lower portion of the stern frame had been blown away, and the rudder stock bent so that the rudder itself was at an angle of some 60 degrees to the vertical. He was in some doubt as to the best course to follow, when a helpful United States Army officer came along and, on hearing of the situation, had the rudder pushed back into position with a bulldozer. At the next high tide *Citrine* floated off and proceeded unaided to the Tyne where she was dry docked for repairs.

As the war in Europe drew towards its close and the Allied armies advanced along the Channel coast, the ships followed them. *Jargoon* (2) is said to have been the first merchant ship to enter the port of Antwerp after its liberation, her master Captain A.H. Fletcher receiving the Croix-de-Guerre from the Belgian King for his work during this period.

Recovery, reorganisation and renewal

When war ended, James Cassels Robertson (known as Jim), who had been serving as a lieutenant in the Royal Naval Volunteer Reserve, returned to Glasgow to join his brother Frank Robertson in the office at 45 West Nile Street. A considerable measure of governmental control was still being exercised over coastal shipping, but slowly the pre-war patterns of trade were re-established and conditions returned to normal, apart from the ever-present risk of mines. The ships which had been requisitioned were gradually returned to their owners and put back into peacetime condition. Captain J.A. Simpson who joined the *Cameo* (3) as mate in July 1945 recalled that: 'The job now was to try and get the ship back to peace-time condition. We knocked off all the cement blocks that had been protecting the wheelhouse and got it scraped and varnished, painted over all the battleship grey and generally smartened her up to look like a Robertsons' coaster again'.[22]

The crews of Robertson vessels about this time were mainly from the West Highlands or from around Carnlough in County Antrim. Ian Walker's memories of his time in these coasters were that he was usually tired, hungry and hard up. He recalls that the ships, like those of other coastal ship owners, were run on a tight budget. They stored up every six months, usually after an overhaul, and then half way to the next dry docking. In the steamers the crew lived in damp, cramped quarters in the forecastle, seemingly in endless bad weather. At times they slept on fiddley gratings in the boiler room when the weather was too bad for them to get forward. They were paid for a 112-hour fortnight, but had to buy all their own food. Ian recalls meeting many ex-Robertson men later in life, especially when he was a master with Sealink.

For almost a century the ships had been registered in the ownership of individuals who owned 64th shares, first William Robertson, and later his sons and senior employee Charles Bell and, until 1949, continued to trade under the founder's name as William Robertson. This gave problems, not least that the individual shareholders had to be consulted before a vessel could be sold, and financing new and increasingly expensive ships on the 64th system meant that individual shares became enormously expensive. Reorganisation was long overdue, as few if any other large fleets persisted with this ownership system, which dated from the days of sailing ships. On 16th April 1949 a private limited company entitled William Robertson Shipowners Ltd. was registered. Its share capital was £239,000, most of which was held in a trust fund on behalf of the Robertson family, with grandsons Jim and Frank Robertson each holding shares of nominal value £37,500. Shares valued £15,200 were given to Alexander Gibb, a long serving employee who had replaced Charles Bell as chartering clerk and the key man in the Glasgow office. Gibb had been made a partner in 1948. On 15th May 1949 all the ships were transferred to William Robertson Shipowners Ltd. A total of 23 ships were involved, 15 of which were steamers all but one of which were over ten years old.

A further reorganization saw the formation of Gem Line Ltd. in 1952 to which ownership of the ships was transferred. No reason for this change has been found in company records, but a possibility is that Gem Line Ltd. was formed as an umbrella company to own ships and other assets. The 1949 company, William Robertson Shipowners Ltd., now became a wholly owned subsidiary of Gem Line Ltd. and continued as managers of the fleet. Also in 1952, the Llanddulas quarrying operation which was bought by Robertsons in 1922, Kneeshaw, Lupton and Co. Ltd., became a wholly owned subsidiary of Gem Line Ltd. A further unexplained change was made on 23rd December 1957 when William Robertson Shipowners Ltd. was renamed Gem Line Ltd. Presumably, the 1952 Gem Line Ltd. was wound up

Seen in the Bristol Channel, *Olivine* (5) set a distinctive style for Robertson's ships, with her conical funnel. This photograph shows that at some time during her 24-year career with the company her hatch coamings were heightened. *[J. and M. Clarkson]*

just prior to this change. The year 1952 was a significant one for the company in another way, marking the centenary of William Robertson beginning ship owning. To mark the occasion gifts were presented to the office staff and to many of the senior seagoing officers and ratings.

Renewal of the fleet was a priority, and Robertsons knew it. A rather downbeat review of the business in 1954 concluded that 'ships were largely inadequate for anything more than short term requirements'. A considerable building programme had been undertaken, but with a fleet whose average age was 17 years, it was only a half-way house, and the company had years of consolidation ahead. However, it was conceded that high allowances for depreciation had helped the building programme.

Four new motor ships had been built between 1949 and 1953: *Sapphire* (4) by Grangemouth Dockyard in 1949 and *Emerald* (3) in 1952; *Olivine* (5) in 1951, *Gem* (5) in 1952, and *Pearl* (5) in 1953 by Ailsa at Troon. *Olivine* (5) was the first ship with the distinctive conical funnel which was to characterize the next ten ships built for Robertsons, eight by Ailsa and one each at Grangemouth and at Groningen.

Although there were significant differences in the sizes of these ships, and of their hull design and cargo gear, their funnels made them instantly recognisable as Robertson vessels. The persistence of the raised quarter deck design, even in *Olivine* and successors with bridge aft, is hard to explain, especially as in his 1953 paper Jim Robertson expressed the opinion that it was an obsolete feature. In steamers with engines aft, a raised quarter deck gave the necessary height for a triple-expansion engine, and the quarter deck was extended as far forward as the bridge to improve capacity. It also helped the vessel to trim evenly when loaded by placing proportionately more of the cargo aft of amidships. In a diesel vessel, neither of these considerations applied, as the engine was lower in height and occupied less space so that the after hold extended further aft, obviating problems of trim. Robertson felt the persistence of the raised quarter deck to 'result merely from custom or tradition', and in the discussion of his paper a speaker made the point that the break in the upper deck on a raised quarter deck vessel made it inherently weaker than one with a straight deck. However, a raised quarter deck remained a feature of the company's new buildings until the *Amber* (2) of 1956 and reappeared with the *Brilliant* (2) of 1958. A welcome feature of the new ships was the greatly improved accommodation, especially that for the seamen, who were provided with one- or two-berth

Amber (2) on trials in 1956. *[Robertson archives]*

Bought in 1929 for a modest £12,000, *Asteria* (2) remained in the fleet until 1954 when a grounding on Drogheda Bar left her fit only for scrap. *[Robertson archives]*

cabins, a mess and a recreation room. A comparison of a 1906 steamer and the *Pearl* (5) of 1953 showed that the area devoted to crew accommodation had increased from 1,230 to 2,190 square feet.

During the early 1950s older steamers including the *Asteria* (2), *Pebble* (2), *Pearl* (4) and *Nugget* (4) were scrapped and others sold. Nevertheless, secondhand steamers were still being added to the fleet, the last being *Girasol* (3), acquired in 1950. The problem of replacing vessels when costs were increasing prompted a review of the company's financial position in 1954. It concluded that the useful life of a vessel was no more than 30 years - a figure that may have been sensible in the 1890s but seems optimistic in the 1950s - but that each vessel had to undergo a complete refit after 16 years. The company aimed at keeping the average age of its fleet at not more than 15 years and, so the report claimed, this would necessitate an annual appropriation towards replacement costs of about £75,000.

The remaining three steamers were sold in 1958, the last being *Girasol* (3) which went to Italian owners for further trading. The company continued to invest in new and larger motor ships. During the 1960s *Gem* (5) was lengthened and renamed *Cameo* (4), and four further ships were added to the fleet: *Topaz* (7), *Tourmaline* (3), and *Sapphire* (5) from Ailsa and *Gem* (6) from Groningen. The 1969 *Gem* was the last ship to be built for the company during its independent existence. She cost £347,342 and at 297 feet overall became the largest in the fleet.

Attempts were made to diversify the company's activities. In 1961, the Robertson Group, as it had become

The sixth *Gem* of 1969. As proudly recounted by George Moore, the company's Superintendent Engineer: 'The engine room of the latest *Gem* is designed to be unmanned for 16 hours a day ... the main engine is controlled from the bridge and the ship is fitted with an automatic pilot'.[23] *[Paul Boot/J. and M. Clarkson collection]*

Family occasions: launches of the motor ships often involved Robertson ladies. Above: Mrs Joan Robertson (wife of Jim Robertson) launches the *Sapphire* (4) at Grangemouth on 12th May 1949, watched by the yard manager. Right: Mrs Harriet Robertson, widow of William F. Robertson (1882-1939), launches the *Gem* (5) at Troon on 26th June 1952.

At Troon on 4th December 1951 is the launch party for *Olivine* (5) (middle left). The ship is sent on its way by Elizabeth Robertson, wife of Frank Robertson (above).
A younger generation takes its turn as Frank's daughter Caryl Robertson launches *Tourmaline* (3) on 18th September 1962 (left and with grandmother and other family members below). *[All: Robertson archives]*

known, had formed the Ailsa Craig Quarrying Co. Ltd. to extract Ailsa Blue Hone stone for curling stone manufacture with advice from its subsidiary Robertson Research (see page 33). In 1964 the Robertson Group acquired the Scottish Curling Stone Company Ltd. to refine the stones using precision engineering equipment. This venture was short lived because cheaper, high-quality stones became available from Canada. Other mineral interests included holdings in the Rodel Quarry in Harris, in Assynt Minerals and rights to prospect in the Gairloch and Conon estates in western Scotland.

Patterns of trade: post-Second World War

Many of the company's surviving freight books for the period from the Second World War to 1960 have been donated to Strathclyde University Archives. These books have been sampled to give an impression of the company's business over this period.

In 1946 the ships made just over 1,000 voyages on Robertson's account, in addition to which five ships spent varying periods on time charter. Coal totally predominated, making up 69% of cargoes, with Llanddulas limestone second at 14%, divided between voyages to the Clyde and the Thames. Next came cement at 4%; phosphate, granite, metals and various foodstuffs (mainly grains) at around 2% each; whilst the number of voyages with rails, scrap, ores, fertilisers, saltcake, or government stores were all in single figures. Time charters included the *Beryl* (2) running for Burns and Laird from January to June and again for part of December, with *Pearl* (4) running for the same company in January; *Cameo* (3) running for Clyde Shipping and Coast Lines for much of the year; and *Empire Fanal* running between Manchester and Belfast for the Belfast, Mersey and Manchester company.

Twelve years later, during the period January to March 1958, the fleet made 235 loaded voyages, which taken over the whole year is equivalent to about 6% fewer than were made in 1946, although there were more relatively long voyages. The most frequent cargo was again coal, now making up 53% of all loaded voyages. The majority of these, 39% of the total number of voyages, were from ports around the Irish Sea, with the remaining cargoes loaded at ports on the east coast of the UK usually for the south coast of England or for Northern Ireland and from Antwerp or Rotterdam for south coast ports. Limestone from Llanddulas was again the second most frequent cargo, accounting for 20% of loaded voyages. In declining order, the other major cargoes were stone (mostly granite from Creetown to Glasgow); cement either from Magheramorne to Scottish ports or occasionally London to Irish Sea ports; basic slag from Middlesbrough to the south coast; steel from Cumbrian ports; general cargo; grain and soda ash. Time on charter to liner companies was considerably reduced compared with 1946, and mainly comprised single voyages, for instance *Pearl* (4) between Antwerp and Liverpool for British and Continental; *Fluor* (2), *Olivine* (5) and *Jade* (1) from Antwerp and Ghent to London or Southampton for General Steam; *Turquoise* (3) from Belfast to the south coast for Dundee, Perth and London. A notable voyage made by *Cairngorm* (3) was from Rotterdam to Troon with the main engine for the new *Amethyst* (4) which had been built by Klockner-Humboldt-Deutz A.G. in West Germany. A trend for making longer voyages is apparent, with occasional voyages to Odda with limestone, a number with timber from the Baltic and (a sign of things to come) with Polish coal, phosphates from Morocco, ore from Spain and timber from Archangel. The honour of making the longest voyage fell to *Gem* (5) - not the largest in the fleet - which loaded pitch from the North Thames Gas Board's works at Beckton for Baie Comeau on the St. Lawrence, returning with pit props from South Nelson in New Brunswick to Acton Grange on the Manchester Ship Canal.

The ships were fully employed in these years, and on occasion 'outside' ships had to be chartered. For instance, in 1945 *Runnelstone* (869/1923) made a voyage carrying cement from London to Glasgow, Gardner's *Saint Oran* (253/1923) sailed from Creetown to Glasgow, and Monks' *Rockville* (481/1922) did some salvage work for the Ministry of Supply on Robertsons' account. The Ellerman Wilson steamer *Dynamo* (870/1926) was chartered to fulfil commitments to carry coal and limestone after *Cameo* (3) was wrecked on Arklow Bank in September 1950. The steamer *Girasol* (3), bought in November 1950, was a stop-gap replacement for *Cameo* (3), allowing the charter of *Dynamo* to be terminated in January 1951.

Coal was carried to Dublin and elsewhere in the Irish Republic for the power stations of the Electricity Supply Board, but in 1954 the contract was lost to Irish Shipping Ltd.

Something of a distress purchase, the 17-year old *Girasol* (3) was acquired in 1950 to fulfil commitments after the loss of the *Cameo* (3). The last steamer bought by Robertsons is seen at Ayr on 15th June 1957. Sold less than a year later, *Girasol* found an Italian buyer who kept her until 1971. *[J. and M. Clarkson]*

as new stations were opened which could take ships beyond the size range of those in the Robertson fleet. Limestone from the quarries of Kneeshaw, Lupton and Co. Ltd. remained a cornerstone of the company's business, producing over 200,000 tons of cargo annually, equivalent to 25% of the fleet's cargo capacity. Limestone continued to be shipped to the Clyde and also to the Thames, where customers included the Lafarge Aluminium Cement Co. Ltd. at Thurrock and the Ford Motor Company at Dagenham. Ships unloading limestone in the Thames would often load cement from there back to the west coast. Quarrying clearly benefited from an alliance with a firm of ship owners: several similar quarries just as dependant on shipping fell into decline because they remained independent.

Some new trades were developed in the post-war years. Between 1951 and 1953 the company used the steamer *Tourmaline* (2) in experiments on the Nigerian coast in conjunction with Polpen Shipping Co. Ltd. The new motor ship *Olivine* (5) made voyages to south Spain and North Africa. During the early 1950s a substantial tonnage of limestone was shipped to Northern Ireland for British Oxygen. This organisation had a similar chemical plant in western Norway and a trial cargo of stone was shipped there in 1956. The experiment went well and a new trade from North Wales began, initially to Northern Ireland and later to Odda in Norway. The trade to Norway reinforced an existing association with local owner Thor Thoresen. In the early 1950s, Robertson ships including *Olivine* (5) were loading at Manchester or Ellesmere Port for this Oslo owner's regular service. When these ships began trading to Odda with limestone, they would when possible load on a Thoresen berth on their way back to the U.K. Robertsons invested in the A/S Thor Thoresen Linje, which ran the steamer *Skotfoss* (1,449/1948), and in the British subsidiary Thor Thoresen Line Ltd. based in Manchester, which acted as ships' agents, cargo forwarders and haulage contractors.

Some years ago, Captain Ian Walker recalled his service in the motor ship *Prase* (2) and the steamer *Topaz* (6) between 1948 and 1951. The former carried coal and limestone, with at least one voyage with salt from Runcorn to Glasgow. *Topaz* had more varied cargoes, including domestic and industrial coal, phosphate, flour, barley, cattle

Olivine (5) discharges limestone at Odda. *[Robertson archives]*

cake, cement, briquettes and, on one unique occasion, lard loaded overside from Anchor Lines' *Egidia* (9,952/1945) at Glasgow and consigned to Bristol. Late in 1959 he was mate on the motor ship *Gem* (5) shortly before she was lengthened. She was on foreign-going articles, and Ian joined her in Hull after she had bought a timber cargo from Duluth in the Great Lakes, no mean voyage in winter for a ship of just 1,600 tons. She then carried the usual Robertson cargoes of coal and limestone, plus briquettes from Norway to the River Foyle.

Tables 5 and 6 list the voyages made by *Spinel* (2) in 1946 and in 1958 respectively and give an interesting indication of how trading patterns had begun to change over this post-war period. In 1958 proportionately more voyages were made from the North Wales quarries than in 1946, presumably because fewer other cargoes were available.

In post-war years Robertsons' motor ships traded regularly to the Mediterranean. Here *Amethyst* (4) loads phosphate at Casablanca. *[Robertson archives]*

Table 5: Voyages by *Spinel* in 1946

After being recovered in the Channel Islands during May 1945, *Spinel* (2) was taken over by the Ministry of War Transport and placed under the management of William Robertson. She spent 12 months laid up or under repair in London, and was not returned to service until May 1946, initially as *Empire Spinel*. Robertsons reacquired her in September, although this seems to have made little difference to her voyage pattern as Robertsons had been running her in their trades since May.

* indicates Coast Lines charter

Sailed	From	To	Cargo
12th May	London	Mostyn	cement
- May	Mostyn	Manchester	-
May: two voyages Manchester-Belfast with general.*			
4th June	Liverpool	Ardrossan	-
5th June	Ardrossan	Dublin	coke
8th June	Dublin	Irwell	-
11th June	Irwell	Rouen	coal
17th June	Rouen	Newlyn	-
20th June	Newlyn	London	granite
27th June	London	Mostyn	cement
2nd July	Mostyn	Birkenhead	-
4th July	Birkenhead	Londonderry	phosphate
9th July	Londonderry	Liverpool	-
22nd July	Liverpool	Sligo	general*
- July	Sligo	Clyde	for repairs
28th September	Port Glasgow	Ardrossan	-
28th September	Ardrossan	Dublin	coke
1st October	Dublin	Waterford	wheat
4th October	Waterford	Trevor	-
5th October	Trevor	Bristol	setts, granite
10th October	Bristol	Barry	-
11th October	Barry	London	coal
18th October	London	Belfast	cement
21st October	Belfast	Llanddulas	-
22nd October	Llanddulas	London	limestone
29th October	London	Glasgow	cement
6th November	Glasgow	Liverpool	coal
10th November	Liverpool	Trevor	-
11th November	Trevor	London	setts, granite
19th November	London	Mostyn	cement
29th November	Mostyn	Llanddulas	-
30th November	Llanddulas	London	limestone
5th December	London	Belfast	pig iron
- December	Belfast	Glasgow	-
12th December	Glasgow	Ayr	-
13th December	Ayr	Liverpool	coal
18th December	Liverpool	Glasgow	maize
21st December	Glasgow	Troon	for repairs
31st December	Troon	Trevor	-

Table 6: Voyages by Spinel in 1958

Sailing dates were not recorded for ballast voyages, and these are not listed below.

Sailed	From	To	Cargo
30th December	Garston	Dublin	804t coal
6th January	Garston	Dublin	831t coal
11th January	Llanddulas	London	830t limestone
21st January	Goole	Hayle	800t coal
1st February	London	Douglas	692t cement
7th February	Llanddulas	Glasgow	820t limestone
- February	Raynes Quarry	Glasgow	826t limestone
18th February	Whitehaven	Belfast	823t coal
21st February	Partington	Dundalk	767t coal
3rd March	Garston	Kingstown	819t coal
6th March	Ayr	Londonderry	819t coal
11th March	Fleetwood	Glasgow	800t soda ash
14th March	Raynes Quarry	Glasgow	814t limestone
19th March	Liverpool	Douglas	626t coal
24th March	Partington	Dundalk	773t coal
28th March	Llanddulas	Dagenham	824t limestone
2nd April	London	Douglas	590t cement
9th April	Llanddulas	Ardrossan	842t limestone
12th April	Ayr	Barrow	656t coal
17th April	Partington	Kingstown	821t coal
20th April	Llanddulas	Glasgow	828t limestone
23rd April	Llanddulas	Ardrossan	862t limestone
26th April	Ayr	Stornoway	702t coal
2nd May	Garston	Dublin	814t coal
7th May	Llanddulas	Glasgow	845t limestone
10th May	Llanddulas	Ardrossan	877t limestone
13th May	Ayr	Barrow	692t coal
17th May	Llanddulas	Glasgow	861t limestone
27th May	Barry	Workington	840t coal
29th May	Workington	Cardiff	644t steel billets
4th June	Llanddulas	Glasgow	865t limestone
6th June	Trevor and Penmaenmawr	Cardiff	860t granite
10th June	Swansea	Rouen	844t coal
16th June	Rouen	Birkenhead	735t wheat
21st June	Raynes Quarry	Glasgow	844t limestone
25th June	Liverpool	Douglas	611t coal
30th June	Cardiff	Honfleur	837t coal
8th July	Treport	Glasgow	poplar logs
31st July	Liverpool	Douglas	629t coal
5th August	Liverpool	Douglas	616t coal
8th August	Raynes Quarry	Glasgow	822t limestone
13th August	Liverpool	Douglas	608t coal
17th August	Llanddulas	Ardrossan	852t limestone
19th August	Raynes Quarry	Glasgow	818t limestone
23rd August	Partington	Dundalk	691t coal
27th August	Penmaenmawr	Liverpool	631t granite
30th August	Liverpool	Douglas	617t coal
3rd September	Llanddulas	Ardrossan	867t limestone
6th September	Troon	Stornoway	611t coal
11th September	Liverpool	Douglas	614t coal
15th September	Liverpool	Douglas	609t coal
18th September	Llanddulas	Dagenham	867t limestone
25th September	London	Douglas	609t cement
2nd October	Liverpool	Douglas	625t coal
6th October	Ayr	Barrow	541t coal
10th October	Cardiff	Rouen	832t coal
15th October	Rouen	Leith	799t wheat
22nd October	Blyth	Bangor	814t coal
30th October	Cardiff	Rouen	832t coal
6th November	Swansea	Amsterdam	819t coal
15th November	Rotterdam	Sharpness	813t grain
20th November	Swansea	Antwerp	817t coal
26th November	Antwerp	Ellesmere Port	539t phosphate

The motor ship *Spinel* (2) post-war but before fitting an extra mast forward in the 1950s. Cargo books from 1958 show that on a good day she could lift a maximum of 877 tons of limestone and a slightly smaller tonnage of coal. *[Roy Fenton collection]*

3rd December	Ayr	Barrow	551t coal
11th December	Manchester	Warrenpoint	liner board
15th December	Liverpool	Douglas	811t coal
22nd December	Swansea	Antwerp	809t coal

Rather anachronistically, the freight books list 'Kingstown' rather than Dun Loaghaire. Raynes Quarry was at Llysfaen, North Wales and was operated by Imperial Chemical Industries Ltd.

End of independence

A report compiled by Frank Robertson in the 1960s lamented that this was a challenging time. It noted that the coastal trades were continuing to decline and that many small companies similar to Robertsons had disappeared. A report on British shipping by a committee under Lord Rochdale is quoted as stressing that many companies were too small and fragmented for effective management. The rise of containerisation was also mentioned as a factor, although this affected general cargoes which Robertson's ships rarely carried. More pertinent was a recognition of a preference amongst shippers for larger vessels which could carry economically-viable consignments to purpose-built terminals specialising in particular cargoes. The report also noted that taxation on small, private companies was unfavourable. Mentioning factors which were not unique to Robertsons, and some which were largely irrelevant, suggests that the report writer had made up his mind that the family should sell out, and was looking for reasons to convince his fellow shareholders. He concluded that the company had to reconsider its strategy: the cost of building new ships was increasing and to continue in business would have required heavy borrowing to fund larger ships. The option of raising additional capital by floating the company on the Stock Exchange had been considered, but it was felt that the shares were not sufficiently attractive to outside investors.

The favoured strategy was to merge the shipping and quarrying interests with a bigger group of companies and accordingly negotiations began with Powell Duffryn Ltd., which owned Stephenson Clarke Shipping Ltd. On 14th October 1970 an offer from Powell Duffryn Ltd. was accepted which gave Robertsons £500,000 in Powell Duffryn shares and £935,000 in cash.[24] The take over involved the assets of Gem Line Ltd., including its subsidiary companies, William Robertson Shipowners Ltd., the quarries of Kneeshaw, Lupton and Co. Ltd. (with 145 employees at Llanddulas), as well as an 80% stake in the Norwegian Thor Thoresen Linje and a 40% stake in Skibs A/S Thor Thoresens Linje.[25] Not included in the sale were other enterprises including Robertson Research and interests in curling stone manufacture. Under Powell Duffryn, the interests of Gem Line Ltd. were amalgamated into one holding company entitled William Robertson Shipowners Ltd. which became a direct operating subsidiary of Powell Duffryn and to which the ownership of the coasters was transferred. At the time of the sale 11 ships were operated, and 140 people were employed at sea with a further 23 office staff in Glasgow. The management of the shipping company initially remained unchanged under Frank and Jim Robertson. Other directors included C.N. Ross (also a director of Kneeshaw, Lupton), R.M. Barge, and G. Jones. The company continued to operate from 45 West Nile Street.

The first few years after the takeover saw the acquisition of two further ships: *Cairngorm* (4) built in Germany in 1973 and *Jade* (2) bought from Norwegian owners in 1974. In 1971 Robertsons took over management of *Kylebank*, which was formally transferred to their ownership in 1975 and renamed *Turquoise* (4); she was the last of 146 sail, steam and motor ships to be acquired by the company. The ships continued to work in Robertsons' traditional trades, complementing the fleet of Stephenson Clarke which, operated in similar trades, and indeed had for

In 1975, William Robertson Shipowners Ltd. were already operating the Stephenson Clarke owned *Cowdray* (top, off South Shields, 4th August 1962) and *Lancing* (middle), and they were asked to try loading *Brightling* (below) at Llanddulas. This was anything but a success, and a report by Robertsons gives an interesting insight into the requirements of the stone trade from this jetty. Five problems were identified. At 17 feet forward compared with 15 feet for *Gem* (6), *Brightling* was too deep for the berth. It was important to spend as little time as possible at the jetty, and the slow rate with which *Brightling* discharged ballast water was considered to reduce the speed of loading, as was the 40 minutes it took to remove her hatch covers. It was impossible to close the hatches until both holds were fully loaded, so *Brightling* had to leave the berth with both open. Lastly, it was considered that her bulbous bow could cause damage to the jetty. *[P.A. Vicary; J.K. Byass; Roy Fenton collection]*

some time loaded at Llanddulas. Although ownership was not formally transferred, at least two ageing Stephenson Clarke ships were operated by Robertsons, *Cowdray* (1,748/1959) and *Lancing* (1,765/1958). By no means all the company's ships were suitable, however, and the Spanish-built *Brightling* (1,600/1972) was singled out for criticism (see caption above).

Reflecting his concern for his employees, Frank Robertson's correspondence with the new owners supported the notion of keeping the Glasgow operation separate, stressing that it was a 'close-knit unit', and maintaining that customers were used to dealing with the Glasgow office. However, pressure for integration became inexorable. In April 1976

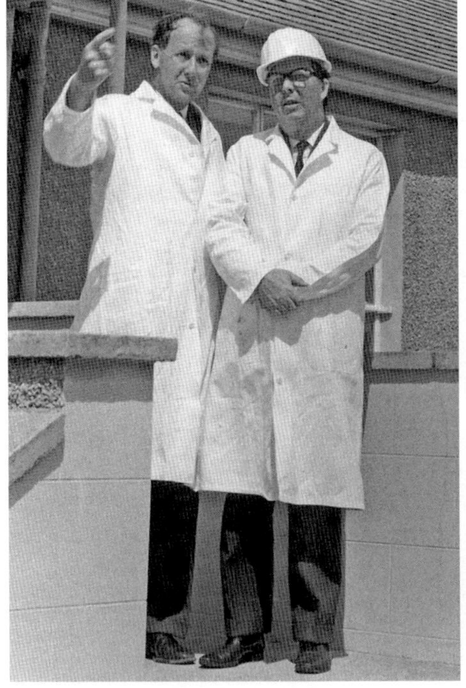

The last two principals of William Robertson Shipowners Ltd., on the left side of the left-hand photograph Jim Robertson (1921-1978) and on the right Frank Robertson (1920-2005) in his robes as first Chairman of the Council of Strathclyde University. *[Robertson archives]*

the Kneeshaw, Lupton operation was absorbed by Powell Duffryn Quarries Ltd. and on 1st November 1976 William Robertson Shipowners Ltd. was formally made a subsidiary of Stephenson Clarke Shipping Ltd., although it continued to trade under its own name. With effect from November 1978 the Gem fleet was integrated with that of Stephenson Clarke. Frank and Jim Robertson resigned from the board and from that of Powell Duffryn Quarries Ltd. and became directors of Stephenson Clarke Shipping Ltd. This was not quite the end of the Robertson story, for the Glasgow offices at 45 West Nile Street remained open until Frank Robertson retired in 1982 when its remaining functions were transferred to Stephenson Clarke offices at Newcastle-upon-Tyne and to London. Some small reminders of the company remained, however: Stephenson Clarke continued to use Gem names for the remaining Robertson ships and also applied them to four others which it built or acquired. These ships are included in an appendix.

Jim Robertson died in December 1978. He had been Chairman of the British Shipping Federation's Scottish and Ulster area, and Chairman of Robertson Research Holdings. He also served as Lord Lieutenant of Dunbartonshire from 1975 until his death, and was a member of the Royal Company of Archers, the Queen's bodyguard in Scotland. He had made a contribution to advancing the design of the coastal tramp, and in reinforcing the importance of its role in the British mercantile marine.[26] His brother Frank Robertson was more closely involved with the day-to-day running of the fleet, and his family remember that a constant concern of his was the weather and particularly the possibility of storms. He showed a great interest, even affection, for the company's employees, and was most anxious that their interests should be looked after following the 1970 takeover by Powell Duffryn. Frank Robertson died in 2005. He had served on committees of Lloyd's Register of Shipping, on the boards of David MacBrayne Ltd., the British Linen Bank, and subsequently that of the Bank of Scotland. He was the first Chairman of the Council of Strathclyde University and served during the years of mergers and consolidation which laid the foundations for its present status. Like their father before them, Frank and Jim Robertson were passionate sailors on the west coast of Scotland.

Three generations of the Robertson family had been deeply involved in coastal shipping over 130 years. During this time 146 sail, steam and motor ships had been owned and others managed. In its early days the company had made a contribution to the development of steam coasters for the bulk trades and – although the company was not amongst the first to exploit the advantages of the diesel engine – it developed a most distinctive-looking motor coaster in post-war years. The company had remained largely true to its founder's

Robertson Research

During the company's final decades, the challenging operating environment in shipping stimulated efforts to diversify into other areas. The most successful venture, Robertson Research, developed from the historic association between William Robertson Shipowners Ltd. and the limestone quarries at Llanddulas. The production of stone for the 1956 contracts with Northern Ireland and Norway called for changes in quarrying practice. The Ships and Quarries Division of the company needed advice because its customers demanded exacting standards for the geological, physical and chemical properties of the stone. The Division was put in touch with Dr Bob Cummings, a geologist at Glasgow University. He was initially employed during his summer holidays as a consultant at Llanddulas, but after a few years he became full time and opened a laboratory at the quarry. In January 1962, after several years of successful consultancy work, a new organisation was formed, Robertson Research. Its roles were to provide advice to Ships and Quarries Division, to seek economically viable new activities suitable for the combined shipping and quarrying group, to carry out scientific research and development, and to provide consultancy in the field of earth sciences. Much of this was made possible through Dr Bob Cummings' contacts worldwide and through the expertise of scientists such as Dr Bill Brown. The company's development coincided with the growth of North Sea oil and gas exploration, and the rapid expansion in this field, combined with consultancy in minerals exploration, formed the core of Robertson Research's activities. The company expanded rapidly, setting up offices worldwide, and was highly successful: in 1975 its turnover was over £2,000,000, and it made a profit of over 40%. Robertson Research was floated on the Stock Exchange in March 1984 and was taken over by Simon Engineering in 1991. During the 1990s, Simon Engineering sold off their Simon Petroleum Technology subsidiaries to a group of directors who re-adopted the Robertson name. Following acquisition by Fugro the company continues to focus on petroleum technology under the title Fugro Robertson Ltd., with laboratories at Deganwy in North Wales[27]

It would be unforgiveable to end this account of William Robertson with a photograph of a ship which, whatever its name, was never owned by the company, so Stephenson Clarke's motor ship *Pearl* built in 1967 (above, in Robertson colours) is contrasted with Robertson's long-lived *Pearl* (4) of 1896 (below at Poole, coincidentally with a Stephenson Clarke up-river collier in the distance). *[Roy Fenton collection (2)]*

principles of operating ships in a variety of mainly coastal and short sea trades, and of building and maintaining them well. A traditional naming scheme was retained throughout its existence, as was a restrained but distinctive livery. Despite undertaking a higher proportion of longer voyages in later years, the fleet remained very familiar around the British coast, and still regularly loaded the limestone which had been a core part of its trade for well over a century. A quarter century after its demise, Gem Line is still remembered with affection.

Notes on the text

1. These and other figures are from Checkland SG, 'The Upas Tree: Glasgow 1875-1975', University of Glasgow, 1981.
2. William Robertson's father is described as a labourer on one certificate, but as a master weaver on another. Quite possibly, he sought work as a labourer during a depression in the cotton industry.
3. This concern was the Scottish branch of Fox, Henderson and Co., which built the Crystal Palace for the 1851 Great Exhibition. The London Works were later taken over by William Simons and Co. who specialised in building dredgers and harbour craft.
4. A list of vessels engaged in the sea-to-sea trade through the Forth and Clyde Canal for the years 1863 to 1866 includes several with gem-type names: *Emerald*, *Gem*, *Garnet*, *Onyx*, and *Opal.* Only *Gem* and *Garnet* are identifiable as Robertson vessels, both making voyages consistent with the size and trading patterns of the vessels he owned in this period; *Garnet* for instance making voyages from Ballachulish to Dundee or Leith with slates and from Carrickfergus to Charleston and Fisherrow with rock salt. Given Robertson's involvement with the canal trade there is a possibility that *Emerald*, *Onyx*, and *Opal* also belonged to him, but in the absence of any confirmatory evidence they have not been included in the fleet list. In any case, no further details of these vessels are known.
5. In the days of the Clyde steam puffer, Garroch Head at the southernmost tip of Bute was regarded as the limit of navigation for the 'shorehead boats', and craft venturing further to seaward had to have a load line. Robertson's first four craft stayed within this limit, suggesting that the term 'lighter' (later applied to the puffers as in 'steam lighters') was reserved for a craft without a load line, rather than without power.
6. This detail is from a hardback notebook entitled 'Debit Day Book 1855', although entries actually start in 1862. By no means all entries are legible. Only one port or harbour is usually named for

each voyage, and light or ballast trips are not listed as the intention is clearly to record freights and costs. It is therefore not always obvious whether the location is the origin or destination of the cargo, and judgement has had to be exercised when drawing up this table.
7. Duckworth CLD, Langmuir GE, 'Clyde Coastal Steamers', Brown, Son and Ferguson, Glasgow, 1939, page 142.
8. There is no *Marchioness of Lorne* listed in the 'Mercantile Navy List' before the 1890s.
9. The newspaper report cites the name of the former as *Vale of Clyde*, but there is no contemporary ship of this name, and almost certainly the vessel referred to is *Vale of Clwyd*, which Duckworth and Langmuir record as being on the Glasgow to Ayr service by 1866.
10. Registration documents rigorously record details of mortgagees, interest rates, dates of opening and discharging of mortgages but do not usually give the amount of the mortgage.
11. These were *The Countess, The Duchess, The Emperor, The Princess, The Queen* and *The Marchioness* (eight shares in each case) plus *The Monarch* and *The Sultan* (both 16 shares).
12. These reminiscences were set down in June 1949 and April 1954, but it is clear that Fred Donaldson's stories (some of which he may well have heard from his father or from colleagues) date back to before the First World War.
13. From a letter by Frank Robertson to the Valhalla museum in the Scilly Isles, following a visit in the 1960s where he saw some timbers from the stern of a boat carrying the legend 'Turquoise, Glasgow' and believed to be from the torpedoed craft.
14. The spade is now in a museum in Renfrew.
15. Scott and Sons continued delivering traditional steam coasters to British owners until after the Second World War. Joseph Fisher's *Balsa* and *Ebony* (both 405/1947) were completed at Bowling in July and October 1947 respectively, by when the type was thoroughly obsolescent. The pair even had counter sterns, unlike the ship that is regarded as the very last steam coaster, the *Hazelfield* (692/1948) delivered from Lytham to Liverpool owners in April 1948.
16. The varied ship owning activities of these families are described in Fenton RS, 'Mersey Rovers: the Coastal Tramp Ship Owners of Liverpool and the Mersey', World Ship Society, Gravesend, 1997, pages 188 to 193.
17. Additional ships were also chartered when necessary; for instance in 1902 the total cost of hiring steamers was £22,716.
18. A brief history of the Coasting Motor Shipping Co. Ltd. appears in Ships in Focus 'Record' No. 26.
19. Robertson JC, Hagan HH, *A Century of Coaster Design and Operation* 'Transactions of the Institution of Engineers and Shipbuilders in Scotland', 1954, XCVII, 204-256. The motor vessel is clearly the *Pearl* (5) of 1953, but the steamer is harder to identify, as Robertson did not build a ship in 1906, never acquired one built in that year, and had none corresponding to the quoted dimensions. It seems likely that the authors went back to the builders of *Pearl*, Ailsa Shipbuilding Co. Ltd., when searching for the detailed data for the comparison made in their paper. This yard did build a ship of the appropriate specification, the *Ailsa Craig* (641/1906) for Hugh Craig and Co. of Belfast. She was torpedoed and sunk in 1918.
20. William F. Robertson achieved distinction in Clyde yachting circles in 1921 when his six-metre yacht *Caryl*, built by Fife of Fairlie, crossed the Atlantic to participate in the British American Cup. In 1929 his eight-metre yacht, also named *Caryl*, beat the US defender *Gypsy* to take the Seawanhaka Cup.
21. Bryans PJ ed, 'Channel Islands Merchant Shipping 1940-1945', Channel Islands Occupation Society, Grouville, n.d.
22. Simpson JA, *Recollections of a Life at Sea* 'Sea Breezes' October 1983, pages 733-738.
23. 'Powell Duffryn News', November 1970.
24. Powell Duffryn's annual report indicates that the owners of the Gem Line Ltd. received 500,000 shares and £935,000 in cash, payable partly on completion and partly in October 1972.
25 'Powell Duffryn News' for November 1970 reported that Thor Thoresen Line was Manchester-based and operated as ships' agents, cargo forwarders and haulage contractors. Skibs A/S Thor Thoresens Linje was an Oslo-based company owning a 15,000-ton bulk carrier.
26. Robertson JC, Hagan HH, *A Century of Coaster Design and Operation.*
27. A summary history of Robertson Research is at http://www.fugro-robertson.com/corporate/history

Fleet lists

Notes on the fleet lists

William Robertson was by no means alone in giving his ships names of gemstones and minerals, and some vessels belonging to other owners have appeared in draft lists of ships attributed to William Robertson. The list below includes only those vessels identified as definitely owned by Robertson from company records, register books or registration documents. It breaks with convention by presenting the fleet list in separate parts for the sail, steam and motor vessels, although their times in the fleet overlap. Doing this allows photographs of similar ships to be grouped together, at least for the steam and motor coasters, permitting comparisons to be made and developments traced.

The fleet list follows the standard Ships in Focus format, shamelessly derived from that excellently developed by the World Ship Society. The first line of each entry gives the ship's name with the notation (1) to (7) to indicate that she is the first to the seventh of that name in the fleet. The dates following are those of entering and leaving the fleet, or when management began and finished. Unless otherwise stated on this line, vessels are steam or motor ships with steel hulls.

On the second line is given the ship's official number (O.N.) in the British Register; then her tonnages at acquisition, gross (g) and net (n), and an estimate of deadweight (d) when this figure is found in company records. The third line gives dimensions: registered length x breadth x draught in feet or, for vessels owned from 1955 onwards, the dimensions are length overall x breadth x draught in feet and in metres for vessels from 1974 onwards. For any substantial rebuild, new dimensions are given on a subsequent line.

For steam and motor ships the following line describes the engine fitted and gives the name of its builder. Steam reciprocating engines may be single- or two-cylinder simple, two-cylinder compound (C. 2-cyl.) or three-cylinder triple-expansion (T. 3-cyl.). For oil engines are given the type where known if different from that of the builder, the number of cylinders, whether two-stroke (2SC) or four-stroke (4SC) cycle, single-acting (SA) or double-acting (DA). Any changes of engine or major modifications are listed, with dates, on the next line. Where known from registration documents figures are given for horsepower which may be nominal (NHP), brake (BHP) or indicated (IHP), and for the ship's speed. Figures for nominal horsepower should be read with caution, as they are calculated from engine dimensions rather than measured, and are liable to change over time independently of any modifications to the machinery. Speeds are also usually estimated rather than measured, and it is noteworthy that, when ships were requisitioned during the First World War, the speeds quoted in official records were often 1 to 2 knots lower than those in registration documents and were more realistic.

Subsequent lines give the details of the hull builder and then the ship's full career. Where dates of completion are known to the nearest month, they are not quoted if they fall within the same month as the registration date. All sales and transfers are noted which lasted for more than a few days. The port indicated after the title of an owning company is the port in which the owners are domiciled. For ships sold to operators using flags of convenience, efforts have been made to indicate the actual owners and the managers (not always the same body). For these vessels, the flag is that of the state in which the ship owning company is domiciled unless otherwise stated. Major non-fatal casualties and all known fates are noted. Dates of entering or leaving British government requisition in the First and Second World Wars are quoted for ships in Robertson ownership or management during these years; more details appear in Tables 3 and 4.

The fleet lists are based wherever possible on registration documents of British ships in Classes BT108, BT109 and BT110 housed in the National Archives at Kew, and from Glasgow ship registers held in the Mitchell Library, Glasgow and in the National Archives of Scotland in Edinburgh. Using these primary sources allows dates of registrations, sales and renamings to be quoted with great precision, and ownership changes to be plotted in much more detail than from publications such as 'Lloyd's Register' or the 'Mercantile Navy List'. Unfortunately, registration documents for ships whose British registry closed after 1955 are not generally available. For the larger motor ships, 'Lloyd's Confidential Index' has provided details of later owners and managers. Not infrequently, this information conflicts with that in 'Lloyd's Register'. Deadweight tonnages, prices and some sale dates have been taken from surviving company records.

1. Non-powered vessels

Despite searches of the shipping registers of Glasgow, Greenock and Port Glasgow, registration details for Robertson's first four vessels have not been found and so their details are incomplete, to say the least. The descriptions of rigs are those given in surviving company records for the first four vessels, and in registration documents for later craft.

Following her sale to owners in Ireland, the *Topaz* (1) was registered in Belfast. Here she is one of three sailing vessels in charge of a paddle tug. *[Robertson archives]*

1. ELLEN 1852-1865 Wooden scow
50t
5.1852: Acquired by William Robertson, Glasgow.
1865: Leaves company records.

2. GEM (1) 1854-1868 Wooden scow
60t
1854: Acquired by William Robertson, Glasgow.
1868: Leaves company records.

3. RUBY (1) 1855- Wooden scow
1855: Built.

4. PEARL (1) 1859-1867 Wooden smack
70d
1859: Acquired by William Robertson, Glasgow.
1867: Sold.

5. TOPAZ (1) 1862-1879 Wooden smack
O.N. 44799 49g 49n 80d
64.5 x 17.0 x 6.7 feet
1862: Launched by J. and R. Swan, Maryhill, Lanark.
6.9.1862: Registered in the ownership of William Robertson, Glasgow as TOPAZ.
23.2.1872: 16/64 shares sold to Duncan McIntyre, Glasgow.
31.10.1879: Remaining 48/64 shares sold to Alexander Miscampbell, Carrickfergus.
21.7.1896: Sold to Archibald Nicholl, Magheramorne, County Antrim.
3.10.1899: Sold to Arthur Murphy, Belfast.
26.10.1900: Sold to James Shiels, Belfast.
19.4.1901: Sold to Jacob W. Keenan, Belfast.
1.11.1901: Sold to Robert Leitch, Glasgow.
26.2.1902: Wrecked near Rubha Salach, Arran whilst on a voyage from Temple, Forth and Clyde Canal, to Lamlash, Arran with a cargo of bricks. The crew of three survived.
17.3.1902: Register closed.

6. GARNET (1) 1864-1868 Wooden yawl
O.N. 48938 49g 47n
65.1 x 17.1 x 7.0 feet
6.1864: Completed by J. and R. Swan, Maryhill, Lanark.
28.6.1864: Registered in the ownership of William Robertson, Glasgow as GARNET. She cost £630.
28.5.1868: Stranded at Langness Point, Isle of Man.
28.8.1868: Register closed.

7. CHRYSOLITE 1874-1879 Wooden schooner
O.N. 68087 60g 54n
69.6 x 18.0 x 8.0 feet
6.3.1874: Launched by the Scottish Ironworks Company, Irvine.
30.3.1874: Registered in the ownership of William Robertson, Glasgow as CHRYSOLITE.
8.11.1879: Wrecked on Tory Island, off County Donegal, whilst on a voyage from Sligo to Ardrossan in ballast. The crew survived.
10.12.1879: Register closed.

8. SAPPHIRE (1) 1875-1881 Wooden schooner
O.N. 73784 81g 75n
76.2 x 12.6 x 9.0 feet
9.1875: Launched by John Duncan, Kingston-on-Spey.
11.10.1875: Registered in the ownership of William Robertson, Glasgow as SAPPHIRE.
19.5.1881: Register closed on sale to E. Hermann, Nantes, France and renamed SAPHIR.
1881: Transferred to C. Hermann, Paris, France.
4.1892: Abandoned at Manahara, Reunion. Her crew were reported to be unable to navigate her after passing through two cyclones.

9. PEARL (2) 1876-1883 Wooden smack
O.N. 73847 50g 47n
64.0 x 18.2 x 7.8 feet
8.1876: Launched by John Duncan, Kingston-on-Spey
25.8.1876: Registered in the ownership of William Robertson, Glasgow as PEARL
5.11.1883: Sold to James McCrone, Rothesay.
30.4.1891: Re-registered as a schooner.
14.9.1900: Sold to John Kirkwood, Rothesay.
13.1.1903: Sold to Charles Robertson, Arran.
6.9.1904: Sold to James Cowie, Thurso.
12.12.1904: Wrecked in a force nine gale at Sandside Bay, Sutherlandshire whilst on a voyage from Loch Broom to Methil with a cargo of pit props. The crew of three survived.
14.3.1905: Register closed.

10. CAMEO (1) 1876-1888 Iron schooner
O.N. 73852 55g 50n
63.7 x 18.0 x 7.5 feet
9.8.1876: Launched by McKellar, McMillan and Co., Dumbarton.
30.8.1876: Registered in the ownership of William Robertson, Glasgow as CAMEO.
10.11.1888: Sold to John Phillips, Port Isaacs, Cornwall.
7.4.1890: Stranded on Atherfield Ledge, Isle of Wight.
11.7.1890: Registered in the ownership of James Witham, Northwood, Isle of Wight.
1.6.1897: Sold to Charles F. Winder, Plymouth.
18.9.1897: Sold to John H. Davis and John C. Brown, Plymouth.
20.5.1897: 22/64 sold to William Fishwick and William Webber, Plymouth.
10.2.1899: Transferred to the Plymouth Mercantile Shipping Co. Ltd. (John H. Davis, manager), Plymouth.
3.3.1905: Struck Paternoster Rocks and sank in St. Onen's Bay, Jersey whilst on a voyage from Southampton to St. Malo with a cargo of pitch.
4.4.1905: Register closed.

11. NUGGET (1) 1876-1885 Wooden schooner
O.N. 76718 48g 44n
63.0 x 18.3 x 7.5 feet
9.1876: Launched by McKellar and Co., Ayr.
15.11.1876: Registered in the ownership of William Robertson (32/64), Glasgow and four others as NUGGET.
15.5.1885: Sold to Alexander McPherson, Glasgow.
3.12.1887: Sold to John Marshall, Drummore, County Wigtown.
28.12.1905: Sold to Rose Reason (Charles Reason, manager), Glynn, near Belfast.
12.11.1910: Sunk in collision with the steamers HUNGARIAN (4,508/1902) and CLAN ALPINE (3,587/1899) about two and a half miles south west of the Cloch Lighthouse whilst on a voyage from Larne to Glasgow with a cargo of lime shell.
16.12.1910: Register closed.

A naïve portrait of the second *Gem*. Built in 1877, this iron topsail schooner had a remarkably long life, and was not broken up until 1940. *[Robertson archives]*

12. GEM (2) 1877-1888 Iron schooner
O.N. 76737 55g 50n
63.6 x 18.0 x 7.4 feet
3.2.1877: Launched by McKellar, McMillan and Co., Dumbarton.
23.2.1877: Registered in the ownership of William Robertson, Glasgow as GEM.
30.5.1888: Sold to Duncan Sinclair, Lochgilphead.
3.7.1918: Re-registered as a ketch.
16.7.1931: Sold to John Orr, Annalong, County Down.
13.3.1940: Sold to George Cohen, Sons and Co. Ltd., London for breaking up.
2.9.1940: Register closed.

The schooner *Jacinth* (1). Despite being built of wood, unlike her immediate predecessor, *Jacinth* also enjoyed a lengthy career, although her fate under the Greek flag is unknown, and she may not have survived the Second World War. The white-hulled steamer clearly named *Britannia* in the background may be the 1885-built cable ship of that name. *[Robertson archives]*

13. JACINTH (1) 1877-1883 Wooden schooner
O.N. 76743 117g 100n
86.3 x 21.7 x 10.5 feet
1912: Paraffin motor 4-cyl. 4SCSA by the Bergius Launch and Engine Company, Glasgow; 30 NHP, 4.5 knots.
3.1877: Launched by John Duncan, Kingston-on-Spey.
21.3.1877: Registered in the ownership of William Robertson, Glasgow as JACINTH. *8.8.1883:* Sold to Joseph Palin and Co., Northwich.
7.9.1886: Stranded on Tory Island whilst on a voyage from Sligo to Westbank.
21.9.1886: Register closed.
1887: Wreck sold to Colhoun Brothers, Londonderry and refloated.
1889: Sold to Jonathan Samuel, Calstock, Cornwall.
8.2.1902: Sold to William Burgoyne (48/64) and Joseph C. Cock (16/64), Plymouth.
6.12.1902: William Burgoyne acquires all 64 shares.
19.11.1912: Re-registered after fitting a paraffin motor.
6.6.1913: Sold to Paul G. Camilleri, Malta.
14.7.1922: Register closed on sale to Greece.
6.10.1922: Re-registered in the ownership of Giovanni Vella, Gozo, Malta.
16.4.1929: Register closed on sale to K. Mavrelos, Schio, Italy, renamed AFOVOS and registered in Calamata, Greece. *1938:* Sold to G.N. Ghikas, Piraeus, Greece.
1955: Deleted from 'Lloyd's Register'.

2. Steam ships

All are steel unless stated.

1. JASPER (1) 1865-1872 Iron
O.N. 53379 42g 36n
65.5 x 16.1 x 5.7 feet
2-cyl. simple by the Canal Basin Foundry Company, Glasgow; 14 NHP.
9.11.1865: Launched by J. and R. Swan, Maryhill, Lanark.
11.12.1865: Registered in the ownership of William Robertson, Glasgow as JASPER. She is recorded as costing £906 0s 5d.
19.11.1872: Sold to William Glen, Dumbarton.
2.2.1875: Transferred to William Glen, Dumbarton (32/64) and John Anderson junior, Glasgow (32/64).
2.5.1878: Sold to Richard Briscoe, Liverpool.
14.10.1878: Transferred to the Ballincollig Royal Gunpowder Mill Co. Ltd., Liverpool.
21.9.1888: Transferred to the British and Irish Gunpowder Manufacturing Co. Ltd. (John G. Briscoe, manager), London.
6.4.1910: Register closed after becoming unfit for use afloat.

2. DIAMOND (1) 1867-1870 Iron
O.N. 60328 63g 50n
65.6 x 18.0 x 8.3 feet
2-cyl. simple by the Canal Basin Foundry Company, Glasgow; 18 NHP.
31.10.1867: Launched by J. and R. Swan, Maryhill, Lanark.
10.12.1867: Registered in the ownership of William Robertson, Glasgow as DIAMOND.
30.3.1870: Sold to Peter Stuart (32/64) and Peter Douglas (32/64), Liverpool.
4.1875: Sold to Alexander McColl, Glasgow.
12.6.1878: Transferred to Alexander McColl, Hugh H. Galloway, George MacFarlane and William Cowan, Glasgow.
28.12.1882: Sold to Andrew Ross (42/64) and Frank Grindlay (22/64), Glasgow.
11.9.1884: Wrecked at Hynish, Tiree whilst on a voyage from Irvine to Hynish with a cargo of coal.
9.10.1884: Register closed.

3. AMETHYST (1) 1870-1882 Iron
O.N. 63788 113g 56n
100.0 x 18.6 x 8.6 feet
C.2-cyl. by the Canal Basin Foundry Company, Glasgow; 25 NHP.
8.8.1870: Launched by J. and R. Swan, Maryhill, Lanark.
4.10.1870: Registered in the ownership of William Robertson, Glasgow as AMETHYST.
16.3.1882: Sold to the General Steam Fishing Co. Ltd., Edinburgh.
2.3.1883: Stranded on May Island, Firth of Forth whilst fishing out of Granton.
21.3.1883: Register closed.

4. AGATE (1) 1878-1911 Iron
O.N. 78596 184g 98n 210d
120.6 x 20.1 x 9.6 feet
C. 2-cyl. by William King and Co., Glasgow; 35 NHP.
5.4.1878: Launched by T.B. Seath and Co., Rutherglen, Glasgow (Yard No. 180).
8.5.1878: Registered in the ownership of William Robertson, Glasgow as AGATE.
18.2.1911: Wrecked on Rowancarry Rock, half a mile from Danish Island in the Kenmare River whilst on a voyage from Cork to Kenmare with a cargo of flour, bran and meal.
7.3.1911: Register closed.

5. JASPER (2) 1880-1888 Iron
O.N. 82329 279g 158n
144.8 x 23.1 x 10.7 feet
C. 2-cyl. by William King and Co., Glasgow; 60 NHP.
6.7.1880: Launched by T.B. Seath and Co., Rutherglen, Glasgow (Yard No. 194).
19.8.1880: Registered in the ownership of William Robertson, Glasgow as JASPER.
11.12.1888: Wrecked between Portyerrock and Garlieston, on the Island of Whithorn, whilst on a voyage from Workington to Glasgow with a cargo of steel rails. The vessel hit rocks in fog, tearing off the rudder and propellor, and drifted for about a mile before sinking in seven fathoms of water. The entire crew of 12 was lost.
19.12.1888: Register closed.

6. SAPPHIRE (2) 1881-1927 Iron
O.N. 85872 343g 171n 435d
160.0 x 23.2 x 10.9 feet
C. 2-cyl. by William King and Co., Glasgow; 56 NHP.
11.1881: Launched by John Fullerton and Co., Paisley (Yard No. 47).
13.12.1881: Registered in the ownership of William Robertson, Glasgow as SAPPHIRE. She cost £7,252, of which £2,500 was for the engines.
18.10.1927: Register closed on sale to Cecil H. Sheppard, Antwerp, Belgium and renamed COCCINELLE.
1932: Broken up at Bruges.

7. AMETHYST (2) 1883-1908 Iron
O.N. 87636 533g 289n 720d
185.1 x 27.1 x 11.5 feet
C. 2-cyl. by William King and Co., Glasgow; 450 IHP.
23.2.1883: Launched by John Fullerton and Co., Paisley (Yard No. 54).
10.4.1883: Registered in the ownership of William Robertson, Glasgow as AMETHYST. She cost £12,072.
4.10.1908: Sank off Wicklow Head after colliding in fog with the steamer DAISY (320/1904) whilst on a voyage from Ayr to Havre with a cargo of coal. The crew was picked up by the DAISY and landed at Dublin.
8.1.1908: Register closed.

The first Robertson ship built by Fullerton, *Sapphire* (3) had a half-height forecastle and a steering position only slightly raised above her quarter deck. *[Glasgow University Archives DC101 0813]*

Two years after *Sapphire* came *Pearl* (3) from Fullerton's yard, slightly longer but with a higher steering position. Unusually, she was photographed with derricks raised, suggesting a short voyage in sheltered waters. Note the sails. *[Glasgow University Archives DC101 0473]]*

8. TOPAZ (2) 1883-1891 Iron
O.N. 87723 353g 168n
160.1 x 23.2 x 11.1 feet
C. 2-cyl. by William King and Co., Glasgow; 60 NHP.
6.11.1883: Launched by T.B. Seath and Co., Rutherglen, Glasgow (Yard No. 237).
4.12.1883: Registered in the ownership of William Robertson, Glasgow as TOPAZ.
4.4.1891: Sold to John J. Mack and Sons, Liverpool.
28.12.1891: Struck Dunany Point and foundered off Dundalk Bay whilst on a voyage from Workington to Dundalk with a cargo of rails.
12.1.1893: Register closed.

9. PEARL (3) 1885-1895 Iron
O.N. 90070 431g 199n
170.0 x 25.1 x 10.2 feet
C. 2-cyl. by William King and Co., Glasgow; 70 NHP.
31.7.1885: Launched by John Fullerton and Co., Paisley (Yard No. 68).
5.9.1885: Registered in the ownership of William Robertson, Glasgow as PEARL.
5.1.1895: Sank off Dungeness after a collision with the barque PRIMERA (619/1875) whilst on a voyage from Portsmouth to Chatham with a cargo of railway plant.
14.1.1895: Register closed.

10. ENSIGN 1885-1897 Iron
O.N. 86734 318g 146n
145.0 x 23.1 x 10.6 feet
1894: 399g 129n
155.5 x 23.1 x 10.6 feet
C. 2-cyl. by J. and T. Young, Ayr; 50 NHP.
11.11.1882: Launched by T.B. Seath and Co., Rutherglen, Glasgow (Yard No. 224).
10.1.1883: Registered in the ownership of James R. Currie and Co., Glasgow as ENSIGN.
29.10.1885: Major shareholder became James Reston, Glasgow, with William Robertson as managing owner.
1894: Lengthened at Bowling.
23.1.1896: Acquired by William Robertson, Glasgow.
22.12.1897: Stranded at Cleats on the south end of Arran whilst on a voyage from Workington to the Clyde with a cargo of pig iron.
24.1.1898: Register closed.
17.6.1898: Re-registered in the ownership of Alexander Ross and James Marshall, Glasgow as LEELITE.
8.2.1900: Sank off Dumbarton following a collision with the Swedish steamer MANNINGHAM (1,988/1880) whilst on a voyage from the Clyde to Bristol.
22.3.1900: Raised.
17.9.1901: Sold to the North Eastern Shipping Co. Ltd. (George Elsmie and Son, managers), Aberdeen.
27.9.1917: Sold to Matthew Taylor, Methil.
3.10.1926: Sank in collision with the steam trawler AMORELLE (202/1919) near the Would Light Vessel off Cromer whilst on a voyage from Ghent to Dundee with a cargo of coal.
14.1.1927: Register closed.

Ensign was unusual in the fleet in that until 1896 William Robertson was not the sole, or even the majority owner, but was designated managing owner on taking 18 shares. In size she was very similar to Robertson's *Jasper* (2), also built at Rutherglen. Note her relatively short funnel in this trials photograph. *Ensign* suffered three serious casualties during her 45 years. *[Glasgow University Archives]*

Diamond (2) on trials (top) and in the Avon (middle). Amongst numerous changes, in the second photograph the funnel has been considerably heightened, the canvas dodger around the bridge replaced with wood, the sails dispensed with and deckhouses painted white. In the trials view, she lacks the distinctive white line below the bridge.

Diamond was Robertson's first from Scotts of Bowling, who went on to be the company's main builder of steamers. Note the large windows below the wheelhouse: vulnerable to heavy seas, these appear to have been closed with external shutters. Distinguishing colour on early photographs is risky, but comparison with the funnel suggests the masts were also black at this period. *[Robertson archives; J. and M. Clarkson]*

Ropes are thrown ashore as a loaded *Gem* (3) prepares to dock in the Cumberland Basin, Bristol. Apart from a few bent rails on the starboard side of the forecastle, she appears in fine exterior condition, with the painted part of the amidships accommodation gleaming. Note Fullerton's builder's plate prominent on the wood panelling. *Gem* was the first Robertson vessel with a triple-expansion engine. *[J. and M. Clarkson]*

11. DIAMOND (2) 1886-1918 Iron
O.N. 93273 444g 186n 540d
175.0 x 25.1 x 10.3 feet
C. 2-cyl. by Ross and Duncan, Govan; 80 NHP.
5.1886: Launched by Scott and Co., Bowling (Yard No. 63).
14.6.1886: Registered in the ownership of William Robertson, Glasgow as DIAMOND. She cost £7,347.
13.4.1918: Sank off Rathlin Island one mile north west of Altacarry Lighthouse after a collision with the steamer LILY (635/1896) whilst on a voyage from Cardiff to Londonderry with a cargo of steel plates. Both were steaming without lights. Three members of the crew were lost, the others were picked up by LILY.
9.5.1918: Register closed.

12. GEM (3) 1887-1914 Iron
O.N. 93393 432g 185n 520d
175.2 x 25.2 x 10.2 feet
T. 3-cyl. by William King and Co., Glasgow; 80 NHP.
9.6.1887: Launched by John Fullerton and Co., Paisley (Yard No. 74).
18.7.1887: Registered in the ownership of William Robertson, Glasgow as GEM.
She cost £7,940.
25.12.1914: Mined and sank three and a half miles south east by a quarter east of Scarborough whilst on a voyage from Mostyn to the Tyne with a cargo of soda ash. Her entire crew was lost. The mine had been laid on 15.12.1914 by SMS KOLBERG.
4.1.1915: Register closed.

13. LARRY BANE 1888-1897 Iron
O.N. 71733 164g 90n
114.8 x 19.7 x 9.1 feet
C. 2-cyl. by William King and Co., Glasgow; 25 NHP.
24.5.1875: Launched by John Fullerton and Co., Paisley (Yard No. 25).
5.7.1875: Registered in the ownership of Frederick S. Herdman, Belfast as LARRY BANE.
21.1.1888: Acquired by William Robertson, Glasgow.
5.1.1897: Stranded at Selkar Rock, St. Bee's Head whilst on a voyage from Whitehaven to the Duddon in ballast.
13.1.1897: Register closed.

14. RUBY (2) 1888-1898 Iron
O.N. 95052 454g 184n
175.0 x 26.6 x 10.5 feet
C. 2-cyl. by William King and Co., Glasgow; 80 NHP.
16.4.1888: Launched by Scott and Co., Bowling (Yard No. 68).
3.5.1888: Registered in the ownership of William Robertson, Glasgow as RUBY.
23.11.1898: Sold to Andrew Weir and Co., Glasgow.
10.10.1905: Sank two miles west of the Forth Bridge following a collision with the steamer PRUDHOE CASTLE (813/1866) whilst on a voyage from Middlesbrough to Grangemouth with a cargo of pig iron.
9.12.1905: Register closed.

15. JACINTH (2) 1888-1929 Iron
O.N. 95079 453g 178n 600d
175.2 x 26.5 x 10.5 feet
T. 3-cyl. by William King and Co., Glasgow; 80 NHP.
13.7.1888: Launched by John Fullerton and Co., Paisley (Yard No. 81).
16.8.1888: Registered in the ownership of William Robertson (32/64) and James Reston (32/64), Glasgow as JACINTH.
She cost £6,164.
23.1.1896: William Robertson became sole owner.
7.12.1928: Struck submerged object and beached near Innishown Pilot Station, Lough Foyle whilst on a voyage from Londonderry to Workington in ballast.
19.12.1928: Refloated and later dry docked at Londonderry.
1.2.1929: Register closed following sale for breaking up.

16. STRATHNESS/ONYX (1) 1888-1891 Iron
O.N. 87733 375g 179n
160.3 x 24.7 x 11.1 feet
C. 2-cyl. by Hutson and Corbett, Glasgow; 70 NHP.
3.11.1883: Launched by Burrell and Son, Dumbarton (Yard No. 26).
29.12.1883: Registered in the ownership of James Hay and Sons, Glasgow as STRATHNESS.
1.1884: Completed.
4.1888: Acquired by William Robertson, Glasgow.
1.3.1889: Renamed ONYX.
10.2.1891: Sold to Edward Packard junior, Ipswich.
19.3.1891: Owners became Edward Packard junior and Henry W. Packard, Ipswich.
31.12.1903: Sold to the Onyx Steamship Co. Ltd. (C.J. Eaglesfield and Co., managers), Swansea.
3.5.1912: Register closed on sale to the Reval Shipping Co. Ltd. (John Pitka and Co., managers), Reval, Russia and renamed EESTIMA.
1919: Reval became part of Estonia.
1919: Sold to Hoyrylaiva O/Y Otava A/B, (John Nurminen, manager), Helsingfors, Finland and renamed KALEVA.
1922: Owners became O/Y Otava A/B.
1926: Sold to Diesen Wood Co.'s Rederi A/B, Sordavala, from 1928 Pitkaranta, and from *1934* Impilahti, all Finland.
1935: Sold to Pitkarannan Laiva O/Y, Impilahti.
1939: Sold to Laiva O/Y Kaleva (John Nurminen) (Scandinavian Chartering A/B, managers), Helsinki, Finland.
10.4.1943: Mined and sunk off Langeland in the Great Belt in position 55.08 north by 11.02 east whilst on a voyage from Aalborg to Abo with a cargo of chalk. One member of the crew was lost.

Two views of *Jacinth* (2). *[World Ship Society Ltd.; Nigel Farrell collection]*

17. STRATHESK 1888-1889 Iron
O.N. 85877 217g 93n
130.1 x 21.2 x 10.0 feet
C. 2-cyl. by J. and T. Young, Ayr.
24.11.1881: Launched by Scott and Co., Bowling (Yard No. 43).
16.12.1881: Registered in the ownership of James Reston, Glasgow as OMNIOPOLIS.
21.7.1882: Sold to Alexander M. Hay, Glasgow (18/64) and eight others.
28.2.1883: Renamed STRATHESK.
7.1888: Acquired by William Robertson, Glasgow.
21.11.1889: Wrecked off Haulbowline Light near Carlingford whilst on a voyage from Glasgow to Newry with a cargo of coal. Her crew of eight was rescued.
10.12.1889: Register closed.

18. CAIRNGORM (1) 1888-1903 Iron
O.N. 87714 376g 182n
160.4 x 24.7 x 11.1 feet
C. 2-cyl. by Hutson and Corbett, Glasgow; 60 NHP.
21.9.1883: Launched by Burrell and Son, Dumbarton (Yard No. 25).
16.11.1883: Registered in the ownership of James Hay and Sons, Glasgow as STRATHNAIRN.
8.1888: Acquired by William Robertson, Glasgow.
29.1.1889: Renamed CAIRNGORM.
1.1.1903: Stranded at the entrance to Harrington harbour whilst on a voyage from the Duddon to Harrington with a cargo of iron ore and became a total loss.
10.8.1903: Register closed.

19. CAMEO (2) 1888-1930 Iron
O.N. 87682 338g 148n
160.2 x 23.2 x 10.9 feet
C. 2-cyl. by J. and T. Young, Ayr; 60 NHP.
8.5.1883: Launched by John Fullerton and Co., Paisley (Yard No. 57).
23.7.1883: Registered in the ownership of James Hay and Sons, Glasgow as STRATHADDER.
8.1888: Acquired by William Robertson, Glasgow.
17.12.1888: Renamed CAMEO.
8.9.1930: Register closed on sale to Hinko Bertossi, Susak, Yugoslavia and renamed PECINE.
1935: Sold to Paparello and Gallo, Molfetta, Italy and renamed PEPPINO C.
1935: Sold to Salvatore Amato, Molfetta.
1938: Sold to Societa Anonima Anglo-Italiana Carboni, Venice, Italy.
1938: Sold to Salvagno Anonima Navigazione (Gino and Egidio Salvagno, managers), Venice and renamed ANGELO EMO.
5.12.1939: Struck rocks and sank at the entrance to Torre Annunziata whilst entering the harbour during bad weather with a cargo of flour.

20. NUGGET (2) 1889-1915 Steel and iron
O.N. 96070 396g 99n 480d
142.6 x 25.1 x 11.1 feet
T. 3-cyl. by Muir and Houston, Glasgow; 60 NHP.
17.5.1889: Launched by Scott and Co., Bowling (Yard No. 74).
18.6.1889: Registered in the ownership of William Robertson, Glasgow as NUGGET.
She cost £5,801.
14.9.1889: 10/64 shares sold to James Reston, Glasgow.
23.1.1896: 10/64 shares sold to William Robertson, Glasgow
23.7.1915: Commissioned as Fleet Messenger No.38.
31.7.1915: Sunk by gunfire from the German submarine U 28, 45 miles south west of the Scilly Isles, whilst on passage to the Dardanelles.
9.8.1915: Register closed.

21. EMERALD (1) 1889-1903 Iron
O.N. 96077 350g 120n
165.2 x 25.1 x 10.9 feet
T. 3-cyl. by Muir and Houston, Glasgow; 60 NHP.
27.6.1889: Launched by John Fullerton and Co., Paisley (Yard No. 85).
10.7.1889: Registered in the ownership of William Robertson, Glasgow as EMERALD.
4.8.1903: Sank off The Smalls after being in collision with the steamer KILMORE (2,215/1890) whilst on a voyage from Dublin to Llanelly in ballast.
12.8.1903: Register closed.

One of Robertson's relatively few secondhand purchases during the early years, *Cameo* (2) shares Preston Dock with a Scandinavian tanker in the 1920s. Note that lack of an ensign staff aft means she is flying her red ensign at the mizzen, and that she still carries a steadying sail on this mast. Typical of earlier steam coasters she has a low forecastle in which the crew were accommodated below main deck level. *[Harry Stewart/J. and M. Clarkson]*

A fine broadside view of *Nugget* (2) on the Clyde, carrying a jib and sails on all three masts. As a relatively small unit of the fleet, her after hatch is significantly shorter than the forward hatch. *[Glasgow University Archives]*

22. GARNET (2) 1889-1890 Steel and iron
O.N. 97584 480g 173n 520d
165.0 x 26.0 x 11.1 feet
T. 3-cyl. by Muir and Houston, Glasgow; 60 NHP.
8.11.1889: Launched by Scott and Co., Bowling (Yard No. 75).
11.1889: Completed.
2.12.1889: Registered in the ownership of William Robertson, Glasgow as GARNET. She cost £7,650.
2.4.1890: Wrecked at Cardrain Point, one mile north of the Mull of Galloway Light Vessel, whilst on a voyage from Llanddulas to Glasgow with a cargo of limestone. Her crew was saved.
15.4.1890: Registered closed.

23. SARD (1) 1890-1906 Iron
O.N. 97595 458g 189n 520d
165.2 x 26.1 x 10.9 feet
T. 3-cyl. by Muir and Houston, Glasgow; 60 NHP, 400 IHP, 10.5 knots.
20.12.1889: Launched by Scott and Co., Bowling (Yard No. 76).
28.12.1889: Completed.
2.1.1890: Registered in the ownership of William Robertson, Glasgow as SARD.
22.3.1906: Wrecked two miles west of Portrush during fog whilst on a voyage from London to Coleraine with a cargo of manure.
10.4.1906: Register closed.

The last of *Sard* (1), wrecked between Portrush and Port Stewart on the north Antrim coast in March 1906. *[Robertson archives]*

The name *Peridot* was used only once, probably because of the tragic circumstances of this vessel's loss in November 1905. *[Glasgow University Archives DC101 0476]*

Pebble (1) arrives light at Bristol (opposite page). *[J. and M. Clarkson]*

Cornelian (1) was a small steamer with a notably short after hatch (below). She gave Robertsons a very creditable 48 years of service. Her register was never formally closed, probably because her final British owner never told the registrar at Glasgow that he had sold her for scrap to Germany. *[J. and M. Clarkson]*

24. PERIDOT 1890-1905 Iron
O.N. 97603 226g 94n
130.2 x 19.9 x 9.7 feet
C. 2-cyl. by Ross and Duncan, Govan; 45 NHP.
11.12.1889: Launched by John Fullerton and Co., Paisley (Yard No. 87).
1.2.1890: Registered in the ownership of William Robertson, Glasgow as PERIDOT.
26.11.1905: Wrecked at Skernaghan Point, Islandmagee whilst on a voyage from Irvine to Carnlough in ballast. Her entire crew of nine was lost, seven of them from the nearby village of Carnlough.
1.2.1905: Register closed.

25. CORNELIAN (1) 1890-1938 Steel and iron
O.N. 97614 408g 139n 455d
142.5 x 25.1 x 11.1 feet
T. 3-cyl. by Muir and Houston, Glasgow; 60 NHP, 450 IHP.
22.2.1890: Launched by Scott and Co., Bowling (Yard No. 77).
3.1890: Registered in the ownership of William Robertson, Glasgow as CORNELIAN. She cost £6,425.
31.12.1938: Sold to William E. Brewer, Hull.
4.1939: Left Hull for Wewelsfleth, Germany where she was broken up by A. Kubatz of Berlin.

26. OLIVINE (1) 1890-1900 Steel and iron
O.N. 98571 454g 185n 535d
165.2 x 26.1 x 10.9 feet
T. 3-cyl. by Muir and Houston, Glasgow; 60 NHP, 400 IHP.
15.8.1890: Launched by Scott and Co., Bowling (Yard No. 79).
10.9.1890: Registered in the ownership of William Robertson, Glasgow as OLIVINE. She cost £9,050 of which £2,850 was for the engine.
6.4.1900: Sold to James S. Hardman, Liverpool for £6,813 11s 5p.
5.5.1900: Renamed YEWDALE.
142.4.1904: Sold to William Postlethwaite, Millom.
11.4.1911: Transferred to George Postlethwaite (William Postlethwaite, manager), Millom.
16.7.1917: Sold to Earl J. Leslie, Dundee.
24.11.1920: Sold Henry W. Renny (Earl J. Leslie, manager), Dundee.
5.6.1923: Sold to John Stewart and Co., Glasgow.
24.7.1925: Stranded on Goswick Sand Ridge whilst on a voyage from Lerwick to Blyth in ballast. Refloated, but declared a constructive total loss and sold for breaking up.
22.10.1925: Register closed.

27. PEBBLE (1) 1890-1919 Steel and iron
O.N. 98580 477g 176n 540d
165.2 x 26.1 x 10.9 feet
T. 3-cyl. by Muir and Houston, Glasgow; 60 NHP, 400 IHP, 10.5 knots.
18.9.1890: Launched by Scott and Co., Bowling (Yard No. 80).
26.9.1890: Registered in the ownership of William Robertson, Glasgow as PEBBLE. She cost £7,861.
24.7.1915: Commissioned as Fleet Messenger No. 31.
23.5.1919: Sold to the Admiralty for £30,000.
11.1919: Abandoned at Mudros as a constructive total loss.
30.2.1920: Register closed.
8.1920: Sold to J. Saparis, Piraeus, Greece and renamed ANGHELIKI SAPARIS.
1922: Sold to P. Mesolongitis, Piraeus.
1925: Sold to the Michalinos Maritime and Commerce Co. Ltd., Piraeus and renamed KERAMIKOS.
1929: Sold to the Spetsioliki Steam Navigation Co. Ltd., Piraeus.
1932: Sold to E.P. Nomikos (Petros M. Nomikos, manager), Piraeus.
26.6.1933: Lost by explosion and fire at Alexandretta on arriving from Constantza with a cargo of kerosene and benzine.
3.1934: Wreck sold.

Pyrope (1) was refloated after stranding off Kettleness Point in 1927, but was declared a constructive total loss. *[Robertson archives]*

28. PYROPE (1) 1890-1927 Steel and iron
O.N. 98592 452g 167n 525d
165.2 x 26.1 x 10.9 feet
T. 3-cyl. by Muir and Houston, Glasgow; 60 NHP, 400 IHP, 10½ knots.
15.11.1890: Launched by Scott and Co., Bowling (Yard No. 81).
5.12.1890: Registered in the ownership of William Robertson, Glasgow as PYROPE. She cost £8,155.
23.12.1927: Stranded in dense fog 500 yards north of Kettleness Point whilst on a voyage from the Tyne to Newlyn with a cargo of coal. Her crew of nine was rescued by the Runswick lifeboat.
8.1.1928: Refloated and dry docked by Smith's Dock Co. Ltd., Middlesbrough.
13.9.1928: Register closed after being sold for breaking up.

29. ASTERIA (1) 1891-1923 Steel and iron
O.N. 98633 493g 199n 630d
175.0 x 26.7 x 10.4 feet
T. 3-cyl. by Muir and Houston, Glasgow; 75 NHP, 675 IHP, 12 knots.
14.5.1891: Launched by Scott and Co., Bowling (Yard No. 83).
26.5.1891: Registered in the ownership of William Robertson, Glasgow as ASTERIA. She cost £8,049.
20.7.1915: Commissioned as Fleet Messenger No. 29 until 22.1.1921.
2.7.1923: Sold to I.M. Galbraith for breaking up.
7.11.1923: Register closed.

30. TOPAZ (3) 1891-1892 Steel and iron
O.N. 98681 502g 198n 620d
175.2 x 26.7 x 10.7 feet
T. 3-cyl. by Muir and Houston, Glasgow; 75 NHP, 675 IHP, 12 knots.
1918: T. 3- cyl. by Douglas and Grant Ltd., Kirkcaldy; 70 NHP, 500 IHP, 10 knots.
5.11.1891: Launched by Scott and Co., Bowling (Yard No. 87).

A well-laden *Asteria* (1) on the Clyde; her sails appear to have been in use recently. This broadside view emphasises the considerably greater length of the fore hatch compared with that aft of the bridge. The position of the foremast about one third back along the forward hatch would appear to preclude the derrick from reaching the forward part of this hold: compare her with the smaller *Nugget* (2) on page 43. *[Glasgow University Archives DC101 0803]*

Topaz (3) was a particularly powerful coaster that was sold soon after completion to Langlands of Glasgow, who were later to buy the *Citrine* (1) for their cargo liner services. *Topaz* became *Princess Sophia,* as seen here in the Avon. She returned to tramping for Glasgow owners as *Clydebrae* in 1912, and survived a submarine attack in late 1917 that left her so badly damaged that she needed a new engine. However, rebuilding gave her 40 more years of life, latterly in the Belfast-based fleet of Hugh Craig and Co. and she survived to become one of the last of the classic steam coasters working on the British coast. *[Robertson archives]*

28.11.1891: Registered in the ownership of William Robertson, Glasgow as TOPAZ.
6.2.1892: Sold to Matthew Langlands and Sons, Glasgow.
24.3.1892: Renamed PRINCESS SOPHIA.
1912: Sold to the Clydeside Steam Ship Co. Ltd. (James B. Couper, manager), Glasgow.
14.8.1913: Renamed CLYDEBRAE.
1916: Sold to Albert Chester, Middlesbrough.
2.10.1917: Torpedoed by the German submarine UB 41 three miles east of Scarborough whilst on a voyage from Calais to Middlesbrough and beached. Five of her crew including her master were killed. Abandoned as a constructive total loss to the North of England Protecting and Indemnity Association (J.S. Todd, manager).
1918: Repaired by Palmer's Shipbuilding and Iron Co. Ltd., Jarrow and fitted with a new engine.
1918: Sold to James Craig, Belfast.
1920: Transferred to Hugh Craig and Co., Belfast.
7.2.1958: Arrived at Dublin to be broken up by the Hammond Lane Metal Co. Ltd.

Onyx at Llanddulas, identified as the short-lived second vessel of the name built in 1891. *[Robertson archives]*

31. ONYX (2) 1891-1898 Steel and iron
O.N. 98688 400g 129n 465d
142.5 x 25.1 x 10.8 feet
T. 3-cyl. by Walker, Henderson and Co., Glasgow; 60 NHP.
15.12.1891: Launched by Scott and Co., Bowling (Yard No. 91).
12.1891: Completed.
6.1.1892: Registered in the ownership of William Robertson, Glasgow as ONYX.
3.11.1898: Foundered 12 miles east south east of the South Arklow Light Vessel whilst on a voyage from Neath Abbey to Dublin with a cargo of coal.
9.11.1898: Register closed.

32. TOPAZ (4) 1892-1895 Steel and iron
O.N. 99817 506g 199n
175.2 x 26.7 x 10.7 feet
T. 3-cyl. by Muir and Houston, Glasgow; 75 NHP, 675 IHP, 12 knots.
26.5.1892: Launched by Scott and Co., Bowling (Yard No. 88).
8.6.1892: Registered in the ownership of William Robertson, Glasgow as TOPAZ.
5.12.1895: Foundered off Start Point whilst on a voyage from Fecamp to Harrington with a cargo of pebbles.
11.12.1895: Register closed.

The first ship for Robertsons from the yard of John Shearer and Sons of Kelvinhaugh, Glasgow was the *Coral* (1) of 1892, seen arriving at Bristol. Of her original full complement of sails, only the jib remains. *[J. and M. Clarkson]*

33. CORAL (1) 1892-1915 Steel and iron
O.N. 99819 477g 170n 600d
165.2 x 26.1 x 10.8 feet
C. 2-cyl. by Ross and Duncan, Govan; 66 NHP, 450 IHP, 11 knots.
28.5.1892: Launched by John Shearer and Sons, Kelvinhaugh, Glasgow (Yard No. 8).
11.6.1892: Registered in the ownership of William Robertson, Glasgow as CORAL. She cost £7,024.
6.2.1915: Sold to James McKelvie (James Steele Smith, trading as Eirinn Steamers Co., managers), Edinburgh for £7,500.
24.5.1915: Renamed ARDRI.
20.7.1916: Sold to William J. Grey, Dublin (James Steele Smith, Edinburgh, manager).
29.5.1917: William J. Grey became manager.
11.10.1923: Sold to John and William Thomas, trading as William Thomas and Sons, Amlwch.
22.1.1936: Sprang a leak and sank 13 miles west of Bardsey whilst on a voyage from London to Glasgow with a cargo of cement.
7.2.1936: Register closed.

34. AMBER (1) 1892-1915 Steel and iron
O.N. 99840 401g 123n 470d
142.5 x 25.1 x 10.8 feet
C. 2-cyl. by Ross and Duncan, Govan; 66 NHP, 530 IHP, 10 knots.
28.7.1892: Launched by Scott and Co., Bowling (Yard No. 93).
10.8.1892: Registered in the ownership of William Robertson, Glasgow as AMBER. She cost £6,076.
8.2.1915: Sold to Kennedy Stewart, Belfast.
5.12.1915: Sold to James McKelvie and Co., Edinburgh for £4,650.
11.2.1916: Sold to William M. Barkley and Sons, Belfast.
12.9.1916: Sold to John Henderson, Belfast.
30.11.1916: Sold to John E. Wellwood, Belfast.
2.5.1917: Captured by the German submarine UC 65 near Skulmartin Lightvessel in Ballyhalbert Bay, County Down and sunk by explosive charges. She was on a voyage from Troon to Waterford with a cargo of coal.
10.5.1917: Register closed.

35. IOLITE 1893-1908 Steel and iron
O.N. 99879 509g 196n
175.0 x 26.6 x 10.7 feet
C. 2-cyl. by Ross and Duncan, Govan; 75 NHP, 700 IHP, 9 knots.
19.1.1893: Launched by Scott and Co., Bowling (Yard No. 96).
1.2.1893: Registered in the ownership of William Robertson, Glasgow as IOLITE.
4.12.1908: Stranded on Grand Lejon Rocks near St. Brieuc whilst on a voyage from Cardiff to St. Brieuc with a cargo of coal.
16.12.1908: Register closed.

36. TURQUOISE (1) 1893-1915 Steel and iron
O.N. 99886 486g 169n 590d
165.2 x 26.1 x 11.1 feet
T. 3-cyl. by Walker, Henderson and Co., Glasgow; 60 NHP.
3.1893: Completed by John Shearer and Sons, Glasgow (Yard No. 11).
24.3.1893: Registered in the ownership of William Robertson, Glasgow as TURQUOISE. She cost £7,640.
22.7.1915: Commissioned as Fleet Messenger No. 30.
31.7.1915: Sunk by gunfire from the German submarine U 28, sixty miles south west of the Scilly Isles, whilst on passage to the Dardanelles.
9.8.1915: Register closed.

37. SPINEL (1) 1893-1933 Steel and iron
O.N. 99895 509g 196n 660d
175.0 x 26.6 x 10.7 feet
T. 3-cyl. by Muir and Houston, Glasgow; 68 NHP, 560 IHP, 10 knots.

6.4.1893: Launched by Scott and Sons, Bowling (Yard No. 97).
24.4.1893: Registered in the ownership of William Robertson, Glasgow as SPINEL.
She cost £8,550.
6.10.1915: Requisitioned by the British Government until 29.6.1920.
22.7.1915: Commissioned as an Admiralty fleet messenger until 29.6.1920.
7.1933: Sold to Smiths, Port Glasgow for breaking up.
14.8.1933: Register closed.

The only known photograph of *Amber* (1), dressed overall (upper right). The name was not used again until 1956. *[Nigel Farrell collection]*

Turquoise (1) was lost whilst on passage to the Dardanelles in 1915 (middle). *[Nigel Farrell collection]*

Spinel (1) has steam to spare as she arrives at Preston (below). Her 40 years of service contrasts with that of her near-sister *Iolite*, wrecked in 1908. *[Ships in Focus]*

Beryl (1) on the Bristol Avon. At 142 feet, she was one of only a handful of Robertson's ships suitable for trading to Ringsend Basin where much of Dublin's extensive coal imports were handled. The shortness of the after hatch is apparent in this view. *[J. and M. Clarkson]*

38. BERYL (1) 1893-1915 Steel and iron

O.N. 102605 402g 122n 470d
142.3 x 25.2 x 10.7 feet
C. 2-cyl. by Ross and Duncan, Govan; 66 NHP, 552 IHP, 9.25 knots.
7.1893: Completed by Scott and Sons, Bowling (Yard No. 98).
12.7.1893: Registered in the ownership of William Robertson, Glasgow as BERYL.
She cost £5,795.
3.2.1915: Sold to James McKelvie trading as Eirinn Steamers Co. (James Steele Smith, manager), Edinburgh for £5,000.
21.5.1915: Renamed FODHLA.
22.6.1921: Manager became John Nicol, Edinburgh.
4.6.1924: Sold to Reuben Burbage-Clark, London.
15.8.1932: Sold to James Mitchell and Co. Ltd., Leith.
1937: Sold to Thomson and McGregor, Bo'ness for breaking up.
25.6.1938: Register closed.

Jargoon (1) in the Avon at Bristol. The shutters have been removed from the large windows fronting the amidships accommodation. Compared with earlier products from Scotts of Bowling, including *Beryl* and *Spinel*, she has considerably shorter masts. *[J. and M. Clarkson]*

39. JARGOON (1) 1893-1917 Steel and iron

O.N. 102649 501g 188n 650d
175.0 x 26.5 x 10.6 feet
C. 2-cyl. by Ross and Duncan, Govan; 81 NHP, 700 IHP, 9.5 knots.
25.11.1893: Launched by Scott and Sons, Bowling (Yard No. 99).
9.12.1893: Registered in the ownership of William Robertson, Glasgow as JARGOON. She cost £7,810.
20.11.1917: Sank eight miles east of the entrance to Belfast Lough after colliding with the steamer TUNISIAN (10,576/1900) whilst on a voyage from Troon to Dublin with a cargo of coal.
4.12.1917: Register closed.

40. OPAL (1) 1894-1916

O.N. 102659 599g 210n 735d
180.0 x 29.1 x 10.6 feet
T. 3-cyl. by Muir and Houston, Glasgow; 120 NHP, 700 IHP, 12 knots.
24.1.1894: Launched by Scott and Sons, Bowling (Yard No. 100).
6.2.1894: Registered in the ownership of William Robertson, Glasgow as OPAL.
She cost £8,086.
18.12.1916: Mined and sunk off the Chicken Rock, Isle of Man whilst on a voyage from Llanddulas to Belfast and the Clyde with a cargo of limestone. The entire crew was lost. The mine was laid by the German submarine U 80.
21.2.1917: Register closed.

41. CITRINE (1)/BRONZITE 1894-1899/1904-1946

O.N. 102687 602g 199n 735d
181.0 x 29.1 x 10.6 feet
T. 3-cyl. by Muir and Houston, Glasgow; 120 NHP, 700 IHP, 12 knots.
21.4.1894: Launched by Scott and Sons, Bowling (Yard No. 104).
8.5.1894: Registered in the ownership of William Robertson, Glasgow as CITRINE.
She cost £8,734.
6.6.1899: Sold to Matthew Langlands and Sons, Glasgow.
4.8.1899: Renamed PRINCESS THYRA.
14.11.1904: Re-acquired by William Robertson, Glasgow for £8,734.
7.12.1904: Renamed BRONZITE.
19.12.1941: Requisitioned by the British government until 5.5.1942, and again from 23.3.1943 until 31.5.1943.
23.3.1946: Sold to Gordon A. Sheves, Fraserburgh and renamed ARCHGROVE.
23.12.1957: Arrived at Antwerp for breaking up by Omer Bulens, Hoboken.

42. DALRIADA 1894-1910 Iron

O.N. 843362 273g 139n 348d
140.0 x 23.0 x 10.5 feet
C. 2-cyl. by William King and Co., Glasgow; 56 NHP.
7.1881: Launched by John Fullerton and Co., Paisley (Yard No. 46).
17.8.1881: Registered in the ownership of Hugh H. Smiley, Paisley as DALRIADA.
20.8.1881: Completed.
6.10.1885: Manager became William Robertson.
22.1.1894: Acquired by William Robertson, Glasgow.
26.4.1910: Wrecked on Russell Rocks, north of The Maidens, whilst on a voyage from Ayr to Larne with a cargo of coal.
28.5.1910: Register closed.

After only five years in the fleet, *Citrine* (1) (top, on trials) was sold to Langlands, Glasgow owners operating cargo liner services, and who probably bought her for her speed. After five years as *Princess Thyra* (upper middle) they sold her back to Robertson, Langlands putting her on a slip at their own expense so that her hull could be examined and her engines opened up. Such had been Robertson's growth that there was now another *Citrine*, so the new name *Bronzite* was taken (lower middle). Her repurchase was a good investment: she served for another 42 years, and in terms of age – 52 – became the second oldest ship ever to work for Robertson. This was not the end of the story, however, as she gave another 11 years of service to Fraserburgh owners as *Archgrove* (bottom), and was 63 years old when broken up. In the final photograph she has gained a closed wheelhouse and lost her mizzen mast - the latter modification probably during the Second World War. *[Glasgow University Archives DC101 0131; World Ship Society Ltd.; Roy Fenton collection (2)]*

A delightful view of *Morion* (1) on the Clyde when relatively new. *[Glasgow University Archives DC101 1379]*

43. MORION (1) 1894-1917 Steel and iron
O.N. 104569 299g 76n 350d
135.0 x 23.1 x 9.9 feet
C. 2-cyl. by Ross and Duncan, Glasgow; 51 NHP, 425 IHP, 9.5 knots.
12.9.1894: Launched by John Shearer and Son, Glasgow (Yard No. 16).
29.9.1894: Registered in the ownership of William Robertson, Glasgow as MORION. She cost £5,250.
2.5.1917: Captured by the German submarine UC 65 and sunk by explosive charges in Ballyhalbert Bay, County Down whilst on a voyage from Dublin to Carnlough in ballast.
12.6.1917: Register closed.

44. MALACHITE (1) 1894-1901
O.N. 104580 605g 196n 740d
180.0 x 29.1 x 10.7 feet
T. 3-cyl. by Muir and Houston, Glasgow; 80 NHP, 600 IHP, 10 knots.
4.10.1894: Launched by Scott and Sons, Bowling (Yard No. 106).
25.10.1894: Registered in the ownership of William Robertson, Glasgow as MALACHITE. She cost £8,829.
9.7.1901: Sold to the Bellambi Coal Co. Ltd., Sydney, New South Wales.
28.4.1915: Sold to Hugh and Roy Cowlishaw, Sydney.
13.7.1915: Sold to Australian Steamships Ltd. (Howard Smith Ltd., managers), Melbourne, Victoria.
31.1.1920: Owner became Australian Steamships Proprietary Ltd., Melbourne, Victoria.
17.7.1928: Capsized whilst lying alongside a wharf at Blackwattle Bay, Sydney.
14.8.1928: Refloated.

In service with Australian Steamships Ltd., a Howard Smith subsidiary, *Malachite* (1) had her masts extended. *[Ian J. Farquhar]*

3.9.1928: Sold to Herbert P. Stacey, Sydney.
22.7.1929: Sold to the Bellambi Coal Co. Ltd., Sydney.
14.4.1930: Re-registered after conversion to a coal hulk.
16.6.1933: Register closed.
28.5.1946: Hulk scuttled off Sydney Heads.

45. ZIRCON 1895
O.N. 104596 605g 196n 740d
180.0 x 29.1 x 10.7 feet
T. 3-cyl. by Muir and Houston, Glasgow; 80 NHP, 600 IHP, 10 knots.
1.12.1894: Launched by Scott and Sons, Bowling (Yard No. 107).
2.1.1895: Registered in the ownership of William Robertson, Glasgow as ZIRCON. She cost £8,820.
23.5.1895: Sank off the Goodwins after a collision with the steamer AHDEEK (1,457/1881) whilst on a voyage from Hamburg to Preston with a cargo of sugar.
15.6.1895: Register closed.

46. GIRASOL (1) 1895-1929
O.N. 104624 602g 197n 725d
180.0 x 29.1 x 10.7 feet
T. 3-cyl. by Muir and Houston, Glasgow; 90

NHP, 650 IHP, 11½ knots.
9.5.1895: Launched by Scott and Sons, Bowling (Yard No. 111).
24.5.1895: Registered in the ownership of William Robertson, Glasgow as GIRASOL. She cost £8,511.
17.3.1918: Requisitioned by the British Government until 21.12.1918.
2.5.1929: Sold to Smith and Co., Port Glasgow.
7.5.1929: Arrived at Port Glasgow to be broken up.
16.8.1929: Register closed.

47. SPHENE (1) 1895-1901
O.N. 105964 411g 95n 465d
142.5 x 25.1 x 10.7 feet
C. 2-cyl. by Muir and Houston, Glasgow; 65 NHP, 450 IHP, 10 knots.
2.11.1895: Launched by Scott and Sons, Bowling (Yard No. 115).
15.11.1895: Registered in the ownership of for William Robertson, Glasgow as SPHENE.
3.9.1901: Sold to Frederick J. Curtis, London.
2.10.1901: Sold to Bernard Byrnes, Sydney, New South Wales.
19.6.1904: Owners became Bernard Byrnes Ltd., Sydney.
6.3.1918: Sold to Roy G. Cowlishaw, Sydney.
17.12.1919: Sold to Australian Steamships Ltd. (Howard Smith Ltd., managers), Melbourne, Victoria.
3.1.1920: Owners became Australian Steamships Propriety Ltd., Melbourne.
16.4.1935: Sold to Alfred Auland, Sydney.
12.7.1935: Renamed DELLIE.
9.7.1936: Owners became Aulco Ltd., Sydney.
8.1.1937: Owners became Aulco Propriety Ltd., Sydney.

Girasol (1), seen at Bristol, probably had a sister in Robertson's shortest-lived ship *Zircon*, as their dimensions match. *[J. and M. Clarkson]*

24.8.1941: Stranded at Fingal Brook, Tweed Heads, New South Wales after striking a reef near Cook Island whilst on a voyage from Hobart to Brisbane with general cargo. Later became a total loss.
15.9.1941: Register closed.

48. NEPHRITE (1) 1896-1927
O.N. 105981 673g 199n 770d
185.0 x 29.1 x 10.8 feet
T. 3-cyl. by Muir and Houston, Glasgow; 90 NHP, 650 IHP, 11.5 knots.
15.2.1896: Launched by Scott and Sons, Bowling (Yard No. 116).
2.1896: Completed.
2.3.1896: Registered in the ownership of William Robertson, Glasgow as NEPHRITE. She cost £8,225.
20.3.1918: Requisitioned by the British Government until 10.3.1919.
2.7.1927: Wrecked on Umfin Island, off Derrybeg, County Donegal, whilst on a voyage from Ayr to Galway with a cargo of coal.
26.8.1927: Register closed.

Sphene (1) had a net tonnage of just 95. Photographed following her sale to Australia, she has additional derricks fitted for the New South Wales coal trade. *[Ian J. Farquhar]*

49. PEARL (4) 1896-1950
O.N. 106026 691g 189n 700d
185.0 x 29.1 x 10.8 feet
T. 3-cyl. by Muir and Houston Ltd., Glasgow; 90 NHP, 650 IHP, 11.5 knots.
8.8.1896: Launched by John Shearer and Son, Kelvinhaugh, Glasgow (Yard No. 19).
31.8.1896: Registered in the ownership of William Robertson, Glasgow as PEARL.
30.3.1915: Requisitioned by the British Government until 12.9.1918.
21.9.1950: Arrived at Llanelly to be broken up by the Rees Shipbreaking Co. Ltd. who began work 30.9.1950. She had been sold for £1,800.
5.10.1951: Register closed.

Costing £5,800 for her hull and another £2,750 for her engines, *Pearl* (4) gave William Robertson an unmatched 54 years of continuous service, a record which merits her both a bow and a stern view. In the latter, taken at Preston, she has a rudimentary covered wheelhouse which was fitted in the 1930s and has lost her mizzen mast. The emergency steering position aft can be seen. She realised £1,800 when sold for scrap in September 1950. *[Ships in Focus; J.and M. Clarkson]*

Topaz (5) on trials, well decorated with flags and – despite the trials being run in November - with a fine turn out of bowler hat wearers on both bridge and forecastle. The short-lived *Kyanite* (1) was a sister. *[Glasgow University Archives DC101 1596]*

50. TOPAZ (5) 1896-1917
O.N. 106049 696g 199n 810d
185.0 x 29.1 x 10.8 feet
T. 3-cyl. by Muir and Houston Ltd., Glasgow; 90 NHP, 650 IHP, 11.5 knots.
7.11.1896: Launched by Scott and Sons, Bowling (Yard No. 122).
30.11.1896: Registered in the ownership of William Robertson, Glasgow as TOPAZ.
She cost £9,006.
12.3.1917: Torpedoed by the German submarine UB 18 in the English Channel 27 miles east by north, half north of Cape Barfleur in position 49.50 north by 00.40 west whilst on a voyage from Honfleur to Port Talbot in ballast. Three members of her crew were lost.
29.3.1917: Register closed.

51. KYANITE (1) 1897-1903
O.N. 106073 712g 235n 840d
185.0 x 29.1 x 10.6 feet
T. 3-cyl. by Muir and Houston Ltd., Glasgow; 80 NHP, 700 IHP, 11 knots.
17.4.1897: Launched by Scott and Sons, Bowling (Yard No. 123).
6.5.1897: Registered in the ownership of William Robertson, Glasgow as KYANITE. She cost £8,807.
17.10.1903: Sank off Dover after colliding with the steamer BUCCLEUGH (785/1885) whilst on a voyage from London to Liverpool with a cargo of bagged cement.
27.10.1903: Register closed.

52. TOURMALINE (1) 1898-1938
O.N. 108705
835g 357n 1,010d
200.0 x 30.1 x 12.1 feet
T. 3-cyl. by Muir and Houston Ltd., Glasgow; 90 NHP, 650 IHP, 11.5 knots.
1.1898: Launched by John Shearer and Son, Kelvinhaugh, Glasgow (Yard No. 20).
16.2.1898: Registered in the ownership of William Robertson, Glasgow as TOURMALINE. She cost £10,832.
26.6.1917: Requisitioned by the British Government until 4.5.1918.
18.11.1938: Sold to the Jenny Steamship Co. Ltd. (George J. Livanos, manager), London
10.1.1939: Renamed BAWTRY.
9.2.1939: Transferred to the Bawtry Steamship Co. Ltd. (George J. Livanos, manager), London.
21.5.1940: Bombed and sunk at Dunkirk where she had arrived 13.5.1940 from the Tees in ballast. There were 14 survivors.
19.7.1940: Register closed.
Later raised by the Germans and renamed RIVAL.
31.12.1944: Sunk at Hamburg during a raid by the Eighth U.S. Army Air Force.

Tourmaline (1) at Avonmouth. *[J. and M. Clarkson]*

The biggest steamer built for Robertsons - larger ones were bought scondhand and managed - *Obsidian* (1) runs trials with house flag flying at the main and name pennant just visible at the fore (above). She was the first vessel for the fleet from the yard of A. Rodger and Co. at Port Glasgow, but was sold within a year. *[Glasgow University Archives DC101 1413]*

Another engines amidships, long quarter deck steamer, *Achroite* enters Preston, possibly on Robertson's only liner route, from Hamburg. Although the larger *Obsidian* and *Corundum* of a similar size were sold soon after delivery, *Achroite* remained in the fleet for 32 years. *[Douglas Cochrane/World Ship Society Ltd.]*

53. FLUOR (1) 1898-1923
O.N. 108712 884g 295n 1,165d
200.0 x 31.1 x 11.9 feet
T. 3-cyl. by Muir and Houston Ltd., Glasgow; 90 NHP, 650 IHP, 11.5 knots.
12.3.1898: Launched by Scott and Sons, Bowling (Yard No. 20).
31.3.1898: Registered in the ownership of William Robertson, Glasgow as FLUOR. She cost £10,932.
1.5.1916: Under British Government requisition whilst on loan to Russia until 31.3.1919.
12.3.1918: Scuttled at Leningrad but later refloated.
19.10.1923: Sold to the Board of Trade (Glover Brothers, managers), London.
1924: Sold to Stelp and Leighton Ltd., London.
2.1924: At Bremen, where she was broken up during the third quarter.
9.2.1925: Register closed.

54. OBSIDIAN (1) 1898-1899
O.N. 108739 1,472g 898n
250.9 x 35.1 x 16.3 feet
T. 3-cyl. by Muir and Houston Ltd., Glasgow; 155 NHP, 1,000 IHP, 10 knots.
25.5.1898: Launched by A. Rodger and Co., Port Glasgow (Yard No. 336).
14.6.1898: Registered in the ownership of William Robertson, Glasgow as OBSIDIAN. She cost £18,008.
3.5.1899: Register closed on sale to Compania Montañesa de Naviera (M. Piñeiro y Compania, managers), Santander, Spain and renamed ASTILLERO.
1902: Manager became M. Piñeiro Bezañilla.
17.2.1913: Sunk after colliding with the French sailing ship ACONCAGUA (1,313/1880) 20 miles north of the Scilly Isles whilst on a voyage from Glasgow to Bordeaux with a cargo of coal.

55. ACHROITE 1898-1930
O.N. 108756 1,196g 710n 1,660d
230.0 x 34.1 x 14.2 feet
T. 3-cyl. by Muir and Houston Ltd., Glasgow; 96 NHP, 700 IHP, 10 knots.
5.8.1898: Launched by John Shearer and Son, Kelvinhaugh, Glasgow (Yard No. 24).
26.8.1898: Registered in the ownership of William Robertson, Glasgow as ACHROITE. She cost £14,850.
28.9.1914: Requisitioned by the British Government until 1.11.1919.
16.4.1930: Sold to the Maryland Shipping Co. Ltd. (Alan Bell, manager), Hull.
6.5.1930: Register closed on sale to Rederi A/B Hannah (G.H. Dalgren, manager), Helsingborg, Sweden and renamed HANNAH.
1935: Manager became Stig Gorthon.
23.10.1940: Wrecked outside Leixoes Harbour whilst on passage from Cardiff to Leixoes with a cargo of coal.

56. CORUNDUM (1) 1899-1900
O.N. 108783 1,202g 728n 1,810d
230.0 x 35.1 x 13.9 feet
T. 3-cyl. by Muir and Houston Ltd., Glasgow; 96 NHP, 700 IHP, 10 knots.
3.11.1898: Launched by Scott and Sons, Bowling (Yard No. 131).
14.1.1899: Registered in the ownership of William Robertson, Glasgow as CORUNDUM. She cost £14,450.
9.10.1900: Register closed on sale to Compania Anonima Maritima La Actividad (E. Munitas, manager), Bilbao, Spain for £4,420 and renamed ACTIVO.
13.5.1912: Registered in the ownership of John Stewart and Walter Fulton, Glasgow as CORUNDUM.
26.5.1913: Transferred to the Corundum Shipping Co. Ltd. (John Stewart and Co., managers), Glasgow.
17.10.1914: Sank after colliding with the steamer KYLENESS (3,444/1901) six miles south west of Helwick Light Vessel whilst on a voyage from Burryport to Rouen with a cargo of coal. There were no casualties amongst the crew of 17.
5.11.1914: Register closed.

57. PRASE (1) 1899-1931 Iron and steel
O.N. 108784 285g 72n 290d
135.1 x 21.1 x 9.4 feet
C. 2-cyl. by Muir and Houston Ltd., Glasgow; 42 NHP, 320 IHP, 9 knots.
17.12.1898: Launched by Carmichael, MacLean and Co., Greenock (Yard No. 22).
31.1.1899: Registered in the ownership of William Robertson, Glasgow as PRASE. She cost £5,280.
1.4.1931: Sold to Thomas Dougall, Glasgow.
21.4.1931: Renamed APPIN.
13.12.1933: Stranded at Carnalea after her anchors had dragged in Belfast Lough whilst on a voyage from Coleraine to Carlingford in ballast.
4.1.1934: Register closed.

The years 1898 and 1899 saw the largest as well as some of the smallest ships delivered to Robertson. The 135-foot *Prase* has a steering position situated no higher than the raised quarter deck, and would give very poor visibility, especially when the ship was unladen and down by the stern. Nevertheless, she remained in the fleet for 32 years and even then could find a new owner, although he took less care of her than Robertson and lost her in December 1933. *[J. and M. Clarkson]*

Plasma gave even better service than her sister *Prase*, lasting 43 years with Robertson, and still finding another buyer. *[World Ship Society Ltd.]*

58. PLASMA 1899-1942 Iron and steel
O.N. 108792 325g 86n 335d
135.4 x 23.0 x 10.0 feet
C. 2-cyl. by Muir and Houston Ltd., Glasgow; 42 NHP, 320 IHP, 9 knots.
17.12.1898: Launched by Carmichael, MacLean and Co., Greenock (Yard No. 21).
1.1899: Completed.
14.2.1899: Registered in the ownership of William Robertson, Glasgow as PLASMA. She cost £5,450.
31.7.1942: Sold to Gordon A. Sheves, Fraserburgh.
23.11.1945: Renamed ARCHELLA.
11.6.1946: Sold to Joseph Barlow and John Sinclair, Dundee.
31.12.1946: Stranded in fog between Whitburn and Marsden, two miles north of Sunderland, whilst on a voyage from Kirkwall to Sunderland and beached in the River Wear at Sunderland.
3.4.1947: Arrived on the Tyne for repairs.
6.12.1950: Register closed, broken up.

59. AXINITE (1) 1899-1912
O.N. 111223 1,744g 1,095n 2,740d
260.0 x 37.4 x 16.9 feet
T. 3-cyl. by Muir and Houston Ltd., Glasgow; 155 NHP.
9.1899: Launched by A. Rodger and Co., Port Glasgow (Yard No. 344).
6.10.1899: Registered in the ownership of William Robertson, Glasgow as AXINITE. She cost £21,250.
12.2.1912: Sold to the Mossgiel Steamship Co. Ltd. (John Bruce and Co., managers), Glasgow for £14,850.
14.2.1912: Renamed ALHAMA.
3.3.1916: Sold to Bolivian General Enterprise Ltd. (Leopold Walford (London) Ltd., managers), London.
26.4.1917: Sank one and a half miles north of Calais pier head after striking a mine whilst on a voyage from Bayonne to Dunkirk with a cargo of pitprops.
10.5.1917: Register closed.

60. CITRINE (2) 1899-1915
O.N. 111237 1,743g 1,095n 2,740d
259.9 x 37.4 x 16.9 feet
T. 3-cyl. by Muir and Houston Ltd., Glasgow; 155 NHP, 1,000 IHP, 10 knots.
30.11.1899: Launched by A. Rodger and Co., Port Glasgow (Yard No. 345).
26.12.1899: Registered in the ownership of William Robertson, Glasgow as CITRINE. She cost £21,250.
23.7.1915: Sold to the Town Line (London) Ltd. (Harrison, Sons and Co., managers), Cardiff for £23,760.
26.7.1915: Renamed AVONTOWN.
22.9.1924: Sold to Percy J. Copeman, London.
10.12.1924: Sold to Hallett, Dixon and Co., Ltd., Cardiff.
18.6.1925: Transferred to G.A. Harrison and Hallett Dixon Ltd., Cardiff.
6.7.1925: Renamed COPEMAN.
25.2.1931: Sold to Lionel W.B. Hitchen, London.
21.5.1931: Renamed POMARON.
4.1936: Sold to Usalduhing Jacobson ja Ko, Parnu, Estonia (Charles Strubin and Co. Ltd., London, managers).
21.1.1938: Captured by the Spanish Nationalist cruiser V. PUCHOL in the Straits of Gibraltar and later renamed BILBAO .
1939: Owners became the Spanish Government, Madrid (Companhia Trasmediterránea, Barcelona, Spain, managers) and renamed CASTILLO BUTRON.
About 1944: Transferred to Empresa Nacional 'Elcano' de la Marina Mercante, Madrid.
1954: Sold to Compania Vasco-Cantabrica de Navegacion, Bilbao, Spain.
1959: Renamed RIO JILOCA.
9.1963: Broken up by Don Jenaro Menendez Cebrian at Santander following stranding.

61. BRILLIANT (1) 1901-1939
O.N. 114003 657g 262n 775d
185.0 x 29.2 x 10.8 feet
T. 3-cyl. by Muir and Houston Ltd., Glasgow; 91 NHP, 600 IHP, 10 knots.
12.12.1901: Launched by Scott and Sons, Bowling (Yard No. 150).
3.1.1902: Registered in the ownership of William Robertson, Glasgow as BRILLIANT. She cost £11,551 5s 0d.
17.1.1915: Requisitioned by the British Government until 25.8.1919.
17.7.1939: Sold to Karl Heinz Kopf and others, Tallinn, Estonia and renamed GAMMA.
10.1940: Expropriated by the USSR during the annexation of Estonia, owners becoming Estonskoye Gosudarstvyennoye Morskoye Parokhodstvo, Tallinn.
26.8.1941: Sunk by German artillery near Juminda during the Russian evacuation of Tallinn.

Brilliant (1) on the Thames with a yellow funnel (top) and on the Mersey (middle). *[Ships in Focus; Basil Feilden/J. and M. Clarkson]*
Olivine (2) on the Clyde (below right). As with *Brilliant* (1) in the top photograph, the unusual yellow funnel has not been explained. *[Glasgow University Archives]*

62. OLIVINE (2) 1902-1915
O.N. 114028 634g 240n 800d
185.2 x 29.2 x 10.8 feet
T. 3-cyl. by Muir and Houston Ltd., Glasgow; 91 NHP, 600 IHP, 10 knots.
20.2.1902: Launched by John Shearer and Son, Kelvinhaugh, Glasgow (Yard No. 31).
8.3.1902: Registered in the ownership of William Robertson, Glasgow as OLIVINE. She cost £11,511 5s 0d.
1.4.1915: Requisitioned by the British government.
4.4.1915: Torpedoed and sunk by the German submarine U 31 thirty miles south of St. Catherine's Point, Isle of Wight whilst on a voyage from Guernsey to Calais with a cargo of granite.
10.4.1915: Register closed.

63. OBSIDIAN (2) 1902-1918
O.N. 115705 742g 310n 990d
195.2 x 30.1 x 11.2 feet
T. 3-cyl. by A. Rodger and Co., Govan; 99 NHP, 750 IHP, 10 knots.
8.8.1902: Launched by A. Rodger and Co., Port Glasgow (Yard No. 364).
28.8.1902: Registered in the ownership of William Robertson, Glasgow as OBSIDIAN. She cost £12,412 5s 0d.
1.5.1916: Under British Government requisition whilst on loan to Russia.
4.4.1918: Scuttled in Sveaborg Roads.
17.3.1902: Register closed.

Obsidian (2) running trials with her firemen working hard. She has light walkways rigged across both hatches, perhaps to make access easier for the those witnessing the trials. *[Glasgow University Archives DC101 1414]*

64. SPHENE (2) 1902-1916
O.N. 115710 740g 309n 990d
195.4 x 30.1 x 11.1 feet
T. 3-cyl. by A. Rodger and Co., Govan; 99 NHP, 750 IHP, 10 knots.
10.9.1902: Launched by A. Rodger and Co., Port Glasgow (Yard No. 365) for the company as SPHENE.
23.9.1902: Registered in the ownership of William Robertson, Glasgow as SPHENE. She cost £11,720.
3.8.1916: Captured by the German submarine UB 18 and sunk by explosives 26 miles south west of St. Catherine's Point, Isle of Wight whilst on a voyage from Honfleur to Newport in ballast.
11.8.1916: Register closed.

65. MALACHITE (2) 1902-1914
O.N. 115713 718g 312n 985d
195.6 x 30.2 x 11.2 feet
C. 2-cyl. by Ross and Duncan, Glasgow; 98 NHP, 850 IHP, 10.25 knots.
8.9.1902: Launched by John Shearer and Son, Kelvinhaugh, Glasgow (Yard No. 32).
30.9.1902: Registered in the ownership of William Robertson, Glasgow as MALACHITE. She cost £12,381 1s 0d.
23.11.1914: Captured by the German submarine U 21 and sunk by gunfire four miles north by west of Cap La Hève whilst on a voyage from Liverpool to Le Havre with general cargo. Her crew was allowed to leave in the ship's boats.
17.12.1914: Register closed.

Despite her considerable length, *Sphene* (2) was of the conventional bridge-amidships, engines-aft design. *[J. and M. Clarkson]*

Malachite (2) arrives at Preston in the years before the First World War. *[Roy Fenton collection]*

66. HEMATITE 1903-1937
O.N. 115741 722g 302n 990d
195.7 x 30.1 x 11.2 feet
C. 2-cyl. by Ross and Duncan, Govan; 98 NHP, 800 IHP, 10 knots.
15.1.1903: Launched by Scott and Sons, Bowling (Yard No. 158).
1.1903: Completed.
2.2.1903: Registered in the ownership of William Robertson, Glasgow as HEMATITE.
She cost £12,381 1s 0d.
9.10.1914: Requisitioned by the British government until 29.4.1919.
13.2.1937: Foundered after striking a rock between the North and South Bishop, Pembrokeshire whilst on a voyage from Dublin to Newport in ballast.
2.3.1937: Register closed.

Notwithstanding damage to the negative, this is a fine view of *Hematite* arriving at Bristol. *[J. and M. Clarkson]*

67. ONYX (3) 1903-1910
O.N. 119063 557g 219n 705d
170.7 x 27.1 x 10.5 feet
T. 3-cyl. by Ross and Duncan, Govan; 81 NHP, 550 IHP, 9 knots.
7.10.1903: Launched by Scott and Sons, Bowling (Yard No. 152).
10.1903: Completed.
2.11.1903: Registered in the ownership of William Robertson, Glasgow as ONYX. She had been ordered by a company based in the north east and was bought on the stocks by Robertson for £8,650, plus £36 14s 0d for work in connection with electric lighting.
17.2.1910: Sold to William D. Whitehead, Vancouver, British Columbia.
18.2.1910: Renamed BRITISH COLUMBIA.
10.2.1915: Transferred to the Coast Steamship Co. Ltd. (William D. Whitehead, manager), Vancouver.
12.5.1916: Sold to Harry F. Bullen, Victoria.
19.6.1916: Sold to the Western Shipping Co. Ltd., Victoria.
19.12.1916: Sold to the Coastwise Steam Ship and Barge Co. Ltd., Vancouver.
6.1.1919: Sold to the Union Steamship Co. of British Columbia Ltd., Vancouver.
13.2.1919: Renamed CHILLIWACK.
1.2.1926: Transferred to Union Steamships Ltd., Vancouver.
7.12.1926: Register closed on sale to USA to be broken up. However, then re-registered.
1927: Sold to Francis Millerd, Vancouver and converted to a floating cannery (one source describes her as a barge, presumably because her engine was removed).
15.6.1927: Sold to the Somerville Cannery Co. Ltd., Vancouver.
23.6.1928: Sold to Markale Fisheries Ltd., Vancouver.
27.7.1928: Resold to Somerville Cannery Co. Ltd., Vancouver.
6.11.1930: Sold to North Western Dredging Co. Ltd., Vancouver and immediately resold to Albert Berquist, Vancouver.
20.1.1931: Sold to John W. Patterson, Vancouver.
18.4.1931: Register closed, vessel dismantled and broken up by John Wilson, Vancouver.

A pristine *Onyx* (3), photographed when new (above). *[Glasgow University Archives DC101 1421]*

On the night of 12th February 1907, a severe north westerly gale in the Irish Sea drove the *Onyx* and another steam coaster, the Glasgow-owned *Moray Firth* (359/1904), on to the beach at Llanddulas. *Onyx* was partly loaded, and had probably stood off from the jetty during the storm: she ended up broadside on to the shingle about 500 yards to the west of the jetty. She was listing about 20 degrees, her seaward side badly beaten in, and with water rising and falling in her hold and engine room. Her stern post was bent, her rudder gone, the propellor damaged and boats washed away. An officer of the Liverpool Salvage Association was quickly on the scene and feared that there was internal damage but, with the cargo thrown over to leewards, he could not carry out a full inspection. Indeed, there was difficulty getting aboard from the landward side, and the Association's salvage steamer *Ranger* (409/1880) could not get alongside. Eventually a lighter drafted steamer was used, named as *Merlin*, and probably the wooden vessel owned by Zillah Shipping and Carrying Co. Ltd., which was a regular trader in the area (124/1895). It was considered possible to refloat *Onyx*, but the operation would be expensive, requiring her cargo to be discharged, the hull to be patched and pumps put aboard.

Anchors were laid out to hold *Onyx* in position, and discharge of her limestone cargo began, being completed by Monday 18th February. The next day pumps arrived by rail, and it was hoped to refloat her on the next spring tide. However, heavy weather continued and on the 21st it was reported that *Onyx* had sustained more damage, with the hull further beaten in on the seaward side; frames, beams and hold stanchions broken or bent; and bilges crushed. Indeed, 'Lloyd's Lists' was told that she was '... rapidly unrivetting herself as heavy seas shake her terribly'. Fortunately the gale moderated, and log beams could be placed in the holds to help support the hull. Pumps were now placed on board and presumably the hull was patched up. Tugs were ordered, and about noon on 27th February *Onyx* was pulled off the beach, and towed away to Liverpool by the paddle tug *Pathfinder* (377/1877) of the Liverpool Steam Tug Co. Ltd.

Not surprisingly in view of the damage, repairs on the Mersey were protracted, and she was not ready for sea again until 20th June 1907.

The saga was recorded in photographs retained by the Robertsons and reproduced on this page. They show the list and the jetty in the background (top), and discharge of her cargo in progress (middle). The most dramatic picture is the bottom one, taken at the time she was pulled off. The pumps on her deck are working hard as are two paddle tugs, the more distant one being the *Pathfinder*. The damage to the rudder post can be clearly seen, and only one of her boats remains. In the low February sunlight a gang of workers watches operations, some from the heap of stone discharged from her hold. *[Robertson archives]*

Ruby (3) approaches Preston in the years before the First World War (above). She is seen again in Queen's Dock, Glasgow (below). *[J. and M. Clarkson; Robertson archives]*

68. RUBY (3) 1904-1936
O.N. 119106 406g 127n 500d
142.5 x 26.1 x 10.9 feet
C. 2-cyl by Muir and Houston Ltd., Glasgow; 91 NHP, 600 IHP, 10 knots.
3.2.1904: Launched by Scott and Sons, Bowling (Yard No. 167).
11.3.1904: Registered in the ownership of William Robertson, Glasgow as RUBY. She cost £8,734.
8.5.1936: Register closed on sale to Karl Heinz Kopf, Tallinn, Estonia and renamed ALFA.
19.2.1939: Damaged by stranding west of Arendsburg Oesel Island whilst on a voyage from Riga to Klaipeda with general cargo. Later refloated and broken up.

69. CAIRNGORM (2) 1904-1936
O.N. 119113 401g 117n 510d
141.7 x 26.1 x 10.9 feet
C. 2-cyl by Muir and Houston Ltd., Glasgow; 91 NHP, 600 IHP, 10 knots.
21.3.1904: Launched by John Shearer and Sons Ltd., Glasgow (Yard No. 36).
31.3.1904: Registered in the ownership of William Robertson, Glasgow as CAIRNGORM. She cost £7,707 5s 0d.
4.1904: Completed.
12.10.1936: Sold to John Psaroudis, London.
1.7.1937: Register closed, sold for breaking up.

Cairngorm (2) on the Clyde as new with stone-coloured superstructure (above) and later, on the Avon, with deck houses partly painted white (below). The foresail has gone: when the original set was no longer serviceable, it was rarely replaced on steam coasters.*[Glasgow University Archives DC101 0991; J. and M. Clarkson]*

70. EMERALD (2) 1904-1944
O.N. 119153 736g 305n 1,010d
195.0 x 30.1 x 11.2 feet
T. 3-cyl. by A. Rodger and Co., Govan; 99 NHP, 750 IHP, 10 knots.
2.8.1904: Launched by A. Rodger and Co., Port Glasgow (Yard No. 379).
16.8.1904: Registered in the ownership of William Robertson, Glasgow as EMERALD.
17.9.1914: Requisitioned by the British government until 4.4.1919.
9.8.1940: Requisitioned by the British government and converted to a dummy corvette by Harland and Wolff Ltd., London.
7.8.1942: Returned to owners, having been reconverted to a cargo vessel by Harland and Wolff Ltd.
28.12.1943: Requisitioned by the British government.
31.1.1944: Torpedoed and sunk by the German motor torpedo boat S 142 south east of Beachy Head in position 50.03.14 north by 00.25.35 east whilst on a voyage from Middlesbrough to Poole with a cargo of coal. Her entire crew of fifteen was lost.
5.2.1944: Register closed.

Emerald (2) in Preston Dock. She was under British government requisition in both world wars. When requisitioned on the second occasion in 1940 she became a dummy corvette, but was back in use as a coaster when torpedoed with heavy loss of life in January 1944. *[J. and M. Clarkson]*

71. KYANITE (2) 1904-1917
O.N. 119156 564g 200n 720d
175.2 x 28.2 x 10.6 feet
T.3-cyl. by Muir and Houston Ltd., Glasgow; 99 NHP, 600 IHP, 10 knots.
10.8.1904: Launched by John Shearer and Son, Kelvinhaugh, Glasgow (Yard No. 37).
26.8.1904: Registered in the ownership of William Robertson, Glasgow as KYANITE.
She cost £9,597 5s 0d.

Remarkably, *Kyanite* (2) was salvaged after coming to grief off the Lizard on 24th June 1915, but was sunk some 20 months later. *[Nigel Farrell collection]*

15.2.1917: Captured by the German submarine UC 65 and sunk by explosive charges 27 miles south south west of Bardsey in position 52.18 north by 04.55 west whilst on a voyage from Fleetwood to Bristol with a cargo of alkali.
15.3.1917: Register closed.

72. ESSONITE (1) 1904-1917
O.N. 119193 589g 211n 635d
174.8 x 28.1 x 10.7 feet
T.3-cyl. by Muir and Houston Ltd., Glasgow; 99 NHP, 600 IHP, 10 knots.
11.11.1904: Launched by Scott and Sons, Bowling (Yard No. 174).
5.12.1904: Registered in the ownership of William Robertson, Glasgow as ESSONITE. She cost £9,597 5s 0d.
1.2.1917: Torpedoed and sunk by the German submarine U 55 three miles north north west of Trevose Head in position 50.35 north by 05.04 west whilst on a voyage from Caernarvon to Rochester with a cargo of stone. Ten of her crew were lost.
16.2.1917: Register closed.

73. SAGENITE 1904-1939
O.N. 119195 712g 288n 1,010d
194.7 x 30.2 x 11.2 feet
T. 3-cyl. by Ross and Duncan, Govan; 99 NHP, 760 IHP, 10.5 knots.
24.11.1904: Launched by John Shearer and Sons Ltd., Kelvinhaugh, Glasgow (Yard No. 38).
9.12.1904: Registered in the ownership of William Robertson, Glasgow as SAGENITE. She cost £11,732 5s 0d.
7.9.1914: Requisitioned by the British Government until 31.3.1919.
11.12.1939: Sold to Benjamin J. Morgan and Co., Cardiff.
19.5.1940: Renamed ELLAROY.
21.7.1940: Sunk by gunfire from the German submarine U.30 about 200 miles west of Cape Finisterre in position 42.30 north by 12.36 west whilst on a voyage from Lisbon to Newport with a cargo of pit wood. Her crew of 16 was rescued and landed at Vigo.
29.10.1940: Register closed.

Essonite (1) in the Avon. *[Robertson archives]*

A flurry of new buildings came to an end with *Sagenite*, after which no new ships entered the fleet for four years. Photographed at Jersey, the 194-foot *Sagenite* was one of the larger members of Robertson's fleet. *[World Ship Society Ltd.]*

At almost 200 feet, *Felspar* was one of Robertson's longest ships to have her engines aft (above), and is also notable as having been requisitioned for war service by the British government for a total of 12 years.

Robertson records show that she cost £12,615, with payments of £3,100 made on 11th March 1908 when framing was completed, a second instalment on 23rd April, a third on her launch on 4th June and a final one on 23rd June when complete. Extras came to £215.

It was money well spent, and even after 32 years' service a new owner considered her worth repairing following a serious collision in May 1950 (opposite page) from which she came off better than her Spanish adversary and she emerged as *Holdernab* (below). *[Above: J. and M. Clarkson; right: Robertson archives; below: Fotoflite incorporating Skyfotos]*

74. FELSPAR 1908-1950
O.N. 128199 799g 331n 1,040d
199.0 x 30.1 x 11.3 feet
T. 3-cyl. by A. Rodger and Co., Govan; 99 NHP, 750 IHP, 9.5 knots.
4.6.1908: Launched by A. Rodger and Co., Port Glasgow (Yard No. 406).
24.6.1908: Registered in the ownership of William Robertson, Glasgow as FELSPAR. She cost £12,615.
1.9.1914: Requisitioned by the British Government until 6.2.1920.
21.5.1940: Requisitioned by the British government until 22.5.1946.
14.5.1949: Transferred to William Robertson Shipowners Ltd., Glasgow.
26.5.1950: Beached two miles west of Deal following a collision with the Spanish steamer CABO ESPARTEL (3,712/1920) (which sank) three miles east of Dungeness whilst on a voyage from Newlyn to London with a cargo of stone.
27.6.1950: Sold to the Holderness Steamship Co. Ltd. (Thomas E. Kettlewell and Son Ltd., managers), Hull for £7,000.
18.7.1950: Renamed HOLDERNAB.
12.11.1951: Transferred to Roberts and Cooper (Hull) Ltd. (Thomas E. Kettlewell and Son Ltd., managers), Hull.
30.1.1955: Arrived at Troon to be broken up by the West of Scotland Shipbreaking Co. Ltd.
26.7.1955: Register closed.

These photographs show the aftermath of the collision between *Felspar* and a much larger Spanish steamer in the English Channel during May 1950. The above shot was taken after she had been beached near Deal, and the remainder after jettisoning part of her cargo, refloating and towing to Dover. From there she was taken to the Tyne for repairs, but within a month of the incident had been sold to owners in Hull who were building up a considerable fleet of superannuated steam coasters. *[Robertson archives].*

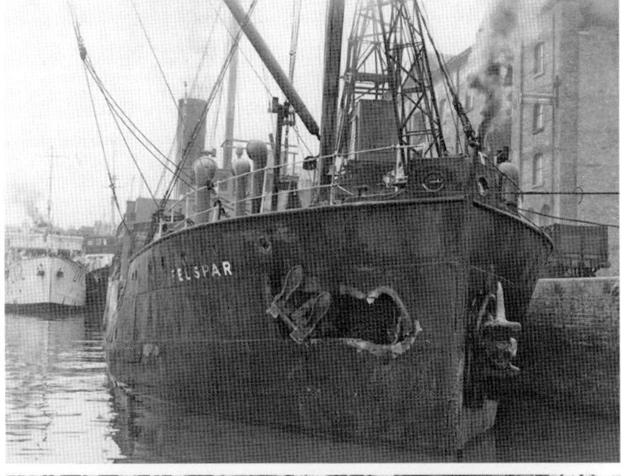

75. SARD (2) 1909-1943
O.N. 128259 410g 155n 500d
142.3 x 26.1 x 11.3 feet
C. 2-cyl. by Muir and Houston Ltd., Glasgow; 91 NHP, 600 IHP, 10 knots.
8.3.1909: Launched by the Ailsa Shipbuilding Co. Ltd., Ayr (Yard No. 219).
6.4.1909: Registered in the ownership of William Robertson, Glasgow as SARD. She cost £7,901.
28.12.1943: Sold to Robert Kinnes and Sons, Dundee.
22.10.1945: Sold to the Tay Sand Co. Ltd. (John Neilson, manager), Dundee.
18.1.1946: Renamed ARCHROYAL.
29.4.1947: Sold to Thomas Stone (Shipping) Ltd., Swansea.
12.6.1947: Renamed FENSTONE.
13.7.1950: Mined and sunk near the Terschelling Light Vessel in position 53.07.49 north by 04.36.44 east whilst on a voyage from Emden to Hull with a cargo of scrap iron. Her crew was rescued.
15.8.1950: Register closed.

Sard (2) just prior to her launch at Ayr on 8th March 1909 (left). The dress of the shipyard hands on board contrasts with that of the launch party below, which undoubtedly includes William Robertson. *Sard* was the first of a large number of Robertson ships from the Ailsa yard. Photographed 30 years later, on 27th April 1939, *Sard's* masts are at odd angles and she has a distinct list to port, probably because of uneven coal distribution in side bunkers (below). *[Robertson archives; Graham Langmuir/Roy Fenton collection]*

76. AMETHYST (3) 1910-1911
O.N. 129472 662g 263n 750d
185.3 x 29.6 x 10.9 feet
T. 3-cyl. by Muir and Houston Ltd., Glasgow; 103 NHP, 850 IHP, 10.5 knots.
10.2.1910: Launched by Scott and Sons, Bowling (Yard No. 219).
1.3.1910: Registered in the ownership of William Robertson, Glasgow as AMETHYST. She cost £11,300.
13.3.1911: Sold to the Grand Trunk Pacific Development Co. Ltd. (C.H. Nicholson, manager), Montreal, Canada.
Rebuilt with passenger accommodation by A. Rodger and Co., Port Glasgow.
5.5.1911: Renamed PRINCE JOHN.
17.5.1911: Sailed from the Clyde for Vancouver.
27.10.1936: Sold to Prince John Ltd. (Canadian National Steamships, managers), Toronto, Canada.
7.6.1940: Sold to Union Steamships Ltd. (Eric W. Sheffield, manager), Vancouver, British Columbia.
15.7.1940: Renamed CASSIAR.
11.4.1951: Register closed on sale to Walter W. Johnson Co., San Francisco, USA.
5.1951: Breaking up began by at Stockton, California, USA.

Just a year after delivery *Amethyst* (3) (above) was sold to Canadian owners and rebuilt with accommodation for 52 first-class passenger mostly in a 70-foot deckhouse as *Prince John* (below). The attraction was her exceptional speed of 12 knots. In later life she was used between Prince Rupert, terminus of the Grand Trunk Railway, and Queen Charlotte Island. During the Second World War she carried spruce for aircraft construction. *[Glasgow University Archives DC101 0876; Robertson archives]*

77. ONYX (4) 1910-1937
O.N. 129501 592g 241n 740d
182.2 x 28.1 x 10.8 feet
T. 3-cyl. by Muir and Houston Ltd., Glasgow; 85 NHP, 750 IHP, 10 knots.
25.5.1910: Launched by Scott and Son, Bowling (Yard No. 221).
14.6.1910: Registered in the ownership of William Robertson, Glasgow as ONYX. She cost £9,875.
31.8.1937: Sold to the Porth Shipping Co. Ltd. (Richard P. Care and Co. Ltd., managers), Cardiff.
7.10.1937: Renamed PORTHMORNA.
7.5.1945: Transferred to Care Lines Ltd. (Richard P. Care and Co. Ltd., managers), Cardiff.
21.2.1948: Sold to George W. Grace and Co. Ltd., London.
22.4.1948: Renamed SUSSEX ASH.
8.4.1952: Arrived at Dunston-on-Tyne to be broken up by Clayton and Davie Ltd.
14.7.1952: Register closed.

Onyx (4) on the Thames in ballast (top) and at Southampton with White Star's *Majestic* (56,551/1921) in the background (middle). The third photograph shows her with her third owner and name, *Sussex Ash*, carrying a timber cargo. She has been fitted with a wheelhouse but has lost her mizzen mast. This modification was usual in coasters that served in the Second World War as this mast tended to reduce the arc of fire of any anti-aircraft guns carried: coasters being particularly vulnerable to Luftwaffe attacks. *[World Ship Society Ltd. (2); Fotoflite incorporating Skyfotos/ Roy Fenton collection]*

Agate (2) was the only ship completed for Robertson during the First World War (left). She had particularly large hatches. Her stranding in December 1940 may have been due to lights round the UK coast being extinguished in wartime. *[Harry Stewart/J. and M. Clarkson]*

Photographed at launch in October 1919 (middle) and at Preston (bottom), *Malachite* (3) was one of many steam coasters built by Dutch yards around the end of the First World War and was the first Robertson ship built outside the United Kingdom, indeed the first from beyond the west of Scotland. Note in the launch photo the non-standard white spirket plate, soon repainted black. *[Robertson archives; Harry Stewart/J. and M. Clarkson]*

78. AGATE (2) 1917-1940
O.N. 137844 824g 397n 990d
199.4 x 30.1 x 11.9 feet
T. 3-cyl. by Ross and Duncan, Govan; 108 NHP, 750 IHP, 10 knots.
22.2.1917: Launched by Scott and Son, Bowling (Yard No. 261).
15.3.1917: Registered in the ownership of William Robertson, Glasgow as AGATE. She cost £20,438.
5.1917: Completed.
30.12.1940: Wrecked four miles north of Oversay Lighthouse, Islay whilst on a voyage from Goole to Belfast with a cargo of coal.
12.2.1941: Register closed.

79. MALACHITE (3) 1920-1939
O.N. 141944 743g 329n 960d
188.0 x 28.1 x 12.2 feet
T. 3-cyl. by Penn and Bauduin, Dordrecht, Netherlands; 650 IHP, 9 knots.
10.1919: Launched by Scheepsbouwwerft v/h T. Nederlof, Sliedrecht, Netherlands (Yard No. 298).
24.2.1920: Registered in the ownership of William Robertson, Glasgow as MALACHITE. She cost £46,750.
30.11.1939: Sold to the Cook Shipping Co. Ltd. (Ambrose, Davies and Matthews Ltd., managers), London.
27.12.1939: Renamed BRYNMILL.
2.11.1941: Damaged by enemy aircraft 210 degrees and four miles from the East Dudgeon Buoy (59A) whilst on a voyage from Blyth to London with a cargo of coal. Taken in tow, but the towrope parted and she sank five miles west of the East Dudgeon Bell Buoy. Her crew was rescued.
22.4.1942: Register closed.

Essonite (2) (above) and *Kyanite* (3) were part of a three-ship order building by Yarrow and Co. Ltd. for Cargo Steamships Ltd. of Dublin, and were sold to Robertson when the shipping market collapsed in 1921. *[Harry Stewart/J. and M. Clarkson]*

80. ESSONITE (2) 1921-1939
O.N. 146265 642g 266n 740d
175.1 x 28.1 x 11.2 feet
T. 3-cyl. by Yarrow and Co. Ltd., Scotstoun; 120 NHP, 750 IHP, 9-10 knots.
29.9.1921: Launched by Yarrow and Co. Ltd., Scotstoun (Yard No. 1460).
16.11.1921: Registered in the ownership of William Robertson, Glasgow as ESSONITE. She cost £47,500.
29.12.1939: Sold to Gilchrist's Traders (Steamships) Ltd. (R. Gilchrist and Co., managers), Liverpool.
2.2.1940: Renamed MEG MERRILIES.
27.3.1941: Bombed and damaged by enemy aircraft one mile south of St. Govan's Light Vessel whilst on a voyage from Newport to Liverpool with tinplate and general cargo. Although taken in tow she sank three and a half miles north north west of St. Govan's Light Vessel. Her crew of 14 was rescued.
10.4.1941: Register closed.

81. KYANITE (3) 1923-1939
O.N. 146271 643g 266n 740d
182.3 x 28.1 x 11.2 feet
T. 3-cyl. by Yarrow and Co. Ltd., Scotstoun; 120 NHP, 750 IHP, 9-10 knots.
3.11.1921: Launched by Yarrow and Co. Ltd., Scotstoun (Yard No. 1461).
2.12.1921: Registered in the ownership of William Robertson, Glasgow as KYANITE. She cost £47,500.
1.1922: Completed.
31.10.1939: Sold to Care Lines Ltd. (Richard P. Care and Co. Ltd., managers), Cardiff.
1.11.1939: Renamed PORTHREPTA.
13.10.1954: Sold to the Holderness Steam Ship Co. Ltd., Hull.
8.11.1954: Renamed HOLDERNETT.
4.4.1955: Handed over to T.W. Ward Ltd. for breaking up at Grays, Essex.

Kyanite (3) at Preston, part of the same order as *Essonite* (2). *[Douglas Cochrane/World Ship Society Ltd.]*

82. NUGGET (3) 1922-1926
O.N. 129471 405g 152n 530d
142.2 x 26.1 x 11.1 feet
C. 2-cyl. by David Rowan and Co., Govan; 96 NHP, 550 IHP, 9.5 knots.
25.1.1910: Launched by John Fullerton and Co., Paisley (Yard No. 213).
2.1910: Completed.
21.4.1910: Registered in the ownership of the Clydeside Steam Ship Co. Ltd. (James B. Couper, manager), Glasgow as CLYDESIDE.
16.2.1917: Transferred to the Western Transport and Trading Co. Ltd. (James B. Couper, manager), Glasgow.
6.2.1920: Sold to the Shields Shipping Co. Ltd. (Joseph B. Cubitt, manager), Newcastle-upon-Tyne.
27.1.1922: Managers became Arthur Stott and Co. Ltd.
13.4.1922: Acquired from the mortgagees in possession by William Robertson, Glasgow for £6,200.
20.5.1922: Renamed NUGGET.
4.3.1926: Stranded south of Ayr whilst on a voyage from Ayr to Dublin with a cargo of coal.
15.3.1926: Refloated.
6.4.1926: Sold for breaking up at Ardrossan.
9.4.1926: Register closed.

The delay between completion and registration of *Clydeside* suggests she was built as a speculation during a lean time for shipbuilders and bought later by James Couper. When he failed to keep up her mortgage payments, Robertson bought *Clydeside* and renamed her *Nugget* (3) (above). *[J. and M. Clarkson]*

83. OLIVINE (3) 1922-1929
O.N. 142744 754g 337n 890d
190.9 x 29.2 x 11.5 feet
T. 3-cyl. by the Forth Shipbuilding and Engineering Co. Ltd., Alloa; 110 NHP.
10.1918: Launched by the Forth Shipbuilding and Engineering Co. Ltd., Alloa (Yard No. 28) for the Shipping Controller, London as WAR CAM.
13.12.1918: Registered in the ownership of Joseph T. Leete and Sons, London as CATHERINE AIDA.
9.1922: Acquired by William Robertson, Glasgow for £14,500 and renamed OLIVINE.
24.3.1929: Stranded at Woodcombe Point, near Prawle Point whilst on a voyage from Rochester to Glasgow with a cargo of cement and became a constructive total loss.
2.6.1929: Refloated.
5.6.1929: Sold to John Kelly Ltd., Belfast, repaired by the Grangemouth Dockyard Co. Ltd. and renamed CARRICKMACROSS.
1952: Renamed BALLYHENRY.
11.6.1959: Arrived at Troon to be broken up by the West of Scotland Shipbreaking Co. Ltd.

A comparison of the £14,500 paid in September 1922 for the four-year old steamer which became *Olivine* (3) and the £47,500 cost of the *Kyanite* and *Essonite*, delivered late in 1921, illustrates how ship prices slumped following the short post-war boom. No images have been found of *Olivine* in Robertson colours, but this photograph of her as *Carrickmacross* was taken at Avonmouth soon after sale to John Kelly Ltd. *[J. and M. Clarkson]*

84. TOPAZ (6) 1922-1956
O.N. 144036 577g 265n 760d
164.8 x 27.0 x 11.1 feet
T. 3-cyl. by John Lewis and Sons Ltd., Aberdeen; 83 NHP.
6.12.1919: Launched by John Lewis and Sons Ltd., Aberdeen (Yard No. 71) for John Kelly Ltd., Belfast as COLLOONEY.
31.1.1920: Completed and registered in the ownership of the Allied Steam Navigation Co. Ltd. (Willmott, Buttle and Co., managers), Hull.
10.1922: Acquired by William Robertson, Glasgow for £12,150 and renamed TOPAZ.
19.4.1944: Requisitioned by the British government until 22.2.1945.
14.5.1949: Transferred to William Robertson Shipowners Ltd., Glasgow.
9.5.1956: Arrived at Port Glasgow to be broken up by Smith and Houston Ltd.

An early photograph of *Topaz* (6) at St. Malo (upper) shows that she originally had a gaff-rigged mizzen. The middle photograph shows her as later in her career with Robertson, now with a wheelhouse. *[Dave Hocquard collection; J. and M. Clarkson]*

85. CORAL (2) 1923-1944
O.N. 141928 638g 300n 760d
175.4 x 28.3 x 10.1 feet
T. 3-cyl. by William Beardmore and Co. Ltd., Coatbridge; 99 NHP, 625 IHP, 10 knots.
7.1919: Launched by the Ardrossan Dry Dock and Shipbuilding Co. Ltd., Ardrossan (Yard No. 272).
21.10.1919: Registered in the ownership of the Ferrum Steam Ship Co. Ltd. (G.T. Gillie and Co., managers), Newcastle-upon-Tyne as CROMARTY FIRTH.
19.3.1923: Acquired by William Robertson, Glasgow for £13,000.
30.4.1923: Renamed CORAL.
23.4.1944: Requisitioned by the British government.
20.8.1944: Torpedoed and sunk by the German submarine U 764 thirty miles south of the Isle of Wight in position 50.13 north by 00.48 west whilst on a voyage in convoy ETC 72 from Arromanches to Southampton in ballast. Six of the 18 on board were lost.
22.11.1945: Register closed.

Coral (2), seen at Preston, was Robertson's only loss to a U-boat during the Second World War. *[Douglas Cochrane/World Ship Society Ltd.]*

86. GEM (4) 1924-1952
O.N. 147915 640g 289n 840d
182.0 x 27.6 x 11.0 feet
T. 3-cyl. by Aitchison, Blair Ltd., Clydebank; 72 NHP, 505 IHP.
1.7.1924: Launched by Scott and Sons, Bowling (Yard No. 295).
9.8.1924: Registered in the ownership of William Robertson, Glasgow as GEM. She cost £17,200.
19.4.1944: Requisitioned by the British government until 26.7.1945.
14.5.1949: Transferred to William Robertson Shipowners Ltd., Glasgow.
1.1952: Sold to the Esplen Trust Ltd. (Springwell Shipping Co. Ltd., managers), London for £35,000 and renamed RED SEA.
1953: Sold to the Lindean Steamship Co. Ltd., Edinburgh and renamed GLENAPP CASTLE.
1958: Sold to the Deeside Shipping Co. Ltd. (Thomas Rose and Co., managers), Sunderland and renamed DEESIDE.
16.11.1959: Arrived in the Nieuw Waterweg for breaking up by N.V. de Koophandel who began work at Nieuw Lekkerland in March 1960.

Gem (4) is seen at Preston in original condition with open wheelhouse (top), in dry dock at Rouen awaiting repair to a crumpled bow after being hit by the Belgian steamer *Flore* (1,020/1913) whilst anchored in the River Seine on 18th April 1934 (middle), and from the air in post-war years with a closed wheelhouse (bottom). *[J. and M. Clarkson; Robertson archives; Roy Fenton collection]*

87. BERYL (2) 1924-1958
O.N. 147932 568g 236n 655d
171.7 x 26.6 x 11.3 feet
T. 3-cyl. by the Ailsa Shipbuilding Co. Ltd., Troon; 88 NHP.
30.9.1924: Launched by the Ailsa Shipbuilding Co. Ltd., Troon (Yard No. 394).
4.11.1924: Registered in the ownership of William Robertson, Glasgow as BERYL. She cost £16,350.
14.5.1949: Transferred to William Robertson Shipowners Ltd., Glasgow.
1.1958: Transferred to Gem Line Ltd. (William Robertson Shipowners Ltd., managers), Glasgow.
1.8.1958: Arrived at Troon for breaking up by the West of Scotland Shipbreaking Co. Ltd.

Beryl (2) with open bridge (upper), and with wheelhouse but no mizzen (lower). *[Robertson archives; World Ship Society Ltd.]*

88. TURQUOISE (2) 1924-1950
O.N. 147938 570g 235n 653d
171.7 x 26.6 x 11.4 feet
T. 3-cyl. by Ailsa Shipbuilding Co. Ltd., Troon; 88 NHP.
30.10.1924: Launched by the Ailsa Shipbuilding Co. Ltd., Troon (Yard No. 391).
11.1924: Completed.
1.12.1924: Registered in the ownership of William Robertson, Glasgow as TURQUOISE. She cost £16,350.
14.5.1949: Transferred to William Robertson Shipowners Ltd., Glasgow.
5.1.1950: Dragged anchor and stranded one mile north east of Maryport whilst on a voyage from Glasgow to Silloth in ballast. She was abandoned as a constructive total loss but was refloated during March 1950.
23.3.1950: Arrived at Peterhead for repair.
1950: Sold to Castle Coasters Ltd., Edinburgh and renamed TYNECASTLE.
10.1959: Sold for breaking up to Metaalhandel & Sloopwerken Heuvelmann, Rotterdam who began work at Krimpen a/d Ijssel later that year.

Turquoise (2) at Preston with an open bridge and three masts (opposite, bottom). She retained the open bridge during the Second World War (above left), but had been given an enclosed wheelhouse by the time of her stranding near Maryport in January 1950 (top and middle right). Abandoned to the underwriters, she was repaired and sold to an Edinburgh owner as *Tynecastle* (below) and survived until 1959. *[World Ship Society Ltd.; Robertson archives (3), Fotoflite incorporating Skyfotos]*

89. OPAL (2) 1925-1931
O.N. 139808 573g 248n 670d
164.8 x 27.0 x 11.1 feet
T. 3-cyl. by John Lewis and Sons Ltd., Aberdeen; 100 NHP, 630 IHP, 10 knots.
30.4.1919: Launched by John Lewis and Sons Ltd., Aberdeen (Yard No. 68). She had been laid down for the Shipping Controller, London as WAR EXE.
7.6.1919: Registered in the ownership of John Lewis Ltd., Aberdeen (Joseph E. Fisher, Liverpool, manager) as RIVER DEE.
29.12.1919: Sold to Herbert H. Merrett, Cardiff.
11.3.1920: Transferred to D.R. Llewellyn, Merrett and Price Ltd. (Merrett Brothers Ltd., managers), Cardiff
4.3.1925: Acquired by William Robertson, Glasgow for £11,500.
11.4.1925: Renamed OPAL.
4.9.1931: Foundered when cargo of bulk maize shifted three miles south west of the Longships whilst on a voyage from Antwerp to Cardiff.
23.9.1931: Register closed.

The short-lived *Opal* (2) arrives at Jersey. *[Ships in Focus]*

90. FLUOR (2) 1925-1958
O.N. 148864 914g 453n 1,217d
207.0 x 32.6 x 13.2 feet
T. 3-cyl. by the Ailsa Shipbuilding Co. Ltd., Troon; 90 NHP.
21.5.1925: Launched by the Ailsa Shipbuilding Co. Ltd., Troon (Yard No. 393).
18.6.1925: Registered in the ownership of William Robertson, Glasgow as FLUOR. She cost £22,750.
29.11.1943: Requisitioned by the British government until 28.12.1943, and again from 23.4.1944 until 1.11.1945.
10.10.1946: Sank following a collision with the turbine steamer STRATHNAVER (22,283/1931) whilst berthed waiting to load grain at New Docks, Southampton.
25.10.1946: Raised by Risdon, Beazley Ltd. She was repaired at Grangemouth and converted to oil burning.
14.5.1949: Transferred to William Robertson Shipowners Ltd., Glasgow.
1.1958: Transferred to Gem Line Ltd. (William Robertson Shipowners Ltd., managers), Glasgow.
18.4.1958: Sold to the Inca Transports Corporation, Panama and renamed INCA.
1970: Sold to Tecnimaritima S.A.E., Panama.
15.10.1973: Breaking up began by Gres Garcia at San Juan de Nieva.

Fluor (2) is seen discharging coal at Dublin on 12th June 1957 (middle right), in the English Channel (bottom), and sunk at her berth following a collision with a P&O liner in 1946 (opposite top left). Despite her age, she was raised (opposite middle) and her boilers modified to burn oil fuel, the first such installation in the Robertson fleet. The final photograph shows her under the Panama flag as *Inca*, as which she survived until 1973, still steam-driven according to 'Lloyd's Register' (opposite bottom). *[Robertson archives; George Osbon/World Ship Society Ltd.; Robertson archives (4); World Ship Society Ltd.]*

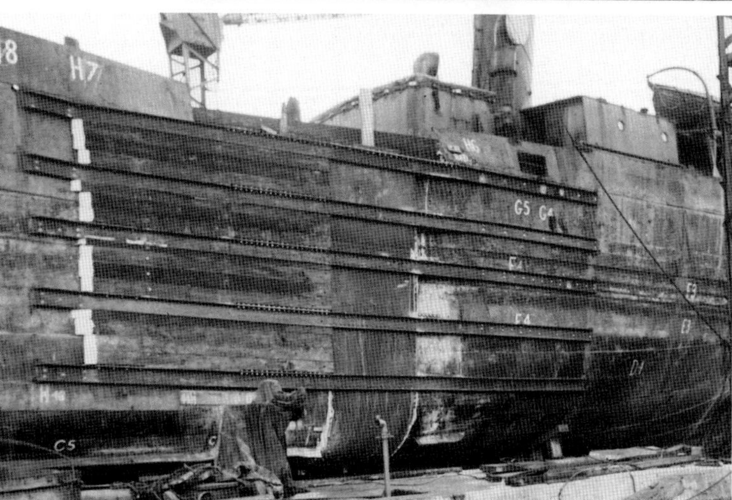
H7
G5 G4

91. OBSIDIAN (3) 1925-1954
O.N. 145709 811g 404n 1,115d
189.2 x 30.3 x 12.5 feet
T. 3-cyl. by William Beardmore and Co. Ltd., Coatbridge, Glasgow; 99 NHP.
14.1.1922: Launched by the London and Montrose Shipbuilding and Repairing Co. Ltd., Montrose (Yard No. 92).
5.1922: Completed.
11.7.1924: Registered in the ownership of D.R. Llewellyn, Merrett and Price Ltd. (Merrett Brothers Ltd., managers), Cardiff as RIVER ELY.
4.3.1925: Acquired by William Robertson, Glasgow for £12,500 and subsequently renamed OBSIDIAN.
11.6.1940: Requisitioned by the British government until 24.6.1940 and again from 21.4.1944 until 5.11.1945.
14.5.1949: Transferred to William Robertson Shipowners Ltd., Glasgow.
1.1.1954: Sold to T. Bagley and Co. Ltd., Middlesbrough for £7,000 and renamed ORO.
1954: Transferred to R.A. Grayson, Middlesbrough.
1955: Transferred to the B. and G. Shipping Co. Ltd., Middlesbrough.
20.12.1957: Arrived at Antwerp for breaking up by Omer Bulens who began work at Hoboken in February 1958.

92. SPHENE (3) 1925-1946
O.N. 143515 815g 413n 1,123d
189.4 x 30.3 x 12.6 feet
T. 3-cyl. by William Beardmore and Co. Ltd., Coatbridge, Glasgow; 79 NHP, 625 IHP, 9 knots.
17.6.1920: Launched by the London and Montrose Shipbuilding and Repairing Co. Ltd., Montrose (Yard No. 85).
8.1920: Completed.
7.9.1920: Registered in the ownership of D.R. Llewellyn, Merrett and Price Ltd. (Merrett Brothers Ltd., managers), Cardiff as RIVER TAWE.
4.3.1925: Acquired by William Robertson, Glasgow for £12,250.
16.5.1925: Renamed SPHENE.
22.4.1944: Requisitioned by the British government until 19.11.1945.
6.2.1946: Struck rocks and sank between Tintagel and Boscastle whilst on a voyage from Barry to London with a cargo of coal.
19.2.1946: Register closed.

Obsidian (3) before (top) and after (bottom) the fitting of a wheelhouse. *[J. and M. Clarkson; Ships in Focus]*

93. CITRINE (3) 1925-1931
O.N. 145704 582g 264n 670d
165.2 x 27.0 x 11.2 feet
T. 3-cyl. by John Lewis and Sons Ltd., Aberdeen; 82 NHP, 580 IHP, 10 knots.
9.1921: Completed by John Lewis and Sons Ltd., Aberdeen (Yard No. 90).
14.2.1922: Registered in the ownership of D.R. Llewellyn, Merrett and Price Ltd. (Merrett Brothers Ltd., managers), Cardiff as RIVER USK.
4.3.1925: Acquired by William Robertson, Glasgow for £11,750.
30.4.1925: Renamed CITRINE.
17.3.1931: Struck rocks and sank off Bradda Head, a half mile from Port Erin, Isle of Man in fog whilst on a voyage from Belfast to Trevor in ballast. There were only two survivors from the crew of 12.
26.3.1931: Register closed.

Sphene (3) on the Thames (top) and at a Penmaenmawr granite quarry jetty (middle) with the tiny steamer *Appliance* (200/1903) owned by the Zillah Shipping and Carrying Co. Ltd. of Liverpool, and a regular visitor to the North Welsh quarry jetties. *[Newall Dunn collection; Robertson archives]*

Citrine (3) at St. Helier, Jersey (below). She was a sister of *Opal* (2), both being acquired from Cardiff owners in 1925, and neither having long careers. *[Robertson archives]*

94. DIAMOND (3) 1927-1939
O.N. 160183 628g 308n 850d
170.0 x 27.7 x 11.2 feet
T. 3-cyl. by William Beardmore and Co. Ltd., Coatbridge, Glasgow; 96 NHP, 650 IHP, 10 knots.
29.8.1927: Launched by the Burntisland Shipbuilding Co. Ltd., Burntisland (Yard No. 143).
21.11.1927: Registered in the ownership of William Robertson, Glasgow as DIAMOND. She cost £16,750.
30.12.1936: Sank in St. Clement's Reach, in the River Thames after colliding with the Norwegian motor vessel HERANGER (4,877/1930). Two of her crew of eight were lost.
3.1.1937: Refloated.
3.2.1937: Arrived at Hull in tow for repair.
21.11.1939: Sold to J.W. Huelin Ltd., St. Helier, Jersey.
6.1.1940: Renamed THORNHILL.
27.4.1940: Sank following a collision with the French steamer CIRCE (2,031/1926) about 50 miles off the Casquets in position 49.50 north by 03.23 west whilst on a voyage from Barry to Caen. One member of her crew was lost.
1.5.1940: Register closed.

95. MORION (2) 1927-1939
O.N. 143608 423g 162n 850d
143.2 x 25.1 x 12.0 feet
C.2-cyl. by Ailsa Shipbuilding Co. Ltd., Troon; 54 NHP, 10 knots.
4.12.1919: Launched by the Ailsa Shipbuilding Co. Ltd., Troon (Yard No. 372).
29.12.1919: Completed.
2.1.1920: Registered in the ownership of the Summerfield Steamship Co. Ltd., Liverpool as JESSIE SUMMERFIELD.
14.3.1927: Sold to the Zillah Shipping and Carrying Co. Ltd. (William A. Savage, manager), Liverpool.
19.3.1927: Acquired by William Robertson Ltd., Glasgow for £6,745.
21.4.1927: Renamed MORION.
21.11.1939: Sold to the Mohochang Exploration Co. Ltd., Manchester (J. Galbraith of Stephenson, Clarke and Associated Companies Ltd, London, manager).
8.12.1939: Renamed GLENBRIDE.
27.5.1942: Sold to Chatterley Whitfield Collieries Ltd. (J. Galbraith, manager), Stoke-on-Trent.
18.2.1946: Sold to the Polgarth Steamship Co. Ltd. (James Macmillan, manager), London.
20.10.1949: Sold to the Alliance and Dublin Consumer Gas Company, Dublin.
10.4.1963: Haulbowline Industries Ltd. commenced demolition at Passage West, Cork.

Diamond (3) was only the second ship new to Robertsons from a yard outside the west of Scotland. The upper photograph shows her launch at Burntisland, Fife on 29th August 1927: note the particularly large letters on her stern, also visible in the lower photograph at Preston. Her engines were probably the only ones in the fleet with poppet valves. She was sold in 1939 to help pay death duties. *[Robertson archives; Douglas Cochrane/World Ship Society Ltd.]*

Morion was a name reserved for relatively small units of the fleet. Photographed in the River Ribble, the second vessel of the name was acquired when her Liverpool owners failed. Sold by Robertsons, again to help pay death duties in 1939, she enjoyed a long career running mainly on the Irish Sea to serve the gas works at Dublin. *[Douglas Cochrane/World Ship Society Ltd.]*

96. PEBBLE (2) 1929-1953
O.N. 148661 597g 303n 846d
170.0 x 27.4 x 11.2 feet
T. 3-cyl. by William Beardmore and Co. Ltd., Coatbridge, Glasgow; 98 NHP, 650 IHP, 9 knots.
3.8.1925: Launched by the Burntisland Shipbuilding Co. Ltd., Burntisland (Yard No. 135).
17.8.1925: Registered in the ownership of H. Harrison (Shipping) Ltd., London as KEMPTON.
8.7.1929: Acquired by William Robertson, Glasgow for £11,000.
16.8.1929: Renamed PEBBLE.
23.4.1944: Requisitioned by the British government until 17.8.1945.
14.5.1949: Transferred to William Robertson Shipowners Ltd., Glasgow.
3.1953: Breaking up began by Smith and Houston Ltd. at Port Glasgow having been sold for £5,100.
3.6.1953: Register closed.

Pebble (2) seems not to have been fitted with a mizzen mast, at least during Robertson ownership. The ratlines are particularly prominent in this Mersey photograph, with a wisp of steam coming from her safety valve. She was later fitted with a wheelhouse, and survived in the fleet until 1953 when she was broken up on the Clyde. *[B. and A. Feilden/J. and M. Clarkson]*

97. JARGOON (2) 1929-1951
O.N. 149706 691g 380n 940d
180.2 x 28.9 x 11.0 feet
T. 3-cyl. by Aitchison, Blair Ltd., Clydebank; 72 NHP, 650 IHP, 9.25 knots.
9.7.1926: Launched by John Fullerton and Co., Paisley (Yard No. 276).
19.8.1926: Registered in the ownership of H. Harrison (Shipping) Ltd., London as TORRINGTON.
8.6.1929: Acquired by William Robertson, Glasgow for £12,000.
14.8.1929: Renamed JARGOON.
27.9.1939: Requisitioned by the British government until 1.11.1939 and again from 21.4.1944 to 31.8.1945.
14.5.1949: Transferred to William Robertson Shipowners Ltd., Glasgow.
7.7.1951: Sank ten miles south of the Owers Light Vessel in position 50.20 north by 00.30 west following a collision in fog with the Spanish steamer TORMES (1,339/1938) whilst on a voyage from Llanddulas to London with a cargo of stone.
13.7.1951: Register closed.

Jargoon (2) was lost in collision in July 1951. *[World Ship Society Ltd.]*

98. ASTERIA (2) 1929-1954
O.N. 149713 649g 319n 850d
171.4 x 27.8 x 11.3 feet
T. 3-cyl. by John Lewis and Sons Ltd., Aberdeen; 70 NHP, 600 IHP, 10 knots.
25.8.1926: Launched by John Lewis and Sons Ltd., Aberdeen (Yard No. 98).
3.9.1926: Registered in the ownership of H. Harrison (Shipping) Ltd., London as SURBITON.
3.7.1929: Acquired by William Robertson, Glasgow for £12,000.
9.8.1929: Renamed ASTERIA.
21.4.1944: Requisitioned by the British government until 18.8.1945.
14.5.1949: Transferred to William Robertson (Shipowners) Ltd., Glasgow.
4.3.1954: Stranded on Drogheda Bar whilst on a voyage from Garston to Drogheda with a cargo of coal.
5.3.1954: Refloated under her own power, but extensively damaged. After being slipped at Irvine declared a constructive total loss and sold for demolition.
26.3.1954: Arrived at Troon for breaking up by the West of Scotland Shipbreaking Co. Ltd.

99. AXINITE (2) 1929-1955
O.N. 160598 724g 369n 1,003d
180.2 x 28.9 x 11.3 feet
T. 3-cyl. by John Lewis and Sons Ltd., Aberdeen; 70 NHP, 575 IHP, 10 knots.
16.10.1928: Launched by John Lewis and Sons Ltd., Aberdeen (Yard No. 105).
29.10.1928: Registered in the ownership of H. Harrison (Shipping) Ltd., London as OKEHAMPTON.
11.1928: Completed.
3.7.1929: Acquired by William Robertson, Glasgow for £15,000.
14.8.1929: Renamed AXINITE.
27.8.1939: Requisitioned by the British government until 28.2.1946.
14.5.1949: Transferred to William Robertson Shipowners Ltd., Glasgow.
7.1955: Sold to Hargeaves Coal and Shipping Ltd. (Comben Longstaff and Co. Ltd., managers), London for £27,500 and renamed HARBROOK.
25.6.1959: Arrived at Hemiksen, Belgium for breaking up by Sorema.
6.8.1959: Work began.

Asteria (2) in the River Suir at Waterford. *[Jimmy Hartery/World Ship Society Ltd.]*

Axinite (2) in as-bought condition loading coal at Preston (left). Completed as *Okehampton* in November 1928, and bought and renamed less than a year later, she was one of several Robertson ships to come from the London-based fleets of H. Harrison (Shipping) Ltd. and the associated Edward T. Lindley who had been too ambitious in their ordering policies. *Axinite* is seen again, post war, in the English Channel, with a wheel house and no mizzen mast (middle) and on the River Ouse in her final guise as *Harbrook* (bottom). Note that her masts are at widely differing angles. *[Harry Stewart/J. and M. Clarkson; Fotoflite incorporating Skyfotos; C.A. Hill]*

100. CORUNDUM (2) 1930-1948
O.N. 148568 929g 496n 1,230d
200.1 x 30.8 x 12.7 feet
T. 3-cyl. by John Lewis and Sons Ltd., Aberdeen; 101 NHP, 800 IHP, 10 knots.
1925: Launched by John Lewis and Sons Ltd., Aberdeen (Yard No. 80).
21.3.1925: Registered in the ownership of Edward T. Lindley, London as BALCOMBE.
14.11.1930: Acquired by William Robertson, Glasgow for £12,000.
30.1.1931: Renamed CORUNDUM.
29.8.1939: Requisitioned by the British government until 8.11.1939, and from 12.6.1941 to 22.10.1945.
28.12.1948: Sold to the Holderness Steamship Co. Ltd. (Thomas E. Kettlewell and Son Ltd., managers), Hull for £50,000.
1949: Renamed HOLDERNAZE.
7.12.1957: Arrived at Antwerp for breaking up by V.F. van Loo.

101. OLIVINE (4) 1930-1941
O.N. 148745 929g 494n
199.8 x 30.9 x 12.7 feet
T. 3-cyl. by John Lewis and Sons Ltd., Aberdeen; 111 NHP, 800 IHP, 10 knots.
13.3.1926: Launched by John Lewis and Sons Ltd., Aberdeen (Yard No. 95).
26.3.1926: Registered in the ownership of Edward T. Lindley, London as HORLEY.
14.11.1930: Acquired by William Robertson, Glasgow for £12,500.
31.1.1931: Renamed OLIVINE.
27.3.1941: Left Glasgow for Sharpness with a cargo of wheat and disappeared.
4.6.1941: Posted missing.
18.8.1941: Register closed.

Corundum (2) (above) and her sister *Olivine* (4) was unusual in the fleet in having her main mast mounted centrally above her after hold. She later lost her mizzen. In 1948 she was one of a collection of superannuated steamers which joined the Holderness fleet, becoming *Holdernaze* (below) and realising over four times what Robertsons had paid for her 18 years earlier. *[Roy Fenton collection; World Ship Society Ltd.]*

In this photograph on the Mersey *Olivine* (4) is, unusually, flying Robertson's house flag. She is passing one of the schooners still working in the Irish Sea during the 1930s. *[B. and A. Feilden/J. and M. Clarkson]*

The short-lived *Girasol* (2) at Bristol (right top), victim of a wartime collision . *[J. and M. Clarkson]*

102. GIRASOL (2) 1930-1940
O.N. 149730 648g 318n 843d
171.2 x 27.8 x 11.3 feet
T. 3-cyl. by John Lewis and Sons Ltd., Aberdeen; 70 NHP, 575 IHP, 10 knots.
22.9.1926: Launched by John Lewis and Sons Ltd., Aberdeen (Yard No. 99).
5.10.1926: Registered in the ownership of Edward T. Lindley, London as OUTWOOD.
14.11.1930: Acquired by William Robertson, Glasgow for £8,150.
14.2.1931: Renamed GIRASOL.
24.4.1940: Sank following a collision with the steamer CONTRACTOR (6,004/1913) off the North Foreland in position 51.28.50 north by 01.22.15 east whilst on a voyage from Penmaenrhos to London with a cargo of limestone.
13.5.1940: Register closed.

103. NEPHRITE (2) 1930-1940
O.N. 149917 927g 493n 1,230d
199.7 x 30.9 x 12.7 feet
T. 3-cyl. by John Lewis and Sons Ltd., Aberdeen; 111 NHP, 800 IHP, 10 knots.
14.9.1927: Launched by John Lewis and Sons Ltd., Aberdeen (Yard No. 104).
11.10.1927: Registered in the ownership of Edward T. Lindley, London as BURSTOW.
14.11.1930: Acquired by William Robertson, Glasgow for £13,000.
26.1.1931: Renamed NEPHRITE.
2.1940: Sold to Stephenson, Clarke and Associated Companies Ltd., London.
8.1.1945: Owners became Stephenson Clarke Ltd., London.
28.6.1946: Renamed PORTSLADE.
10.3.1954: Sold to the Ouse Steamship Co. Ltd. (E.P. Atkinson and Sons, managers), Goole and subsequently renamed ROSEFLEET.
29.10.1956: Wrecked at Mardyck eight kilometres west of Dunkirk whilst on a voyage from Dunkirk to Goole in ballast.
27.12.1956: Wreck sold to M. Vincent of Liege who broke it up *in situ*.

Nephrite (2) is seen under her original name *Burstow* (upper middle), as *Nephrite* at Jersey (lower middle) and after sale to Stephenson Clarke as *Portslade*, when she lost her mizzen and derricks but gained a closed wheelhouse (bottom). She went on to have yet another British owner, but was wrecked near Dunkirk in 1956. *[J. and M. Clarkson; H.A. Breton; World Ship Society Ltd.]*

104. NUGGET (4) 1934-1952
O.N. 126984 515g 205n
182.3 x 27.4 x 10.3 feet
T. 3-cyl. by MacColl and Co. Ltd., Belfast; 85 NHP, 750 IHP, 10.75 knots.
12.11.1912: Launched by the Dublin Dockyard Co. Ltd., Dublin (Yard No.78).
16.1.1913: Registered in the ownership of the Sligo Steam Navigation Co. Ltd., Sligo as SLIGO.
19.10.1917: Sold to the Limerick Steamship Co. Ltd., Limerick.
26.1.1918: Renamed MUNGRET.
7.3.1934: Acquired by William Robertson, Glasgow for £2,300.
27.4.1934: Renamed NUGGET.
27.4.1944: Requisitioned by the British government until 4.4.1945.
14.5.1949: Transferred to William Robertson Shipowners Ltd., Glasgow.
11.7.1952: Arrived at Port Glasgow for breaking up by Smith and Houston Ltd., having been sold for £4,500.
24.1.1953: Register closed.

105. PYROPE (2) 1936-1953
O.N. 164088 500g 213n 560d
171.0 x 25.3 x 9.7 feet
T. 3-cyl. by Aitchison, Blair Ltd., Glasgow; 86 NHP.
1961: Oil engine 4SCSA 6-cyl. by Motorenwerke Mannheim A.G., Mannheim, West Germany.
4.6.1936: Launched by Scott and Sons, Bowling (Yard No. 338).
10.7.1936: Registered in the ownership of William Robertson, Glasgow as PYROPE. She cost £15,630.
14.5.1949: Transferred to William Robertson Shipowners Ltd., Glasgow.
6.5.1951: Stranded off Rhum whilst on a voyage from Ayr to Stornoway with a cargo of coal. Refloated, repaired and returned to service.
9.10.1953: Sold to the Thorn Line Ltd. (S. William Coe and Co. Ltd., managers), Liverpool for £12,500 and later renamed BANNPRIDE.
1954: Transferred to S. William Coe and Co. Ltd., Liverpool.
1961: Sold to G.M. Mancino, Torre del Greco, Italy, renamed CONSIGLIA M. and re-engined.
1967: Sold to Medimar, Mediterraneo Marritima S.r.L., Naples, Italy and renamed CUMA.
5.1.1970: Stranded at Cape Corvo. Refloated under her own power but her hull and machinery were badly damaged.
9.1970: Demolition began by S.I.V. Societa Industrie Varie, La Spezia.

Nugget (4) was a bargain: acquired by Robertson in 1934 from the Limerick Steamship Co. Ltd. for just £2,300 (above). *[J. and M. Clarkson]*

Pyrope (2) was the last steamer to be built for the company, although not the last to be acquired (middle). Note the prominent rim to her funnel. In 1954 she was sold to S. William Coe and Co. Ltd. of Liverpool who renamed her *Bannpride* (bottom). *[Robertson archives; Roy Fenton collection]*

106. TOURMALINE (2) 1948-1955
O.N. 162285 569g 274n 716d
165.5 x 27.2 x 9.7 feet
T. 3-cyl. by John Lewis and Sons Ltd., Aberdeen made in 1931; 70 NHP.
6.9.1933: Launched by John Lewis and Sons Ltd., Aberdeen (Yard No. 129).
29.9.1933: Registered in the ownership of the Border Shipping Co. Ltd. (G.T. Gillie and Blair Ltd., managers), Newcastle-upon-Tyne as DEEMOUNT.
1945: Renamed OLNA FIRTH.
1948: Acquired by William Robertson, Glasgow for £45,000 and renamed TOURMALINE.
14.5.1949: Transferred to William Robertson Shipowners Ltd., Glasgow.
3.1955: Sold to the Bann Shipping Co. Ltd. (S. William Coe and Co. Ltd., managers), Liverpool for £22,500 and later renamed BANNPRINCE.
12.11.1955: Sank in collision with the Swedish tank steamer JUNO (8,422/1945) in the Queen's Channel, River Mersey.
24.11.1955: Raised and beached at Wallasey.
3.4.1956: Sold to Stolk's Handels, Hendrik-ido-Ambacht to be broken up. During 1957 they were reported to be removing the engines so that the hull could be re-used, presumably on inland waterways.

Tourmaline (2) was unusual for a relatively large steam coaster in having her bridge aft. The two upper photographs were taken in West Africa soon after the Second World War: note the presence of floats. The barrels on deck have clearly not been well secured. The upper middle photograph is also unusual in showing her with a walkway rigged across her well deck. In this and the next photograph in the Bristol Channel, the prominent cowl top to her funnel is apparent. She is seen finally in the colours of S. William Coe and Co. Ltd., to whom she was sold in 1955, but she has not yet received her new name of *Bannprince*. She retains her mizzen mast but its gaff has been moved lower. *[Robertson archives (3); J. and M. Clarkson; Roy Fenton collection]*

107. GIRASOL (3) 1950-1958
O.N. 163204 869g 457n 1,240d
197.7 x 30.7 x 12.1 feet
T. 3-cyl. by John Lewis and Sons Ltd., Aberdeen; 103 NHP.
1959: 7-cyl. 2 SCSA oil engine by British Auxiliaries Ltd., Glasgow made in 1941.
23.8.1933: Launched by John Lewis and Sons Ltd., Aberdeen (Yard No. 128).
7.9.1933: Registered in the ownership of John Kelly Ltd. (William Clint, manager), Belfast as ROSAPENNA.
7.1937: Sold to P. Hawksfield and Son Ltd., Dover and renamed KATHLEEN HAWKSFIELD.
10.1941: Sold to the Brussels Steamship Co. Ltd., London.
1942: Renamed CITY OF CHARLEROY.
4.1947: Sold to the Williamstown Shipping Co. Ltd. (Comben Longstaff and Co. Ltd., managers), London and renamed CHESTERBROOK.
6.11.1950: Acquired by William Robertson Shipowners Ltd., Glasgow for £42,000 and later renamed GIRASOL.
1.1958: Transferred to Gem Line Ltd. (William Robertson Shipowners Ltd., managers), Glasgow.
5.1958: Sold to Ubaldo Gennari fu Torquato e Compagni, Pesaro, Italy and renamed HIERAX.
7.1971: Breaking up began by S.I.V. Societa Industrie Varie at La Spezia.

Built as *Rosapenna* for John Kelly Ltd. of Belfast (right), this collier had two further owners before becoming *Girasol* (3), the last steamer bought by William Robertson, and amongst the last to be sold in 1958 (below). *[Douglas Cochrane/ World Ship Society Ltd.; Robertson archives]*

3. Motor vessels

1. SAPPHIRE (3) 1935-1939
O.N. 164062 933g 501n 1,320d
200.2 x 32.6 x 12.4 feet
Oil engine 2SCSA 5-cyl. by Atlas Diesel A/B, Stockholm, Sweden; 81 NHP, 710 BHP, 10.25 knots.
3.7.1935: Launched by the Ailsa Shipbuilding Co. Ltd., Troon (Yard No. 420).
2.9.1935: Registered in the ownership of William Robertson, Glasgow as SAPPHIRE. She cost £24,350.
12.4.1939: Sank seven miles off the South Bishop Lighthouse after colliding with the steamer CLAN CAMERON (7,255/1937) whilst on a voyage from Penmaenrhos to Dagenham with a cargo of limestone.
9.5.1939: Register closed.

Robertson's first motor ship, the short-lived *Sapphire* (3) on the stocks (left), immediately after launch (middle) and on trials (bottom). In the trial's photograph, note the exceptionally long derricks needed to serve the hatches on this 200-foot ship, and the unusually large funnel for a motor coaster. *[Robertson archives]*

2. CAMEO (3) 1937-1950
O.N. 164109 946g 504n 1,324d
210.8 x 32.8 x 12.7 feet
Burmeister & Wain-type oil engine 2SCSA 8-cyl. by Harland and Wolff Ltd., Glasgow; 87 NHP, 725 BHP, 950 IHP, 10.5 knots.
2.12.1936: Launched by A. and J. Inglis Ltd., Glasgow (Yard No. 979).
27.1.1937: Registered in the ownership of William Robertson, Glasgow as CAMEO. She cost £25,600.
2.1937: Completed.
7.9.1939: Requisitioned by the British government until 8.8.1940, and again from 22.4.1944 until 7.2.1946.
15.5.1949: Owners became William Robertson Shipowners Ltd., Glasgow.
10.9.1950: Wrecked on Arklow Bank in position 52.45.51 north by 05.57.30 west whilst on a voyage from Port Talbot to Dublin with a cargo of coal.
27.9.1950: Register closed.

Although from a different yard to the earlier *Sapphire* (3), *Cameo* (3) was built to much the same design and was just ten feet longer, but her scantlings were increased to carry cargoes of heavy equipment and steel. The accommodation had electric light and radiators, but separate entrances for officers and for the hands. She is seen on trials (top). Ironically, the best photographs found of *Cameo* show her aground (middle) and breaking up (left) after hitting Arklow Bank in September 1950. Her crew of 11 was rescued with considerable difficulty by the Wicklow lifeboat. *[Robertson archives]*

3. SPINEL (2) 1937-1940/1946-1970
O.N. 165917 650g 332n 900d
185.0 x 28.7 x 11.4 feet
Oil engine 2SCSA 7-cyl. by British Auxiliaries Ltd., Glasgow; 61 NHP.
1957: Oil engine 2SCSA 7-cyl. by British Polar Engines Ltd., Glasgow; 650 BHP, 9.5 knots.
8.9.1937: Launched by Henry Robb Ltd., Leith (Yard No. 244).
19.10.1937: Registered in the ownership of William Robertson, Glasgow as SPINEL. She cost £30,000.
6.9.1939: Requisitioned by the British government.
25.5.1940: Bombed by German aircraft and abandoned by her crew at Dunkirk, where she had arrived from Poole with a cargo of cased petrol on 21.5.1940.
4.7.1940: Salvaged by the Germans.
15.9.1940: Following repairs at Granville put into service with Hafenschutzflotille Bordeaux supplying the Channel Islands, arriving at St. Helier for the first time on 4.10.1940.
9.5.1945: Recovered in the Channel Islands and renamed EMPIRE SPINEL by the Ministry of War Shipping, London (William Robertson, Glasgow, managers).
27.9.1946: Re-acquired by William Robertson, Glasgow and renamed SPINEL.
15.5.1949: Owners became William Robertson Shipowners Ltd., Glasgow.
1957: Fitted with new engine.
1958: Owners became Gem Line Ltd. (William Robertson Shipowners Ltd., managers), Glasgow.
11.3.1970: W.H. Arnott, Young and Co. (Shipbreakers) Ltd. began demolition at Dalmuir.

Spinel is seen first on the stocks at Leith. Her adventures during the Second World War do not seem to have affected her adversely, and she gave Robertson 33 years' service. She is shown on the Thames in August 1953 (above) and in the Bristol Channel after fitting a light foremast, required to carry a navigating light following changes in regulations (below). *[Robertson archives; Roy Fenton collection; Fotoship/J. and M. Clarkson]*

4. JACINTH (3) 1937-1970
O.N. 165923 650g 332n 900d
185.0 x 28.7 x 11.4 feet
Oil engine 2SCSA 7-cyl. by British Auxiliaries Ltd., Glasgow; 61 NHP.
1957: Oil engines 2SCSA 7-cyl. by British Polar Engines Ltd., Glasgow; 650 BHP, 9 knots.
20.11.1937: Launched by Henry Robb Ltd., Leith (Yard No. 246).
9.12.1937: Registered in the ownership of William Robertson, Glasgow as JACINTH. She cost £24,100.
6.9.1939: Requisitioned by the British government until 12.9.1939, and again from 24.4.1940 until 15.8.1944.
15.5.1949: Owners became William Robertson Shipowners Ltd., Glasgow.
1957: Fitted with new engine.
1958: Owners became Gem Line Ltd. (William Robertson Shipowners Ltd., managers), Glasgow.
11.3.1970: W.H. Arnott, Young and Co. (Shipbreakers) Ltd. began demolition at Dalmuir.

Jacinth (3) had minor differences from her sister *Spinel* (2), including the treatment of the plating just below the bridge. After re-engining in 1957, she too gave 33 years' service to the company. The first two photographs show her largely as built, and in the third, taken on the Manchester Ship Canal on 29th March 1968, she has a light signal mast installed forward. *[Robertson archives (2), Roy Fenton]*

5. PRASE (2) 1938-1966
O.N. 165940 374g 193n 500d
145.8 x 24.7 x 9.0 feet
Oil engine 4SCSA 8-cyl. by Humboldt-Deutzmotoren A.G., Koln-Deutz; Germany; 49 NHP, 400 BHP, 9 knots.
7.4.1938: Launched by A. Vuijk en Zonen, Capelle, Netherlands (Yard No. 644).
24.6.1938: Registered in the ownership of William Robertson, Glasgow as PRASE. She cost £16,334.
26.4.1944: Requisitioned by the British government until 9.2.1945.
15.5.1949: Owners became William Robertson Shipowners Ltd., Glasgow.
1958: Owners became Gem Line Ltd. (William Robertson Shipowners Ltd., managers), Glasgow.
25.4.1966: Sold to M. Gigilinis and Dimitrios Kalkassinas, Thessalonica, Greece for £10,500 and renamed THESSALONIKI.
1971: Owner became Dimitrios Kalkassinas, Thessalonica.
1987: Reported broken up in Greece.

In keeping with Robertson's philosophy of ordering ships of various sizes for different trades, the Dutch-built *Prase* (2) was just 146 feet long, much smaller than the company's earlier motor ships, giving her a capacity of just over 400 tons of coal. Her smallness is emphasised by the diminutive funnel and superstructure, which suggests she was designed to have a low air-draft, which the hinged mast tends to confirm. The first photograph shows her running trials, and shows the white-painted spirket plate right forward which was not part of Robertson's paint scheme and was quickly painted over. The second photograph also shows a unique livery variation. It may well have been taken in 1939, as she carries what appears to be a mourning band on her hull, presumably applied following the deaths of John and William Robertson that year. No other photographs have been found with this feature, which is virtually unknown amongst British ships. In the third photograph minor changes from new include additional supports for wireless aerials, with a stump mast aft and cross trees on her mainmast. *[Robertson archives; J. and M. Clarkson (2)]*

6. JADE (1) 1938-1967
O.N. 165943 930g 495n 1,321d
213.0 x 32.6 x 12.4 feet
Oil engine 4SCSA 6-cyl. by Humboldt-Deutzmotoren A.G., Koln-Deutz; Germany; 75 NHP, 10 knots.
9.1955: Oil engine 4SCSA 6-cyl. by Humboldt-Deutzmotoren A.G., Koln-Deutz, West Germany; 800 BHP, 10 knots.
8.6.1938: Launched by A. Vuijk en Zonen, Capelle, Netherlands (Yard No. 645).
13.7.1938: Registered in the ownership of William Robertson, Glasgow as JADE. She cost £32,082.
8.1938: Completed.
4.9.1939: Requisitioned by the British government until 23.11.1945.
15.5.1949: Owners became William Robertson Shipowners Ltd., Glasgow.
9.1955: Fitted with new oil engine.
1958: Owners became Gem Line Ltd. (William Robertson Shipowners Ltd., managers), Glasgow.
1967: Sold to M. Gigilinis and Dimitrios Kalkassinas, Thessalonica, Greece and renamed KOSTAS. 'Lloyd's Register' spells the name COSTAS from 1973.
1971: Sold to Zoulias Brothers, Piraeus, Greece.
1972: Transferred to Georgios Stavrou, Nikolaos Zoulias and Co. (Dionisios A. Stavrou O. E. Shipping Enterprises), Piraeus.
1978: Transferred to Georgios Stavrou and Evangelos Malkogiorgos (Stavrou Management Co. S.A.), Piraeus.
26.5.1984: Arrived at Perama, Greece.
4.1986: Breaking up began by Aneva Epe.

Robertsons came up with a new name for their second Dutch-built motor ship, *Jade* (1). The Dutch had a reputation for building lighter, and hence cheaper, ships than British yards, and Robertson's four motor ships from the Netherlands did not enjoy quite such long lives as their Scottish-built contemporaries. At around 1,300 tons of coal, *Jade's* carrying capacity was similar to that of the earlier motor ships *Sapphire* (4) and *Cameo* (3). Differences between the upper and lower photographs include a canvas dodger around the exposed upper steering position in that above and in the lower stern view a light mast aft, a radio aerial and changes to the chimneys and water tanks abaft the funnel. *[Robertson archives; Roy Fenton collection.]*

7. CAIRNGORM (3) 1938-1962
O.N. 165950 394g 202n 540d
145.8 x 25.5 x 9.2 feet
Oil engine 4SCSA 8-cyl. by Humboldt-Deutzmotoren A.G., Koln-Deutz, Germany; 49 NHP, 9 knots.
1956: Oil engine 4SCSA 6-cyl. by Humboldt-Deutzmotoren A.G., Koln-Deutz, West Germany; 500 BHP, 9 knots.
19.7.1938: Launched by A. Vuijk en Zonen, Capelle, Netherlands (Yard No. 646).
28.9.1938: Registered in the ownership of William Robertson, Glasgow as CAIRNGORM. She cost £16.411.
11.9.1939: Requisitioned by the British government until 16.10.1939, and again from 22.4.1944 until 19.7.1945.
15.5.1949: Owners became William Robertson Shipowners Ltd., Glasgow.
1956: Fitted with new oil engine.
1958: Owners became Gem Line Ltd. (William Robertson Shipowners Ltd., managers), Glasgow.
4.12.1962: Sold to Surdo Giovan Battista, Trapani, Sicily, Italy for £19,500 and renamed NUOVA AUSILIATRICE.
1975: Sold to Angelo Ribaudo, Palermo, Sicily.
1998: Deleted from 'Lloyd's Register' as continued existence in doubt.

Cairngorm (3) was a near sister of *Prase* (2) with a slightly higher capacity and other minor differences, the most noticeable of which is an ensign staff set at a jaunty angle. *[Ships in Focus; Robertson archives; J. and M. Clarkson]*

After ordering three ships from Capelle, Robertsons turned to a Hardinxveld yard for *Citrine* (4) which, with her taller wheelhouse, was more like the company's Scottish-built motor coasters. In the second photograph a light mast has been added to her funnel to carry an additional navigating light. *Citrine* (4) had the unhappy distinction of being the last Robertson ship to be lost (see Appendix 1). *[Robertson archives; Fotoflite]*

8. CITRINE (4) 1939-1956
O.N. 165956 783g 416n 1,015d
199.6 x 29.2 x 11.4 feet
Oil engine 4SCSA 6-cyl. by Humboldt-Deutzmotoren A.G., Koln-Deutz, Germany; 74 NHP.
11.8.1938: Launched by N.V. Scheepswerf 'De Merwede' v/h Van Vliet and Co., Hardinxveld, Netherlands (Yard No. 386).
7.1.1939: Registered in the ownership of William Robertson, Glasgow as CITRINE. She cost £26,640.
16.1.1939: Completed.
28.3.1944: Requisitioned by the British government until 12.10.1944.
15.5.1949: Owners became William Robertson Shipowners Ltd., Glasgow.
2.1.1956: Foundered in heavy seas four miles north east of the Lizard in position 49.59.40 north by 05.08.40 west whilst on a voyage from Llanddulas to London with a cargo of stone. One member of her crew was lost.

A crumpled *Citrine* awaiting repair following a collision with the steamer *Hendonhall* (5,244/1944) in the Manchester Ship Canal on 16th July 1950. *[Robertson archives]*

9. MORION (3) 1946-1951
O.N. 180369 410g 190n 463d
142.2 x 27.0 x 8.5 feet
Oil engine 2SCSA 6-cyl. by Petters Ltd., Loughborough; 22 NHP.
8.1956: Oil engine 4SCSA 6-cyl. by Blackstone and Co. Ltd., Stamford; 324 BHP.
18.11.1944: Launched by the Goole Shipbuilding and Repairing Co. Ltd., Goole (Yard No. 432).
4.1.1945: Registered in the ownership of the Ministry of War Transport, London (William Robertson, Glasgow, managers) as EMPIRE FANG. It was intended to name her CHANT 39, and later FABRIC 39.
24.7.1946: Acquired by William Robertson, Glasgow for £7,600 and later renamed MORION.
15.5.1949: Owners became William Robertson Shipowners Ltd., Glasgow.
3.8.1951: Sold to Peter Lockett and John Wilson, London for £14,000.
10.1951: Sold to Nevill Long and Co. Ltd. (Benjamin Ackerley and Son Ltd., managers), London.
5.1952: Renamed LONGBOAT.
10.1954: Sold to Gerard Harvey, Quebec, Canada.
8.1956: Fitted with new oil engine.
5.1963: Transferred to Maritime Harvey Ltee., Quebec.
4.1972: Sold to Edgar Lavoie et frères, Quebec.
9.1972: Renamed DE LAVOYE.
10.1972: Transferred to Joseph A. Lavoie, Quebec.
11.1975: Owners became Lavoie, Lavoie et Fils Inc., Quebec.
4.1978: Sold to Vapores Orinoco S.A., Panama
1979: Put under the Honduras flag.
1995: Deleted from 'Lloyd's Register' as continued existence in doubt. No owners had been listed since 1979.

The prefabricated coaster *Morion* (3) was not appreciated by Robertsons, who described her as 'a wartime production of a poor design' and disposed of her after only 29 months in service. As they had previously managed her, it is surprising that they did not realise her deficiencies before they bought her. Despite their opinion, she gave at least 33 years of service to a variety of owners. *[Robertson archives].*

Sapphire (4) was Robertson's only motor ship with the traditional layout of a bridge and officers' accommodation amidships, a design which the builders insisted upon against Robertsons' better judgement, and which the latter regarded as a mistake.

Sapphire could load just under 1,300 tons of coal, making her one of Robertson's largest ships at the time and a candidate for early installation of radar and a Decca Navigator. This improved safety and consequently reduced insurance premiums. *[Robertson archives (2)]*

10. SAPPHIRE (4) 1949-1958
O.N. 182134 1,000g 518n 1,340d
213.6 x 34.2 x 12.1 feet
Oil engine 2SCSA 6-cyl. by British Polar Engines Ltd., Glasgow; 97 NHP, 1,320 BHP, 11 knots.
12.5.1949: Launched by the Grangemouth Dockyard Co. Ltd., Grangemouth (Yard No. 488).
26.9.1949: Registered in the ownership of William Robertson Shipowners Ltd., Glasgow as SAPPHIRE. She cost £118,945.
28.9.1949: Completed.
24.10.1958: Sold to Arthur S. Davidson Ltd., Belfast for £67,500 and later renamed MAYFAIR SAPPHIRE.
1971: Transferred to Cawood's Fuel (Northern Ireland) Ltd., Belfast.
1973: Sold to Comexim Maritime Financial Co. Ltd., Limassol, Cyprus (P.J. Angouras, Piraeus, Greece, managers) and renamed IOULIA K.
1974: Renamed BABI.
1974: Sold to Kappa Shipping Co. Ltd., Limassol, Cyprus (Sissiar Lines S.A. (M.L. Raissis), Piraeus, managers).
23.5.1979: Laid up at Piraeus.
24.6.1983: Breaking up began by Stavros Vamvounakis at Piraeus.
12.10.1983: Work completed.

11. AGATE (3) 1950-1961
O.N. 164909 873g 459n 1,124d
202.8 x 30.2 x 11.6 feet
Oil engine 2SCSA 7-cyl. by British Auxiliaries Ltd., Glasgow; 61 NHP, 525 BHP.
2.12.1940: Launched by the Goole Shipbuilding and Repairing Co. Ltd., Goole (Yard No. 358).
3.3.1941: Registered in the ownership of the Ministry of Shipping, later the Ministry of War Transport, London (Frederick T. Everard and Sons Ltd., managers) as EMPIRE FORELAND.
8.1942: Managers became Comben, Longstaff and Co. Ltd., London.
20.10.1945: Sold to Woodtown Shipping Co. Ltd. (Comben, Longstaff and Co. Ltd., managers), London and later renamed NORFOLKBROOK.
2.1946: Transferred to Williamstown Shipping Co. Ltd. (Comben, Longstaff and Co. Ltd., managers), London.
28.2.1950: Acquired by William Robertson Shipowners Ltd., Glasgow for £53,150.
29.4.1950: Renamed AGATE.
1958: Owners became Gem Line Ltd. (William Robertson Shipowners Ltd., managers), Glasgow.
8.1961: Sold to Di Guido Pio Tomei, Viareggio, Italy for £25,650 and renamed SILVANA TOMEI.
1970: Transferred to Paolo Tomei, Viareggio.
1971: Sold to Navalprotector, Rome, Italy and renamed SABBIATORE PRIMO.
1984: Deleted from the register as no longer self- propelled.

A wartime product of the Goole Shipbuilding and Repairing Co. Ltd., *Agate* (3) was one of the very few Robertson ships built in England. The total cost of her purchase and the alterations required by Robertson was £58,599. Judging by her 11 years of service with the company, she was more useful than their other war-built motor ship *Morion* (3). She could lift just over 1,000 tons of coal. In the upper photograph her hatch boards are being lifted off. The lower photograph shows the *Norfolkbrook* receiving the new name *Agate* in Queen's Dock on 29th April 1950. Moored alongside is the tiny *Taransay* (166/1930), a former motor yacht converted to a cargo vessel. *[Robertson archives; Graham Langmuir]*

Olivine (5) from Ailsa (opposite) began a series of ten distinctive motor ships for Robertson, similar in size but with significant structural differences. *Olivine* was the biggest motor ship yet built, with a capacity for up to almost 1,700 tons of coal, and when new made voyages south to Spain and North Africa. The signal mast fastened to the funnel, and at a different angle to the fore and main masts, looks like an afterthought. She gave Robertsons 28 years of service, but succumbed within months of being sold to Greek owners, foundering in the Mediterranean during October 1976. *[Robertson archives (2); Shipbuilding and Shipping Record]*

12. OLIVINE (5) 1952-1976

O.N. 184962 1,354g 685n 1,354d

244.8 x 38.2 x 13.2 feet

Oil engine 2SCSA 7-cyl. by British Polar Engines Ltd., Glasgow; 1,310 BHP, 10.5 knots.

4.12.1951: Launched by the Ailsa Shipbuilding Co. Ltd., Troon (Yard No. 475).

18.2.1952: Registered in the ownership of William Robertson Shipowners Ltd., Glasgow as OLIVINE. She cost £143,292.

21.2.1952: Commenced trading.

1958: Owners became Gem Line Ltd. (William Robertson Shipowners Ltd., managers), Glasgow.

29.4.1971: Transferred to William Robertson Shipowners Ltd., Glasgow.

20.2.1976: Sold to G. Stavrou, E. Malkogiorgos and Co., Piraeus, Greece and renamed LIZA.

28.10.1976: Foundered south east of Cape Bon, Tunisia in position 36.55 north by 11.44 east after being abandoned by her crew on a voyage from Eleusis to Algeria with a cargo of cement.

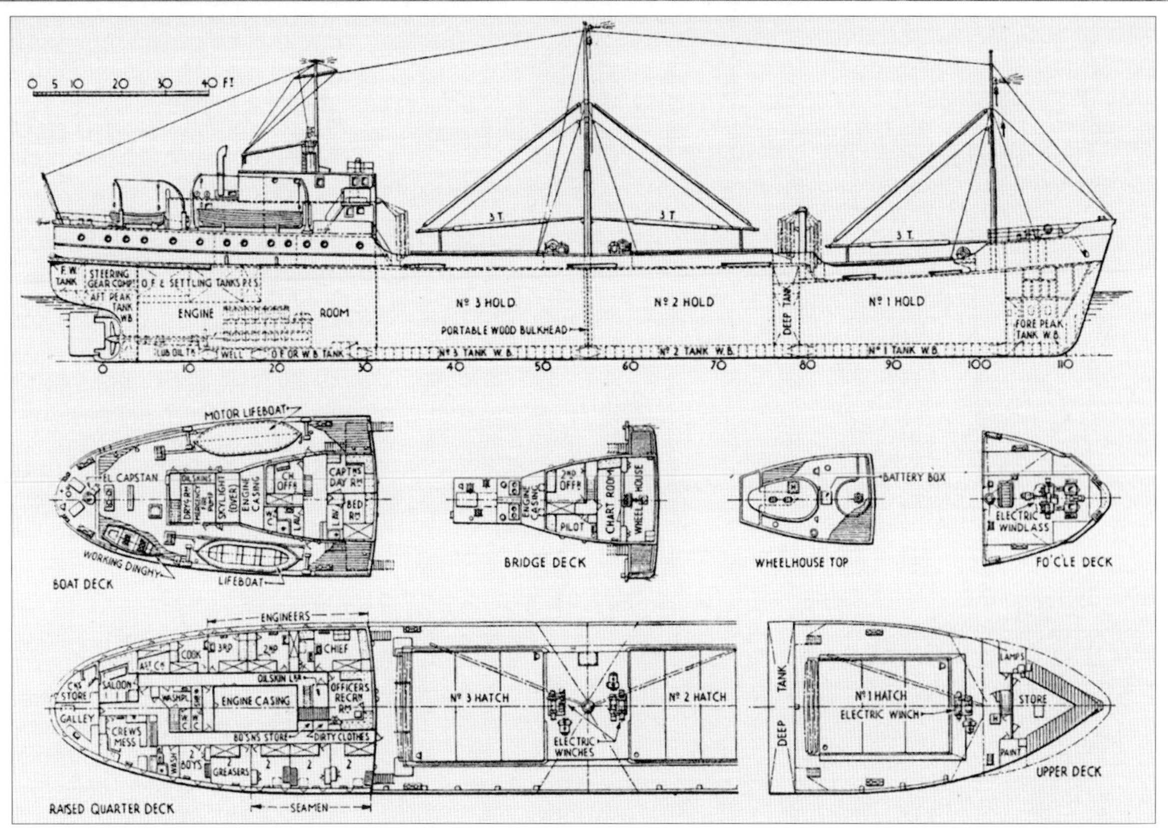

Built at Grangemouth, *Emerald* (3) was virtually a repeat of *Olivine* (5), and although slightly shorter she could load almost as much. She is seen at launch (left), on trials (upper middle), at anchor on the Thames with raised hatch coamings, an anchor ball correctly hoisted on her forestay and with what seems to have been a one-off paint scheme on her bridge front (lower middle). *[Robertson archives (2); Roy Fenton collection]*

13. EMERALD (3) 1952-1975
O.N. 184970 1,382g 678n 1,850d
233.0 x 38.1 x 13.2 feet
Oil engine 2SCSA 7-cyl. by British Polar Engines Ltd., Glasgow; 1,310 BHP, 10.5 knots.
26.2.1952: Launched by Grangemouth Dockyard Ltd., Grangemouth (Yard No. 498).
16.6.1952: Registered in the ownership of William Robertson Shipowners Ltd., Glasgow as EMERALD. She cost £152,850.
17.6.1952: Commenced trading.
1958: Owners became Gem Line Ltd. (William Robertson Shipowners Ltd., managers), Glasgow.
29.4.1971: Transferred to William Robertson Shipowners Ltd., Glasgow.
1975: Sold to Daglas Brothers, Piraeus, Greece and renamed IOANNIS D.
1977: Sold to Sea and Land Transport Co. 'Marina' S.a.r.L., Beirut, Lebanon and renamed HANADI.
1984: Sold to Rachid Kabbara, Tripoli, Lebanon and renamed RANIA.
5.11.1985: Arrived at Perama, Greece.
8.1986: Breaking up began by C. Courtidis S.A.

14. GEM (5) 1952-1960/CAMEO (4) 1960-1976
O.N. 184977 1,354g 685n 1,850d
244.8 x 38.2 x 13.2 feet
1960: 1,597g 796n 2,132d
274.7 x 39.8 x 14.6 feet
Oil engine 2SCSA 7-cyl. by British Polar Engines Ltd., Glasgow; 1,310 BHP, 10.5 knots.
26.6.1952: Launched by the Ailsa Shipbuilding Co. Ltd., Troon (Yard No. 476).
20.8.1952: Registered in the ownership of William Robertson Shipowners Ltd., Glasgow as GEM. She cost £151,749.
2.9.1952: Completed.
1958: Owners became Gem Line Ltd. (William Robertson Shipowners Ltd., managers), Glasgow.
8-11.1960: Lengthened by the Ailsa Shipbuilding Co. Ltd., Troon and renamed CAMEO.
29.4.1971: Transferred to William Robertson Shipowners Ltd., Glasgow.
20.2.1976: Sold to Stamalco Shipping Co. Ltd., Limassol, Cyprus (Dionisios A. Stavrou O. E. Shipping Enterprises, Piraeus, Greece) and renamed MANIA.
1984: Transferred to Patrae Shipping Company (Dionisios A. Stavrou O. E. Shipping Enterprises), Piraeus.
9.1986: Broken up at Eleusis.

Gem (5) was a repeat of *Olivine* (5), although in practice her capacity was slightly less, at about 1,650 tons of coal (left, at anchor on the Thames). *[World Ship Society Ltd.]*

In 1960 *Gem* went back to her builders to be lengthened by 30 feet. The photographs on this page show the lengthening process, which involved putting her into dry dock to be watched intently by Ailsa's work force (right), undoing rivets to cut her in two, pulling the pieces apart, and adding new scantlings, decks and plates (below). She emerged as *Cameo* (4) (bottom). *[Robertson archives]*

Third of the motor ships from Ailsa, *Pearl* (5) was smaller than her predecessors, and could load about 1,200 tons of coal. She saw a rethink of the masting arrangements, with a substantial mast just ahead of the bridge carrying a radar scanner and a navigation light. *[Ships in Focus; Robertson archives]*

15: PEARL (5) 1953-1972
O.N. 184993 1,093g 528n 1,350d
212.2 x 34.1 x 13.2 feet
Oil engine 2SCSA 6-cyl. by British Polar Engines Ltd., Glasgow; 1,120 BHP, 10.5 knots.
14.5.1953: Launched by the Ailsa Shipbuilding Co. Ltd., Troon (Yard No. 482).
10.9.1953: Registered in the ownership of William Robertson Shipowners Ltd., Glasgow as PEARL She cost of £154,632.
15.9.1953: Completed.
1958: Owners became Gem Line Ltd. (William Robertson Shipowners Ltd., managers), Glasgow.
29.4.1971: Transferred to William Robertson Shipowners Ltd., Glasgow.
1972: Sold to Seabright Shipping Ltd., Barking, Essex (Briggs Shipbrokers and Agents Ltd., London, managers) for £30,000 and renamed PAULINE H.
1978: Sold to Richard Whitehead, London.
1978: Sold to Desio Shipping Co. S.A. , Panama (A.H. Watts and Co. Ltd., Exmouth, managers) and renamed MAYMOORE.
1980: Sold to Arios Line Shipping Co. S.A., Panama and renamed ARIOS.
1981: Sold to Uniship Ltd., Panama (United Shipping Corporation Ltd., Dacca, Bangladesh) and renamed SIMUL.
2.7.1983: Broke anchor chain and ran ashore on Manora Beach, Karachi whilst laid up under arrest, having arrived at Karachi in September
1982: Sold to Sambals, Karachi for demolition *in situ*.

16. TURQUOISE (3) 1955-1966
O.N. 183432 547g 319n 716d
170.5 x 28.5 x 9.7 feet
Deutz-type oil engine 2SCSA 8-cyl. by Nydquist and Holm A/B, Trollhattan, Sweden; 91 NHP.
1956: Oil engine 4SCSA 6-cyl. by Motorenfabriek Deutz A.G., Koln-Deutz, West Germany; 800 BHP, 12.5 knots.
24.10.1946: Launched by Kalmar Varv, Kalmar, Sweden (Yard No. 356).
4.1947: Completed for Rederiaktieb Ruth (Leopold Glucksman, manager), Gothenburg, Sweden as ARNE.
18.3.1950: Registered in the ownership of J.R. Rix and Sons, Hull as JARRIX.
20.4.1955: Acquired by William Robertson Shipowners Ltd., Glasgow for £55,000 and later renamed TURQUOISE.
1956: Fitted with new oil engine.
1958: Owners became Gem Line Ltd. (William Robertson Shipowners Ltd., managers), Glasgow.
1966: Sold to Helena T. Vavatsioula and others, Thessaloniki, Greece and renamed HELLINIKOS VORRAS.
1979: Sold to Georgios Hatzielenis, Piraeus, Greece and renamed GEORGIOS.
1980: Sold to Green Parrot S.A., Panama and renamed PAOLA X.
2001: Deleted from 'Lloyd's Register' as continued existence in doubt.

Turquoise goes cruising
In May 1957, soon after the National Trust for Scotland acquired the island of St. Kilda, Robertsons lent the *Turquoise* and her crew to enable members of the Trust's board to investigate their new acquisition on a weekend cruise. Ronald Barge recalled the conversion of the *Turquoise* into a passenger vessel.

'There was no accommodation for passengers so cargo space had to be used for this purpose. Fortunately, we had a great man, Bob Yates, as Marine Superintendent, and he undertook to convert the ship's hold into a men's dormitory. He got hospital beds from the shipbreakers in Faslane, lined the sides of the hold with huge code-flags, laid canvas on the rough boards and even fitted electric lamps and shaver points by the beds.

Turquoise's captain, David Millar, a big cheerful man, was very co-operative and gave up his night quarters for the lady guests, and his day quarters as mess and dining room. The crew entered into the spirit of things...'

Even with ships to their own design coming from the Ailsa yard, Robertsons still bought secondhand coasters, including the Swedish-built *Turquoise* (3). This was probably because she filled a gap in the size of coasters owned. She could load up to 640 tons of coal, more than the motor ships *Cairngorm*, *Beryl* and *Prase* but less than *Jacinth* or *Spinel*. In the middle photograph she has taken the ground in the inner harbour at Douglas, Isle of Man on 22nd July 1959 whilst a Bedford OB coach passes along the quayside. The occasion for dressing *Turquoise* overall in the bottom photograph has not been recorded. *[Roy Fenton collection (2); Robertson archives]*

17. AMBER (2) 1956-1978
O.N. 185045 1,596g 858n 2,440d
267.8 x 39.0 x 17.0 feet
Oil engine 4SCSA 8-cyl. by Klockner-Humboldt-Deutz A.G., Koln-Deutz, West Germany; 1,650 BHP, 12.5 knots.
27.3.1956: Launched by the Ailsa Shipbuilding Co. Ltd., Troon (Yard No. 493).
11.6.1956: Registered in the ownership of William Robertson Shipowners Ltd., Glasgow as AMBER. She cost £208,886.
15.6.1956: Completed.
1958: Owners became Gem Line Ltd. (William Robertson Shipowners Ltd., managers), Glasgow.
29.4.1971: Transferred to William Robertson Shipowners Ltd., Glasgow.
1978: Transferred to Stephenson Clarke Shipping Ltd., London.
30.8.1978: Sold to Simri Compania de Navegacion S.A., Panama (Pan Nautic S.A. (Rafael Vecchiati), Lugano, Switzerland) and renamed SIMRI.
24.12.1980: Foundered in bad weather one mile south east of Capo Boi, off Cape Carbonara, Sardinia during a voyage from Spezia to Benghazi with a cargo of steel bars.

A further variation on the Ailsa design, *Amber* (2) was easily the biggest motor ship owned so far, loading over 2,200 tons of coal. She abandoned the long raised quarter deck design and introduced a third mast, keeping the heavier mizzen with its radar scanner. Klockner-Humboldt-Deutz engines replaced the British Polar units. *[Robertson archives; World Ship Society Ltd.; Shipping and Shipbuilding Record]*

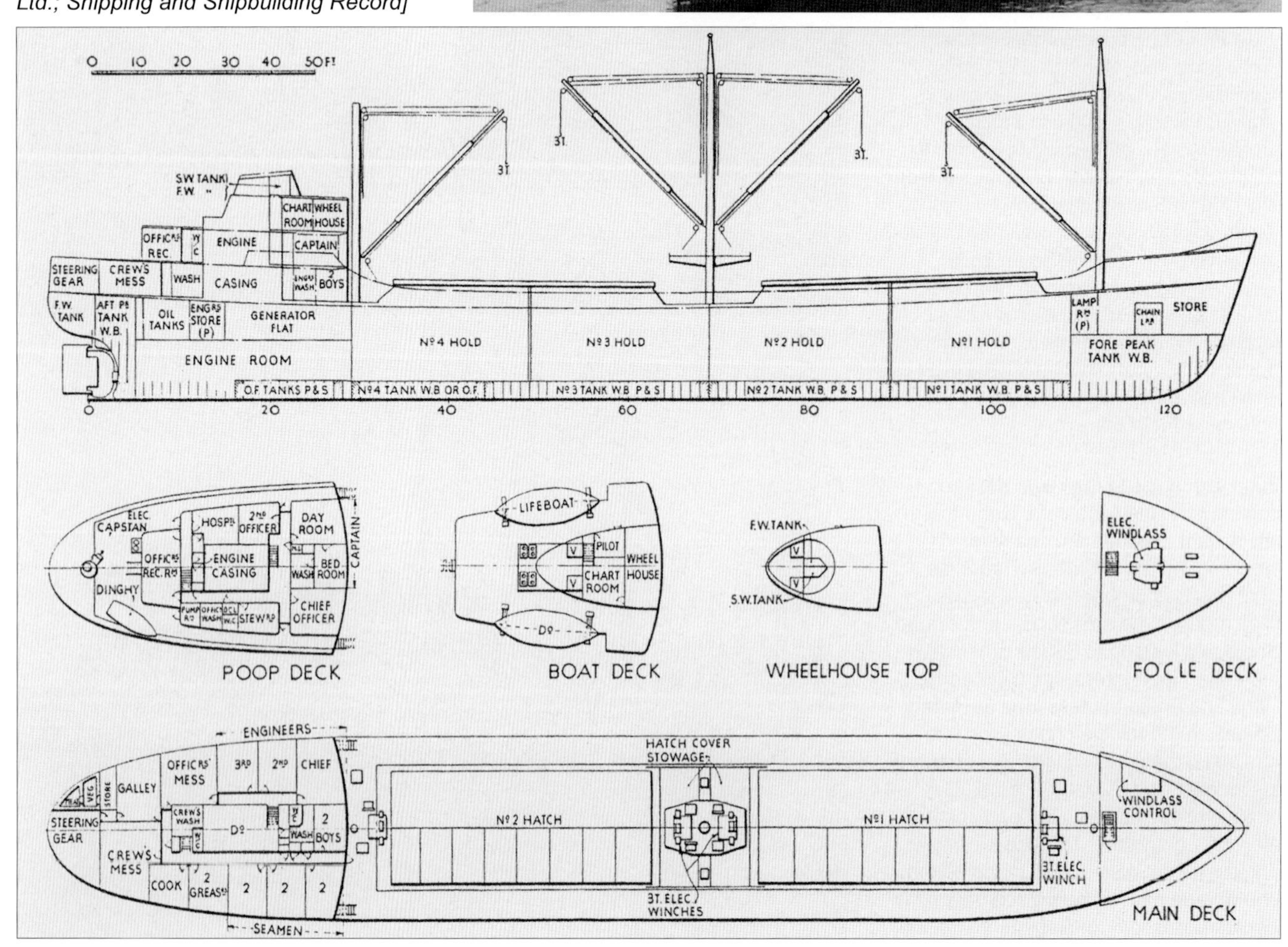

18. **AMETHYST (4) 1958-1978**
O.N. 300208 1,548g 856n 2,319d
258.0 x 39.5 x 17.1 feet
Oil engine 4SCSA 6-cyl. by Klockner-Humboldt-Deutz A.G., Koln-Deutz, West Germany; 1,400 BHP, 12 knots.
6.5.1958: Launched by the Ailsa Shipbuilding Co. Ltd., Troon (Yard No. 502).
14.7.1958: Completed for William Robertson Shipowners Ltd., Glasgow as AMETHYST. She cost £252,667.
1958: Owners became Gem Line Ltd. (William Robertson Shipowners Ltd., managers), Glasgow.
29.4.1971: Transferred to William Robertson Shipowners Ltd., Glasgow.
1978: Transferred to Stephenson Clarke Shipping Ltd., London.
7.3.1980: Sold to the Surbuvan Shipping Co. S.A., Panama (Sutas Shipping Services Ltd., London, managers), and renamed FAITH.
1981: Managers became Hanro Shipping B.V., London.
1982: Managers became Deniz Nakliyat ve Ticaret Barbaros Bulvari (A.O. Saribas), Istanbul, Turkey.
1984: Sold to Mariteco Navigation Co. Ltd., Limassol, Cyprus and renamed TASOS under the Panama and later Honduras flags.
1987: Sold to Jupiter Shipping Co. S.A., Panama (Nini Shipping Company (Vassilios Andreou), Piraeus) remaining under the Honduras flag.
1998: Sold to Astra Shipping Company, Bahamas (Pyrsos Managing Company, Piraeus) remaining under the Honduras flag.
2000: Sold to Swan Navigation S.A., Majuro, Marshall Islands and renamed SILVER STAR II under the Honduras flag.
12.5.2009: Still listed by 'Lloyd's Register'.

Further tinkering with the Ailsa design saw *Amethyst* (4) emerge with just two cargo-handling masts and a radar mast mounted on the superstructure. She was built for trading to Goole, an 'Ousemax' design. The launch (top) and trials shots (bottom) sandwich a photograph taken on 20th January 1969 when her cargo of paper pulp shifted near Vinga Lighthouse during a voyage from Gothenburg to Marseilles. Initially abandoned by her crew, she was towed into Gothenburg after much deck cargo had been jettisoned. *[Robertson archives (2); Newall-Dunn collection]*

19. BRILLIANT (2) 1958-1978
O.N. 300211 1,143g 563n 1,442d
224.3 x 33.8 x 14.5 feet
Oil engine 4SCSA 8-cyl. by Klockner-Humboldt-Deutz A.G., Koln-Deutz, West Germany; 1,060 BHP, 11 knots.
14.6.1958: Launched by Scheepswerf 'Gideon' v/h J. Koster Hzn., Groningen, Netherlands (Yard No. 240).
10.1958: Completed for William Robertson Shipowners Ltd., Glasgow as BRILLIANT. She cost £159,304.
1958: Owners became Gem Line Ltd. (William Robertson Shipowners Ltd., managers), Glasgow.
1968: Transferred to Scotspark Shipping Co. Ltd., Edinburgh (Charles R. Connell, Glasgow) (William Robertson Shipowners Ltd., managers), Glasgow.
1970: Transferred to Gem Line Ltd. (William Robertson Shipowners Ltd., managers), Glasgow.
29.4.1971: Transferred to William Robertson Shipowners Ltd., Glasgow.
1978: Transferred to Stephenson Clarke Shipping Ltd., London.
25.4.1978: Sold to Inishmoyle Shipping Ltd., Belfast (Shamrock Shipping Co. Ltd, Larne, managers) and renamed SLEMISH under the Panama flag.
1978: Transferred to the Shamrock Shipping (S) Pte. Ltd. (Shamrock Shipping Co. S.A., managers), Panama.
1979: Sold to Polybus Shipping Co., Panama.
1980: Renamed BRILLIANTE.
25.11.1982: Sank off French Guiana in position 04.56.30 north by 52.10 west after her cargo had shifted and pierced her hull whilst on a voyage from Cayenne to Maracaibo.

Built in the Netherlands, *Brilliant* (2) appears to have been to the same Ailsa design as *Pearl* (5). The bottom photograph of *Brilliant* loading limestone at Llanddulas shows she has a lighter mainmast with the radar scanner now on the superstructure. Comparison with *Olivine* (5) shows that the funnel casing is smaller.

Photographs opposite taken on 11th February 1969 show *Briiliant* ashore in the Sound of Islay during a voyage from Tofte in Norway to Barrow-in-Furness with pulp. *Amethyst* (4) is standing by, the tug *Flying Foam* (184/1962) is giving assistance, and the *Glen Shiel* (195/1959) offloads cargo. She was refloated on the 12th. *[Robertson archives]*

BRILLIANT
GLASGOW

BRILLIANT
GLASGOW

20. TOPAZ (7) 1962-1978
O.N. 304135 1,597g 835n 2,440d
267.8 x 39.8 x 17.1 feet
Oil engine 4SCSA 8-cyl. by Klockner-Humboldt-Deutz A.G., Koln-Deutz, West Germany; 2,000 BHP, 13 knots.
5.4.1962: Launched by the Ailsa Shipbuilding Co. Ltd., Troon (Yard No. 512).
29.6.1962: Completed for Gem Line Ltd. (William Robertson Shipowners Ltd., managers), Glasgow as TOPAZ.
She cost £274,907.
29.4.1971: Transferred to William Robertson Shipowners Ltd., Glasgow.
1978: Transferred to Stephenson Clarke Shipping Ltd., London.
1982: Sold to Universal Seaways Inc., Panama (Sutas Shipping Services Ltd., London) and renamed SUTAS.
4.9.1983: Laid up at Istanbul.
1984: Managers became Safak Uluslararasi Denizcilik ve Nakliyati A.S., Istanbul, Turkey.
1985: Sold to Naz Shipping Ltd., Valletta, Malta (Ege Deniz Nahliyat ve Ticaret Ltd. (Irfan and Nazli Altinel), Istanbul) and renamed NAZ.
1986: Sold to Ayanoglu Denizcilik ve Ticaret A.S. Istanbul and renamed YILOS under the Maltese flag.
1988: Sold to Sirketi Cavusoglu Denizcilik Turizm ve Ticaret, Istanbul, remaining under the Maltese flag.
1989: Sold to Sparta Shipping Co. Ltd., Kingstown, St. Vincent (Al Jowder International Shipping Shipping Agency, Dubai, United Arab Emirates) and renamed PANAYOTIS.
1990: Renamed AMAFHH TWO.
7.6.2009: Still listed by 'Lloyd's Register', although no owners or flag recorded since 1994.

21. TOURMALINE (3) 1962-1978
O.N. 304147 1,581g 855n 2,440d
267.8 x 39.8 x 17.1 feet
Oil engine 4SCSA 8-cyl. by Klockner-Humboldt-Deutz A.G., Koln-Deutz, West Germany; 1,800 BHP, 13 knots.
18.9.1962: Launched by the Ailsa Shipbuilding Co. Ltd., Troon (Yard No. 513).
28.11.1962: Completed for Gem Line Ltd. (William Robertson Shipowners Ltd., managers), Glasgow as TOPAZ.
She cost £276,164.
29.4.1971: Transferred to William Robertson Shipowners Ltd., Glasgow.
1978: Transferred to Stephenson Clarke Shipping Ltd., London.
1982: Sold to Concord Leasing Ltd., Brentford (Trafalgar Marine Ltd., Stratford-on-Avon) (Shamrock Shipping Co. Ltd., Larne, managers) and renamed PROBA.
1985: Ownership of Concord Leasing Ltd. transferred to Proba Shipping Ltd., Georgetown, Cayman Islands (Captain G. Courtney, Bangor, County Down and others).
1986: Sold to Plaza Shipping Ltd., Gibraltar (Joseph Hawes, Cobh) (Sprante Schiffahrts, Brunsbuttel, West Germany, managers) and renamed FERGUS H under the Honduras flag.
1987: Sold to Socotra Steamship Inc., Panama (Arab African Shipping Company, Abu Dhabi) and renamed SOCOTRA under the St. Vincent and later the Cyprus flag.
1990: Sold to Sorocco Shipping Co. Ltd. Valletta, Malta (Pilar Shipping Co. Ltd., Limassol, Cyprus) and renamed SOROCCO.
9.7.1993: Sold by auction at Rotterdam to Mondail Shipping B.V., Rotterdam (Mohamud Mehiddin Tumeh and Abdelkader Abu Bakr) (Akram Shipping Company, Lattakia, Syria) and renamed AKRAM V under the Honduras flag.
1997: Transferred to Syrian flag.
17.6.2009: Still listed by 'Lloyd's Register', although no owners or flag have been recorded since 1997.

Topaz (7) was a development of *Amber* (2) sharing a similar hull design, but with cargo-handling gear rethought. The masts now have high crosstrees and support pairs of derricks, with the radar scanner moved to the superstructure. The mast table amidships is a much more sturdy structure to support the extra winches. *[Robertson archives; Ships in Focus]*

Tourmaline (3) was a repeat of *Topaz* (7). *[All Robertson archives except bottom W.D. Harris/J. and M. Clarkson]*

Sapphire (5) marked a return to the design of *Pearl* (5), built by Ailsa 12 years previously, but without the long raised quarter deck. The other external difference is that the black paint of the hull has been carried higher on the poop. Despite the many differences in size, hull design and cargo equipment, the sequence of ten motor coasters that had begun with the *Olivine* from Ailsa in 1952 were distinctive enough for each to be recognisable as a Robertson ship, largely because of the treatment of the superstructure and the 'flowerpot' funnel. *Sapphire* was the last to be so distinguished. She was the first Robertson ship to be designed so that the engine room could be unmanned for 16 hours each day, which required an enhanced lubrication system. *[Robertson archives (2)]*

22. SAPPHIRE (5) 1966-1978
O.N. 307643 1,286g 625n 1,682d
227.8 x 36.5 x 14.8 feet
Oil engine 4SCSA 8-cyl. by Klockner-Humboldt-Deutz A.G., Koln-Deutz, West Germany; 1,320 BHP, 11 knots.
24.11.1965: Launched by the Ailsa Shipbuilding Co. Ltd., Troon (Yard No. 521).
7.3.1966: Completed for Gem Line Ltd. (William Robertson Shipowners Ltd., managers), Glasgow as SAPPHIRE. She cost £244,876.
29.4.1971: Transferred to William Robertson Shipowners Ltd., Glasgow.
1978: Owners became Stephenson Clarke Shipping Ltd., London.
19.3.1981: Sold to the Apollonia Shipping Co. Ltd., Cyprus (Spyridon Alexandratos, Piraeus, Greece) and renamed APOLLONIA VIII.
1981: Transferred to Diochris Compania Naviera S.A., Cyprus (Apollonia Shipping Co. Ltd. (Spyridon Alexandratos), Piraeus) and renamed APOLLONIA VII.
1987: Sold to Twilight Navigation Co. Ltd., Nicosia, Cyprus (Sacon Marine Co. Ltd., Piraeus) and renamed SARJO.
1989: Renamed OLGA S.
1993: Sold to Elfin Shipping Co. Ltd., Nicosia, Cyprus and renamed NANA.
1995: Sold to Nissos Giali Naftiki, Piraeus, Greece and renamed NISSIROS.
21.1.2009: Still listed by 'Lloyd's Register'.

***Sapphire* rescues a lifeboat crew**
In 1980 *Sapphire* (5) came to the aid of the Barra lifeboat which sank while going to rescue the Danish motor vessel *Lone Dania* (300/1968). Captain D. Mackinnon and his first mate John McLeod exhibited exceptional seamanship, towing the Barra lifeboat to safety. Company records state that both men were 'from the Outer Hebrides and in the best tradition of that area are first class seamen who no doubt got a kick out of being able to assist fellow Islanders'

23. GEM (6) 1969-1978
O.N. 335059 1,599g 1,194n 2,911d
304.2 x 43.8 x 17.0 feet
Oil engine 4SCSA 8-cyl. by Klockner-Humboldt-Deutz A.G., Koln-Deutz, West Germany; 2,150 BHP, 12 knots.
25.6.1969: Launched by Nieuwe Noord Nederlandsche Scheepswerven N.V., Groningen, Netherlands (Yard No. 363).
10.1969: Completed for Gem Line Ltd. (William Robertson Shipowners Ltd., managers), Glasgow as GEM. She cost £347,342.
29.4.1971: Transferred to William Robertson Shipowners Ltd., Glasgow.
1978: Transferred to Stephenson Clarke Shipping Ltd., London.
1988: Registered in the Isle of Man.
1990: Sold to Mediterranean Express Forwarding Ltd., Gibraltar (Haykal Shipping Company (Abdul Salam Haykal and Mohammad Abdul Salam Haykal)(Cunard Ellerman Shipping Services Ltd., managers) and renamed DAMASK ROSE under the Bahamas flag.
1992: Registered in Tartous, Syria.
1993: Transferred to Haykal Sea Transport Company (Haykal Shipping Company), Tartous, Syria.
1995: Sold to Mohamad Anis Dabha (Riamar Shipping Co. Ltd., managers), Tartous, Syria and renamed ANIS ROSE.
30.1.1996: Foundered 40 miles south east of Olbia in position 40.45 north by 10.37 east when her cargo of chrome ore shifted whilst on a voyage from Durres to Sete. Two of her crew died and a third went missing.

24. CAIRNGORM (4) 1973-1977
O.N. 357617 1,598g 892n 3,386d
315.8 x 46.3 x 17.0 feet
Oil engine 4SCSA 8-cyl. by Klockner-Humboldt-Deutz A.G., Koln-Deutz, West Germany; 3,600 BHP, 14.5 knots.
27.2.1973: Launched by Martin Jansen G.m.b.H & Co. K.G. Schiffswerf & Maschinefabriek, Leer, West Germany (Yard No. 101).
14.5.1973: Completed for Gem Line Ltd. (William Robertson Shipowners Ltd., managers), Glasgow as CAIRNGORM. She cost of £884,822.
22.3.1977: Sold to North Africa Line Ltd. (F.T. Everard and Sons Ltd., managers), London and renamed NORTHRIDGE.
1986: Sold to Fastnet Shipping Co. Ltd.,

Nicosia, Cyprus (Sea River Line N.V., Essen, Belgium) and renamed FASTNET.
1988: Sold to Global Marine Lines Inc., Panama and renamed GENESIS I.
1.1989: Renamed GLOBE.
1.1990: Sold to P.T. Pann Multi Finance, Jakarta, Indonesia and renamed SULTENG 1.
18.7.2000: Broke in two and sank 75 nautical miles north west of Christmas Island after taking in water the previous day in position 09.17.55 south by 105.20.05 east whilst on a voyage from Christmas Island to Indonesia with a cargo of phosphate. The crew of 24 was rescued.

The Groningen builders of *Gem* (6) produced a larger version of the *Topaz* (7) with taller superstructure, higher bulwarks on forecastle and poop, and distinctive cross trees, with only one derrick at each hold. She was the last ship built for Robertsons, and was still recognisable as such. Seen leaving Eastham in ballast, above, the white marks on her hull suggests she has just discharged a cargo of China clay at Runcorn. *[J.K. Byass]*

The only Robertson ship built for the company in Germany, *Cairngorm* (4) was also unique in the fleet in being a shelter decker (below). She found employment outside the owner's usual trades, for instance, carrying Volkswagen cars between Spain and Germany. She was also chartered at times to Ellerman's Wilson or Prince Line, but Robertsons found it difficult to cover their commitments with just one vessel of this type, and after only four years she was sold together with a charter. *[Roy Fenton collection]*

Jade (2) was a standard Polish B459 hull which had been lengthened in 1970. *[Ships in Focus]*

25. JADE (2) 1974-1978
O.N. 361621 1,200g 850n
244.0 x 42.8 x 16.3 feet
1970: 1,498g 1,173n 2,790d
287.3 x 42.9 x 15.8 feet
Oil engine 4SCSA 8-cyl. by Atlas-Mak Maschinenbau G.m.b.H., Kiel, West Germany; 1,500 BHP, 12 knots.
6.1967: Completed by Stocznia Gdanska, Gdansk, Poland (Yard No. B459/01) for Gerner Mathisen Rederi A/S (Arild Gerner-Mathisen, manager), Sandvika, Norway as GDANSK.
1970: Lengthened.
1973: Sold to I/S Fondship (Erik Nuest, manager), Jar, Norway and renamed FONDAL.
1974: Acquired by Gem Line Ltd. (William Robertson Shipowners Ltd., managers), Glasgow for £665,426 and renamed JADE.
1978: Transferred to Stephenson Clarke Shipping Ltd., London.
13.3.1981: Sold to the Dernal Shipping Co. Ltd., Nicosia, Cyprus (Nicolaos Hadjidakis, Piraeus, Greece) and renamed EVANGELIA.
1988: Sold to Coastalight Shipping Co. Ltd., Limassol, Cyprus (P. Pitsiliadadis, Piraeus) and renamed PANAGIOTA P.
1989: Sold to Hilal Shipping Co. Ltd., Cyprus (Laza Shipping and Trading Co. Ltd., Piraeus) and renamed PEPY L.
1991: Sold to Missoni Shipping Co. S.A., Panama (Kavadas GNK Maritime Co., Piraeus, Greece) and renamed KYRIAKI under the Honduras flag.
1993: BAM Lines International (BAM Shipping, managers), Spain and renamed DANY M.
1995: Sold to Wafic Begdache, Beirut, Lebanon (J.E. Papakostantis Successors Shipping Co. Ltd., Piraeus, Greece).
1996: Transferred to Mody Shipping Co. S.a.r.l. (Wafic Begdache), Beirut.
9.2002: Renamed MARZOOQAH under the Cambodian flag.
8.2006: Renamed PRINCE under the Bolivian flag.
19.1.2009: Still listed by 'Lloyd's Register' although no owners have been recorded since 2002.

26. TURQUOISE (4) 1975-1978
O.N. 301374 1,143g 550n
228.0 x 35.9 x 15.1 feet
Oil engine 4SCSA 6-cyl. by Mirrlees, Bickerton and Day Ltd., Stockport; 1,050 BHP, 11 knots.
1960: Launched by Clelands Shipbuilding Co. Ltd., Wallsend-on-Tyne (Yard No. 249).
3.1961: Completed for the Kyle Shipping Co. Ltd. (Monroe Brothers, managers), Liverpool as KYLEBANK.
1970: Managers became Stephenson Clarke Shipping Ltd., London.
1.8.1971: Managers became William Robertson Shipowners Ltd., Glasgow.
1975: Acquired by William Robertson Shipowners Ltd., Glasgow and renamed TURQUOISE.
1978: Transferred to Stephenson Clarke Shipping Ltd., London.
20.4.1979: Sold to Estland Maritime Inc., Panama (Shamrock Shipping Co. Ltd., Larne, managers) and renamed ESTLAND.
1982: Sold to Estrella Maritime Inc., Panama (J. Wood, Swanage) (Charles M. Willie and Co. (Shipping) Ltd., Cardiff, managers) and renamed BARNEY MAC.
1983: Sold to Diplari Shipping Co. S.A., Panama (Lindsay Terminals and Trading Co. Ltd., Leith, managers) and renamed ROSELAND.
3.10.1984: Arrived at Barking Creek for breaking up by G.W. Tutt. She had been arrested earlier that year.

Kylebank was managed by Robertsons on behalf of Kyle Shipping Co. Ltd. from 1971 to 1975, when she was acquired and renamed *Turquoise* (4). *[Roy Fenton collection]*

6. Managed ships

Managed for James Reston, Glasgow
Ship broker James Reston had financial interests in a number of ships which feature in this book. His *Ensign* appears in the list of owned steamers, as William Robertson had a minority shareholding from 1885 and acted as managing owner. Reston's *Omniopolis* was sold to the Hays to become *Strathesk* and came Robertson's way when he bought four of the Hay family's fleet in 1888. Robertson had no financial involvement in *Pennon*, listed below, acting only as manager for several years before her loss. Reston also held 32 shares in Robertson's *Jacinth* (2) of 1888 and from September 1889 to January 1896 held ten shares in *Nugget* (2).

PENNON 1885-1889 Iron
O.N. 87646 318g 147n
145.0 x 23.1 x 10.6 feet
C. 2-cyl. by J. and T. Young, Ayr; 50 NHP, 180 IHP.
3.1883: Launched by T.B. Seath and Co., Rutherglen (Yard No. 221).
27.4.1883: Registered in the ownership of James Reston, Glasgow as PENNON.
26.9.1885: Manager became William Robertson.
23.1.1889: Stranded on Ailsa Craig whilst on a voyage from Duddon to Glasgow with a cargo of iron ore.
5.3.1889: Register closed.

Managed for Hugh H. Smiley, Paisley
A thread manufacturer in the cotton town of Paisley, Hugh Houston Smiley owned three coasting steamers, probably bought as an investment. From November 1885 management was put in the hands of William Robertson, who would have run them alongside his own fleet. The size of the Smiley ships, varying from the 124-foot *Olderfleet* to the 175-feet *Latharna*, reflected a similar ship owning policy to Robertson's, in having a diversity of vessel sizes for different trades. Indeed, Robertson took the *Dalriada* into his owned fleet in 1894, and may have been instrumental in the sale of *Olderfleet* to the Carnlough Lime Co. Ltd., as he continued to manage her. The loss of *Latharna* off Nova Scotia in 1890 is an interesting example of a Robertson-controlled ship trading on the Atlantic coast of North America.

1. OLDERFLEET 1885-1891 Iron
O.N. 82338 213g 118n
124.3 x 21.2 x 9.7 feet
1894: 257g 78n
134.3 x 21.2 x 9.7 feet
C. 2-cyl. by William King and Co., Glasgow; 50 NHP, 350 IHP, 10 knots.
23.8.1880: Launched by T.B. Seath and Co., Rutherglen, Glasgow (Yard No. 197).
30.9.1880: Registered in the ownership of Hugh H. Smiley, Paisley as OLDERFLEET.
6.10.1885: Manager becomes William Robertson.
7.2.1891: Sold to the Carnlough Lime Co. Ltd., Carnlough, County Antrim (William Robertson, Glasgow, manager).
1894: Lengthened by J. Shearer and Son, Kelvinhaugh, Glasgow.
17.12.1920: Manager became John H. Martin.
15.5.1924: Sold to Thomas Dougall and Andrew R.W. Dougall, Glasgow.
3.5.1938: Register closed after she had been broken up.

2. DALRIADA 1885-1894 Iron
See No 42 in steamer fleet list.

3. LATHARNA 1885-1890 Iron
O.N. 89916 511g 265n
175.0 x 27.1 x 11.2 feet
C. 2-cyl. by William King and Co., Glasgow; 85 NHP.
31.3.1884: Launched by John Fullerton and Co., Paisley (Yard No. 61).
4.1884: Completed.
10.5.1884: Registered in the ownership of Hugh H. Smiley, Paisley as LATHARNA.
6.10.1885: Manager became William Robertson.
22.8.1890: Stranded on Soldier's Ledge, near Yarmouth, Nova Scotia whilst on a voyage from Philadelphia to Labrador in ballast.
16.9.1890: Register closed.

Managed for William King, Paisley
In January 1886 the Glasgow coaster owner James Macfarlane was declared bankrupt and three of his ships were acquired from the liquidator by William King. The engines for all three had been built by King's Dock, Engine and Boiler Works, Paisley. To trade the vessels he appointed William Robertson as manager. Possibly in ill health, King began to sell the ships early in 1888 and after his death in August 1888 his executors disposed of the third. The steamers were small in comparison with William Robertson's own vessels, and he took just one, the *Argus*, and then sold her within weeks – a period so short that she has not been counted as an owned vessel for the purposes of the fleet lists in this book.

Although not part of the Robertson story, it is interesting to note that two of the vessels, *Trojan* and *Scythian*, remained under British registry for some years following sale to owners who were domiciled abroad. There is some evidence that *Scythian* was used as a yacht by owners in the USA. Almost uniquely amongst the fleet owned or managed by Robertsons, full details of the fates of all three former King vessels are obscure.

1. TROJAN 1886-1888
O.N. 90014 240g 88n
130.6 x 21.1 x 9.8 feet
C. 2-cyl. by William King and Co., Glasgow; 70 NHP.
28.1.1885: Launched by Murdoch and Murray, Port Glasgow (Yard No. 87).
1.1885: Completed.
18.3.1885: Registered in the ownership of James Macfarlane, Glasgow as TROJAN.
23.2.1886: Acquired by William King, Paisley (William Robertson, Glasgow, manager).
25.1.1888: Sold to William G. Westcott, London.
31.1.1888: Sold to George S. Blunt, trading as the Salonica (British) Steam Ship Company, Salonica but remaining under British registry.
25.10.1890: Sold to Vincent S.E. Grech, Constantinople, Turkey.
2.8.1892: Register closed on sale to the Ottoman Government, Constantinople and

Olderfleet at Preston in the 1930s, when owned by the Dougall family of Glasgow. *[Harry Stewart/J. and M. Clarkson]*

renamed INEBOLU.
1899: Owners became Idarei Massousieh [Ottoman Steam Navigation Co.], Constantinople and name now given as INEBOLI.
1911: Owners became the Administration de Navigation à Vapeur Ottomane, Constantinople.
1923: Owners became the Administration de Navigation à Vapeur Turque, Constantinople and name now given as INEBOLOU.
1926: Deleted from 'Lloyd's Register'.

2. SCYTHIAN 1886-1888
O.N. 90016 240g 88n
130.6 x 21.1 x 9.7 feet
C. 2-cyl. by William King and Co., Glasgow; 70 NHP.
17.2.1885: Launched by Murdoch and Murray, Port Glasgow (Yard No. 88).
27.3.1885: Registered in the ownership of James Macfarlane, Glasgow as SCYTHIAN.
23.2.1886: Acquired by William King, Paisley (William Robertson, Glasgow, manager).
9.8.1888: Sold to Walter F. Irvine, Dublin but resident in Norfolk, Virginia, U.S.A.
9.8.1889: Sold to James B. Hamilton, Hopewell, New Brunswick, Canada.
24.11.1894: Sold to Thomas C. Watson, Pensacola, Florida, U.S.A.
2.11.1899: Register closed on sale to the United Fruit Company, Boston, U.S.A.
1903: Sold to the Belize Royal Mail and Central American Steamship Co., Boston.
1904: Sold to the Haitian Government, Port au Prince, Haiti.
1914: Deleted from 'Lloyd's Register'

3. ARGUS 1886-1889 Iron
O.N. 87644 189g 79n
115.0 x 21.1 x 9.0 feet
C. 2-cyl. by William King and Co., Glasgow; 40 NHP, 200 IHP.
3.1883: Launched by John Fullerton and Co., Paisley (Yard No. 56).
27.4.1883: Registered in the ownership of Hugh Keith, Glasgow as ARGUS.
18.6.1885: Sold to James Macfarlane, Glasgow.
22.3.1886: Acquired by William King, Paisley (William Robertson, Glasgow, manager).
28.2.1889: Acquired by William Robertson, Glasgow.
15.3.1889: Sold to Gregory B. Wadsworth, Goole.
23.12.1889: Sold to William Elemore (Edward H. Ritherdon, manager), London.
21.7.1891: Register closed on sale to A. Areizaga and Co., Bilbao, Spain and renamed CHIMBO.
1895: Owners became Compania Maritima Cantabria (A. Areizaga, manager), Bilbao.
1902: Sold to Victo de Ugarte, Bilbao.
1902: Sold to Compania Vapor Katalin (Ramon de Abrisqueta, manager), Bilbao and renamed KATALIN.
1918: Sold to Santos Lopez e Compania, Bilbao.
1921: Sold to C. Garrastasu e Compania, Bilbao, Spain.
4.1923: Went missing under the name KERT.

Former Hay ships managed
Contemporaries of William Robertson, the Hay family were possibly even more ambitious, although their fortunes were mixed. Alexander M. Hay built up his fleet very quickly to include both coasters and deep-sea steamers, although losses were very heavy. Interestingly, the first two steamers in the Hay fleet were named *Emerald* (370/1879) and *Pearl* (352/1880), although there appears to have been no financial connection with Robertson, and the ships came from yards which Robertson never used, making it unlikely that they were taken over by Hay whilst building. Hays later used the *Strath* prefix despite William Burrell having adopted such a naming scheme for his ocean-going ships as early as 1871. In May 1888 Alexander Hay was declared bankrupt and in the following September 1888, as part owners or mortgagees, Rudolph Feldtmann and John Anderson placed two of the ships, *Strathavon* and *Strathgarry*, under the management of William Robertson. Both the ships were sold within two years.

The Hay dynasty survived the setback of Alexander's bankruptcy, and went on to own two distinct fleets: a group of steam coasters named after orders of nobility with the prefix *The*, and a large fleet of Clyde puffers mostly named after tribesmen. The family also had a small shipyard on the Forth and Clyde Canal at Kirkintilloch which built and maintained its puffers. The coasters were sold to F.T. Everard and Sons Ltd. in 1956 and the puffer fleet went through a series of mergers to end up as a constituent of Glenlight Shipping Ltd.

1. STRATHAVON 1888-1890 Iron
O.N. 58343 252g 141n
137.8 x 19.7 x 11.8 feet
2-cyl. by the Greenock Foundry Company, Greenock; 47 NHP.
7.2.1881: C. 2-cyl. by Walker, Henderson and Co., Glasgow; 42 NHP.
6.1867: Launched by William and John Swan, Maryhill, Glasgow.
6.9.1867: Registered in the ownership of William Swan, Maryhill as PALERMO.
19.11.1867: Sold to John E. Swan, Maryhill (32/64) and Thomas Fell, Greenock (32/64).
12.2.1869: Sold to John Anderson, Glasgow (32/64) and Thomas Fell, Greenock (32/64).
22.12.1869: Sold to Thomas Fell, Greenock (32/64), James Hay, Glasgow (28/64) and Alexander M. Hay, Glasgow (4/64).
29.9.1880: Sold to Alexander M. Hay, Glasgow (32/64) and Rudolph Feldtmann, Glasgow (32/64).
10.1881: Renamed STRATHAVON.
23.4.1888: James Hay became manager.
6.9.1888: William Robertson, Glasgow, appointed manager by Rudolph Feldtmann who had acquired the 32 shares of Alexander M. Hay on his bankruptcy.
29.9.1890: Sold to Edward Hall, Cardiff.
28.10.1890: Register closed on sale to Manuel Camara, Pasajes, Spain and renamed SIXTO CAMARA.
1912: Owners became Viuda y Sobrinos de Manuel Camara, Passajes, Spain.
1923: Sold to Luis Vives-Garcia, Malaga, Spain.
1926: Sold to Eulogio Vives, Malaga.
1930: Sold to Jose Fradero, Barcelona, Spain.
1943: Deleted from 'Lloyd's Register', no trace.

2. STRATHGARRY 1888-1889 Iron
O.N. 82326 347g 160n
143.9 x 21.7 x 12.0 feet
C. 2-cyl. by Fleming and Ferguson, Paisley; 65 NHP.
6.1880: Launched by William Hamilton and Co., Port Glasgow (Yard No. 49).
14.8.1880: Registered in the ownership of Alexander M. Hay, Glasgow as PEARL.
11.11.1881: Renamed STRATHGARRY.
23.4.1888: James Hay appointed manager.
6.9.1888: William Robertson, Glasgow, appointed manager by shareholder John Anderson following Alexander M. Hay being declared bankrupt on 3.5.1888.
11.11.1889: Sold to James Mawson and Son, Barrow.
20.3.1893: Wrecked at the south end of Arran whilst on a voyage from Castletown to Ardrossan.
4.4.1893: Register closed.

Managed for Carnlough Lime Co. Ltd., Carnlough, County Antrim
Robertson's longest involvement as manager was with this lime quarrying company in Northern Ireland, reflecting Robertson's interest in the limestone trade.

1. OLDERFLEET 1891-1920 Iron
See No. 1 in Hugh H. Smiley fleet above.

Managed for the British Government
Although the ultimate owner of the six prizes listed below was the British Government, sources differ as to whether ownership was actually vested in the Shipping Controller or the Admiralty. In addition, registration documents do not always record managers for these vessels, and evidence for Robertson's involvement comes largely from other sources, including the 'Service List' (published by the Admiralty), 'Lloyd's Register' and 'Lloyd's Confidential Index'. Dates for management are therefore not as exact as the authors would wish, although the dates given in the 'Service List' offer a useful indication of when each entered service.

1. HUNTSHOLM 1917
O.N. 139166 2,073g 1,203n
290.7 x 41.2 x 16.9 feet
T. 3-cyl. by Ottenser Maschine Fabriek G.m.b.H., Altona, Germany; 191 NHP, 11 knots.
30.5.1914: Launched by Schiffswerft v. Henry Koch, Lübeck, Germany (Yard No. 226).
1.7.1914: Completed for Oldenburg-Portugiesische Dampfschiffs Rhederei, Oldenburg, Germany as TELDE.
8.1914: Laid up at Teneriffe.
3.5.1916: Drifted seaward after her anchor chain parted in a gale, boarded by a prize crew from HMS ESSEX and taken to Gibraltar. Later condemned as a prize.
7.11.1916: Registered in the ownership of the Admiralty, London (J.J. Denholm Ltd., Greenock, managers) as HUNTSHOLM.
8.11.1916: Became Expeditionary Force Transport G 1826.
1917: Manager became William Robertson, Glasgow.
11.6.1917: Torpedoed and sunk by the German submarine UB 40 four miles east by south of the Owers Light Vessel whilst on a voyage from Dieppe to Southampton in ballast.
8.8.1917: Register closed.

2. HUNSGROVE 1917-1918
O.N. 127056 3,063g 1,978n 5,411d
335.0 x 46.8 x 22.7 feet
T. 3-cyl. by the Newport News Shipbuilding and Dry Dock Co., Newport News, U.S.A.; 309 NHP, 11 knots.
25.1.1913: Launched by the Newport News Shipbuilding and Dry Dock Co., Newport News (Yard No.163).
2.1913: Completed for the New York and Porto Rico Steamship Company, New York, U.S.A. as LORENZO.
12.9.1914: Captured by H.M.S. BERWICK off the Windward Islands and taken to St. Lucia. She was on charter to the German Navy and acting as a collier to S.M.S. KARLSRUHE. Later condemned as a prize.
17.6.1915: Registered in the ownership of the Admiralty (Farrar, Groves and Co. Ltd., managers) , London
28.10.1915: Renamed HUNSGROVE.
4.11.1915: Became Expeditionary Force Transport G 268.
1917: Transferred to the Shipping Controller, London (William Robertson, Glasgow, manager).
8.6.1918: Torpedoed by the German submarine U 82, 6.5 miles off Trevose Head whilst on a voyage from Cardiff to Blaye, France with a cargo of coal.
6.8.1918: Register closed.

3. HUNSGATE 1917-1920
O.N. 136815 3,220g 1978n
365.9 x 49.8 x 20.4 feet
T. 3-cyl. by Bremer Vulkan, Vegesack, Germany; 244 NHP, 9.5 knots.
3.11.1911: Launched by Bremer Vulkan, Vegesack (Yard No. 550).
12.1911: Completed for Dampfschiffahrt Gesellschaft 'Argo', Bremen, Germany as ALTAIR.
11.8.1914: Captured by HMS DUKE OF EDINBURGH in the Red Sea and taken to Port Said. Later condemned as a prize.
13.3.1915: Registered in the ownership of the Admiralty (Lawther, Latta and Co., managers), London.
21.6.1915: Became Expeditionary Force Transport C 6082.
28.6.1915: Renamed HUNSGATE.
1917: Transferred to the Shipping Controller, London (William Robertson, Glasgow, manager).
17.2.1920: Sold to A/S Det Selmerske Rederi, Trondhjem, Norway and renamed GURTH.
1924: Sold to Les Cargos Algeriens S.A., Dunkirk, France and renamed MOGHREB ASCA.
14.7.1928: Wrecked near Honfleur whilst on a voyage from Algiers to Rouen with a cargo of wine.

4. HUNTSCAPE 1917-1920
O.N. 136795 2,933g 1,778n
338.8 x 48.2 x 20.5 feet
T. 3-cyl. by Bremer Vulkan, Vegesack, Germany.
25.4.1911: Launched by Bremer Vulkan, Vegesack (Yard No. 545) for Deutsche Levante Linie, Hamburg, Germany as PINDOS.
26.8.1911: Delivered.
1.8.1914: Captured at Alexandria.
1915: Taken over by the Admiralty and renamed HUNTSCAPE.
1916: Sold to Andrew Weir and Co., Glasgow.
1916: Sold to Elder, Dempster and Co. Ltd., Liverpool.
1917: Transferred to the Shipping Controller, London (William Robertson, Glasgow, manager).
17.2.1920: Sold to A/S Det Selmerske Rederi, Trondhjem, Norway and renamed WILFRID.
1929: Sold to A/S Norasiatic Coal Transports Ltd. (E.M. Nilsen Moe, manager), Oslo, Norway.
1934: Sold to Nils E.A. Moller (Moller and Co., managers), Shanghai, China and renamed DAISY MOLLER.
1936: Owners became the Moller Line Ltd.
14.12.1943: Torpedoed and sunk by the Japanese submarine Ro-110 in position 16.21 north by 82.13 east whilst on a voyage from Bombay and Colombo to Chittagong and Vizagapatam with army stores including guns and ammunition. Of the 127 persons on board, 55 were killed when the submarine rammed and straffed her rafts and boats.

5. CLUTHA 1917-1922
O.N. 98897 3,426g 2,171n
328.4 x 42.3 x 21.4 feet
Q. 4-cyl. by Wigham, Richardson and Co., Low Walker, Newcastle-upon-Tyne; 400 NHP, 1,500 IHP, 10 knots.
13.12.1890: Launched by Wigham, Richardson and Co., Newcastle-on-Tyne (Yard No. 255).
17.2.1891: Registered in the ownership of George Tweedy, London as HOLKAR.
16.8.1892: Sold to Philip W. Richardson, London.
10.7.1893: Transferred to London Steamers Ltd. (Philip W. Richardson, manager), London.
16.10.1897: Register closed on sale to the Hungarian Levant Steamship Co. Ltd., Fiume, Austria-Hungary and renamed ATTILA.
1905: Managers became S. and W. Hoffman.
24.8.1914: Intercepted by the Royal Navy off the Shetland Islands whilst on a voyage from Port Talbot to Bergen in ballast, taken to Kirkwall where she was seized the next day, and subsequently Glasgow. Later condemned as a prize.
22.5.1915: Registered in the ownership of the Donaldson Line Ltd. (Donaldson Brothers Ltd., managers), Glasgow as CLUTHA.
28.5.1917: Transferred to the Shipping Controller, London (William Robertson, Glasgow, manager).
12.9.1921: Register closed on sale to Societa Levante di Navegacion Marittima, Budapest, Hungary and Rome, Italy.
1922: Owners became the Italian Government, Rome.
1923: Sold to Cantiere Navali e Acciaiere di Venezia, and broken up at Trieste.

6. HUNTSLAND 1918
O.N. 123519 2,871g 1,757n 2,871d
338.7 x 48.2 x 20.5 feet
T. 3-cyl. by Bremer Vulkan, Vegesack, Germany; 195 NHP, 1,900 IHP, 11 knots.
3.8.1911: Launched by Bremer Vulkan, Vegesack (Yard No. 546).
15.9.1911: Completed for Deutsche Levante-Linien, Hamburg, Germany as ERYMANTHOS.
3.8.1914: Captured near Malta by the British gunboat H.M.S. HUSSAR.
7.2.1915: Registered in the ownership of the Governor of Malta.
6.6.1915: Registered in the ownership of the Admiralty, London (James Knott and Co. Ltd., Newcastle-upon-Tyne, manager) and registered in Malta.
18.11.1915: Became Expeditionary Force Transport G 610.
1915: Renamed HUNTSLAND.
1918: Transferred to the Shipping Controller, London (William Robertson, Glasgow, manager).
6.6.1918: Torpedoed by the German submarine UC 77, 23 miles north by west of Le Havre in position 49.50 north by 00.10 west whilst on a voyage from Le Havre to Portsmouth in ballast.
6.8.1918: Register closed.

Managed for the Ministry of Shipping and Ministry of War Transport, London

1. DAGMAR 1940-1941
O.N. 167450 844g 498n
212.9 x 31.4 x 13.6 feet
T. 3-cyl. by N.V. Machinefabriek Delftshaven, Rotterdam, Holland; 85 NHP, 800 IHP, 9 knots.
12.4.1922: Launched by N.V. Werf 'Zeeland', Hansweert, Holland (Yard No. 64) for Dampskibsselskabet 'Vesterhavet' A/S (J. Lauritzen, manager), Esbjerg, Denmark as DAGMAR.
26.10.1922: Completed for the builder's own account (J.H. Jensen, Flensburg, Germany, manager) as LEONORA.
13.4.1923: Sold to Dampskibsselskabet 'Vesterhavet' A/S (J. Lauritzen, manager), Esbjerg and renamed DAGMAR.
9.4.1940: In Glasgow when Germany invaded Denmark.
4.5.1940: Owners became the Ministry of Shipping, later Ministry of War Transport, London (William Robertson, Glasgow, manager).
9.6.1941: Bombed and sunk about seven miles from Anvil Point Lighthouse off Bournemouth in position 50.35 north by 01.48 west whilst on a voyage from Cardiff to Shoreham with a cargo of coal. Of her crew of 16 and two D.E.M.S. gunners, three were lost, the remainder being picked up by French naval craft.
3.7.1941: Register closed.
Some sources claim she was renamed DAGMAR II in May 1940.

2. EMPIRE BEACON 1941
O.N. 168695 872g 465n
203.0 x 33.2 x 11.7 feet.
5-cyl. 2SCSA Polar-type oil engine by British Auxiliaries Ltd., Glasgow; 80 NHP, 800 BHP, 1,026 IHP, 10 knots.
24.9.1941: Launched by Scott and Sons, Bowling (Yard No. 358) for the Ministry of War Transport, London (William Robertson, Glasgow, managers) as EMPIRE BEACON.
18.10.1941: Registered in the ownership of the Ministry of War Transport, London (John Stewart and Co. (Shipping) Ltd., Glasgow, managers).
11.1941: Completed.
5.4.1942: Sank after hitting a floating mine six miles from St. Ann's Head in position 51.41 north by 05.10 west whilst on a voyage from Cardiff to Belfast with a cargo of coal. Register closed.
23.4.1942: Register closed.

3. EMPIRE CAPE 1941-1943
O.N. 168681 872g 458n
211.0 x 33.2 x 11.7 feet
Oil engines 2SCSA 5-cyl. by British Auxiliaries Ltd., Glasgow; 800 BHP.
27.3.1941: Launched by Scott and Sons, Bowling (Yard No. 359).
19.6.1941: Registered in the ownership of the Ministry of War Transport, London (William Robertson, Glasgow, manager) as EMPIRE CAPE.
7.1941: Completed.

Photographed as *Lochee*, *Empire Cape* was managed by Robertsons for the British government. *[J. and M. Clarkson]*

1943: Managers became the Tyne-Tees Steam Ship Co. Ltd., Newcastle-upon-Tyne.
7.1944: Managers became the Dundee, Perth and London Shipping Co. Ltd., Dundee.
22.11.1945: Sold to the Dundee, Perth and London Shipping Co. Ltd., Dundee and later renamed GOWRIE.
1948: Renamed LOCHEE.
8.1966: Sold to D. and S. Zoulis Brothers and D. Vlachos, Piraeus, Greece and renamed AGHIOS SPYRIDON.
1968: Sold to S.C. Vazeos and Co., Piraeus.
1970: Sold to Abdel Razzak Sattout, Tripoli, Lebanon and renamed ANWAR.
2.1995: Deleted from 'Lloyd's Register' as continued existence in doubt.

4. ALCYONE 1944-1945
359g 170n 420d
137.0 x 24.8 x 8.1 feet
Oil engines 4SCSA 6-cyl. by Motorenwerke Mannheim A.G., Mannheim, Germany; 295 BHP, 9 knots.
1961: Oil engine 2SCSA 5-cyl. by Alpha Diesel A/S, Frederikshavn, Denmark.
14.9.1938: Launched by N.V. Scheepswerf 'Foxhol' v/h Gebroeder Muller, Foxhol, Holland (Yard No. 48),
2.12.1938: Completed for Derk Schothorst, Hansweert, Holland (N.V. 'Carebeka', Groningen, managers) as ALCYONE.
16.5.1940: Taken over by the Netherlands Shipping and Trading Committee (Freight Express Ltd., managers), London.
29.5.1940: Time chartered by the Ministry Shipping, later the Ministry of War Transport, London
1944: Manager became William Robertson, Glasgow.
1.6.1945: Returned to owners.
15.7.1945: Charter ended.
15.1.1951: Sold to N.V. Hollandsche Kustvaart Maatschappij (Tjark van Dirk, Jurrien Kruidhof and Abraham Kuyper) (A. van Dijk, manager), Delfzijl, Holland and renamed ARION.
12.7.1955: Sold to Hendrik Paap and Wrister J. van Wijk (N.V. Scheepvaartbedrijf 'Gruno', managers), Groningen, Holland and renamed CITO.

Cito photographed at Portsmouth in August 1955. As *Alcyone* she was one of many Dutch coasters which came over to Britain during the Second World War. *[Tom Rayner/J. and M . Clarkson]*

18.5.1960: Sold to N.R. Christensen (A.E. Sorensen, manager), Svendborg, Denmark and renamed PATRICIA.
1.8.1961: Transferred to I/S Jensen and Villadsen (A.E. Sorensen, manager), Svendborg and renamed PROCYON.
1961: Fitted with new oil engine.
1.1970: Sold to Holger Asmussen, Graasten, Denmark and renamed HOAN.
1.1973: Sold to Hans Johannsen, Egernsund, Denmark and renamed YVONNE.
4.1974: Sold to Mohamed W. El-Sohl, Beirut, Lebanon and renamed RIYAD.
1976: Sold to Nizar Gandour, Beirut and renamed MOHAMED.
1978: Renamed SHEREEN.
2.10.1978: Towed into Messina following an engine breakdown in position 37.25 north by 17.50 east.
24.9.1994: Last reported as sailing from Olbia.
9.1997: Deleted from 'Lloyd's Register' as continued existence in doubt.

5. CATARAQUI PARK 1944-1946
O.N. 169936 2,877g 1,652n
328.0 x 46.5 x 22.9 feet
T.3-cyl. by Canada Iron Foundries Ltd., Three Rivers, Quebec, Canada; 1,176 IHP; 10-11 knots.
20.4.1944: Launched by Foundation Maritime Ltd., Pictou, Nova Scotia, Canada (Yard No. 14) for the Government of the Dominion of Canada (Park Steamship Co. Ltd., managers) for bareboat charter to the United Kingdom as CATARAQUI PARK.
30.4.1944: Completed.
8.8.1944: Registered in the ownership of the Ministry of War Transport, London (William Robertson, Glasgow, managers)
22.2.1946: Register closed and returned to the Government of the Dominion of Canada (Park Steamships Ltd., managers).
1946: Sold to Centre d'Approvissionnement de l'Indochine, Tongking, Indo China (Compagnie des Messageries Maritimes, Paris, France, managers), renamed PIGNEAU DE BEHAINE and registered at Saigon.
1948: Transferred to Compagnie de Transports Océaniques, Paris.
1955: Sold to Compagnie Asiatique de Navigation, Djibouti, French Somaliland and renamed AMBOULI.
1958: Renamed MUKALI.
1963: Sold to Neptune Marine Corporation, Monrovia, Liberia (P.S. Li, Hong Kong) and renamed WAYWIND.
1967: Sold to Hiwind Navigation Co. Ltd., Monrovia (Deh Ling Wu, Hong Kong).
25.10.1969: Arrived Hong Kong for demolition by Lee Sing Co.

6. EMPIRE DORRIT 1944-1945
O.N. 169422 965g 536n
197.6 x 34.1 x 13.2 feet
T. 3-cyl. by Aitchison, Blair Ltd., Clydebank.
4.10.1944: Launched by Scott and Sons, Bowling (Yard No. 372).
4.11.1944: Registered in the ownership of the Ministry of War Transport, London (William Robertson, Glasgow, manager) as EMPIRE DORRIT.
12.1944: Completed.
15.12.1944: Maiden voyage.
27.9.1945: Sold to the French Government (Ministere de la Marine Marchande), Paris (Société Navale Caennais, Caen, France, managers) and renamed LIEUTENANT LANCELOT.
1946: Sold to Société Navale Caennais, Caen.
1954: Sold to the Holderness Steamship Co. Ltd., Hull and renamed HOLDERNITH.
17.1.1957: Abandoned and sank after grounding on Whitton Sand in the River Humber whilst on a voyage from Goole to London with a cargo of wool.
19.1.1957: Refloated and taken to Hull for dry docking and repairs.
3.1963: Sold to BISCO Ltd. and allocated to T. W. Ward Ltd. for breaking up at Grays, Essex.

7. EMPIRE FANAL 1944-1946
O.N. 180319 411g 190n 450d
142.2 x 27.0 x 8.5 feet
Oil engines 4SCSA 7-cyl. by Blackstone and Co. Ltd., Stamford; 324 BHP.
3.1954: 2SCSA 6-cyl. 'G' type Sirron oil engine by the Newbury Diesel Co. Ltd., Newbury.
10.1944: Launched by Henry Scarr Ltd., Hessle (Yard No. S455).
17.11.1944: Completed for the Ministry of War Transport, London (William Robertson, managers) as EMPIRE FANAL.

Seen with her final name *Holdernith*, *Empire Dorrit* was managed for a little over nine months during the Second World War, including a period from April to August on what is described as 'Government service', although she was of course owned by the government. Before and after this service she made 16 loaded voyages during Robertson's management. Half of these were with coal or coke from west coast ports, three with limestone from Llanddulas, two from the Thames with grain, and one each with rails, steel and empty boxes. She was handed over to the French Government on arrival at Rouen in September 1945 after a voyage from Swansea with coal. The Admiralty 'Service List' mistakenly spells her name '*Empire Dorritt*'. *[Roy Fenton collection]*

Two Empire F-type prefabricated coasters were managed during the Second World War, including E*mpire Fanal*, seen here as *Futurity. [Roy Fenton collection]*

Managed by Robertsons as *Empire Congham* from 1945, this steamer returned to her former German owners and resumed the name *Söderhamn* in 1946. *[J. and M. Clarkson]*

It was intended to name her CHANT 46, and later FABRIC 46.
1.4.1946: Owners became the Ministry of Transport, London.
23.9.1946: Sold to F.T. Everard and Sons Ltd., Greenhithe.
27.11.1946: Renamed FUTURITY.
3.1954: Fitted with new engine.
7.1960: After partial dismantling by her owners at Greenhithe, sold to BISCO Ltd., London, and allocated to T.W. Ward Ltd. for breaking up at Grays, Essex.
21.7.1960: Work began.

8. EMPIRE FANG 1945-1946
See MORION (3) in motor vessel list.

9. EMPIRE CONGHAM 1945-1946
O.N. 180762 1,499g 945n
240.8 x 34.1 x 15.1 feet
T. 3-cyl. by Helsingors Jernskibs-og Maskinbyggeri A/S, Elsinore, Denmark.
11.3.1899: Launched by Helsingors Jernskibs-og Maskinbyggeri A/S, Elsinore, Denmark (Yard No.76).
3.5.1899: Completed for H.M. Gehrckens, Hamburg, Germany as SÖDERHAMN.
5.1945: Captured by Allied Forces at Kiel.
22.7.1945: Arrived at Methil.
23.7.1945: Registered in the ownership of the Ministry of War Transport, London (William Robertson, Glasgow, manager) as EMPIRE CONGHAM.
4.1946: Owners became the Ministry of Transport, London.
21.8.1946: Transferred to the Allied Control Commission (H.M. Gehrckens, Hamburg, manager) and renamed SÖDERHAMN.
1947: Returned to H.M. Gehrckens, Hamburg.
17.8.1958: Arrived at Hamburg to be broken up by Eisen und Metall K.G. Lehr und Co.
It is doubtful if *Empire Congham* actually operated under Robertson's management as at the time of her return to the former German owner in 1947 she was laid up in the Gareloch.

10. EMPIRE SPINEL 1945-1946
See SPINEL (2) in the motor vessel list.

11. EMPIRE CONCLYDE 1945-1946
O.N. 180740 1,409g 649n
240.8 x 38.7 x 15.2 feet
T. 3-cyl. by A.G. 'Weser', Bremen, Germany.
1.1925: Completed by A.G. 'Weser', Bremen (Yard No. 394) for Dampfschiffahrts Gesellschaft 'Neptun', Bremen as KLIO.
8.1945: Taken over by Allied Forces.
19.11.1945: Transferred to the Ministry of War Transport, London (William Robertson, Glasgow, manager) and renamed EMPIRE CONCLYDE.
15.2.1946: Transferred to the U.S.S.R. and renamed SHOTA RUSTAVELI.
1960: Deleted from 'Lloyd's Register' as no movements reported since 1950.

In 1968 *Brilliant* (2) was transferred to the Scotspark Shipping Co.Ltd., but this made no difference to her livery, crewing or trading. *[Robertson archives]*

Managed for Scotspark Shipping Co. Ltd., Edinburgh
From 1968 to 1970 the *Brilliant* was transferred from the Robertson fleet to Scotspark Shipping Co. Ltd., a company associated with shipbuilder Charles Connell and with Denholms of Greenock.

1. BRILLIANT (2) 1968-1970
See motor vessel list.

Managed for Kyle Shipping Co. Ltd., Liverpool

1. KYLEBANK 1971-1975
See TURQUOISE (4) in the motor vessel list.

Working for Robertsons in the 1940s

In October 1983, 'Sea Breezes' published the reminiscences of Captain J.A. Simpson. Having been a deep-sea master, he wanted a job with a pilotage authority, and decided to work on the coast to be on hand if a position as a pilot came available. In 1945 he went round various shipping offices in Leith and Glasgow looking for a berth, and was employed by William Robertson. This is a lightly-edited account of his three years in Robertson's service as mate and master, reproduced with kind permission of the publisher.

The Superintendent of William Robertson, Captain Mitchell, offered me a mate's job and asked when I could join. I told him right away, whereupon he told me to join their *Jacinth* (3) in Ayr, the following morning.

On arrival in Ayr I found the *Jacinth* to be a smart little motor coaster built just before the war. The master was Captain McLeod who hailed from Tarbert, Loch Fyne. He was an elderly man, near retirement, a fine man who had been on the coast all his life and knew it like the palm of his hand.

The ship was still on charter to the Ministry of War Transport and was engaged in the transport of coal to Northern Ireland. I joined her on 4th April 1945. I found it a hard life and my hands soon had blisters on them with chucking hatches on and off. She did not carry a big crew and the mate could not stand around with his hands in his pockets.

It stood me in good stead, however, as I heard afterwards that the old captain was very taken with the young 'deep-sea' master who wasn't afraid to work and get his hands dirty. He told the owners so.

We mostly ran between Ayr and the power station at Ballylumford, near Larne. It was almost like being in a ferry boat. After a trip or two my wife and family came through to Ayr and stayed in lodgings there and I saw quite a lot of them. We were loading in Ayr on VE-Day; the captain hung on as long as possible waiting for the declaration as we knew there was to be two days' holiday declared. However, Ayr harbour is tidal and he couldn't wait any longer, so we had to sail for Belfast. We were not long on our way when the Prime Minister, Mr. Churchill, declared the war in Europe over. We got our two days' holiday in Belfast which was not much good to us. The captain flew home.

In July 1945 I was sent through to Grimsby to go mate in the *Cameo* (3). She was trading foreign and needed a mate with a foreign ticket. I joined her on 4th July. The master was William McLeod, from Skye, another elderly man nearing retirement. He was a big man, a real Highland gentleman, and a first-rate seaman too. The *Cameo* was a bigger ship than the *Jacinth* - she carried about 1,200 tons and was also a motor ship. We loaded case oil and aviation spirit for Copenhagen.

There was not much to do in Copenhagen. They still had German prisoners in cages on the quay. The shops were bare, and you could see the Danes had had a rough time during the occupation.

After discharge we came back to Glasgow and then went down to the Bristol Channel to load case oil for La Pallice in France. We returned to Liverpool and took another cargo to Rouen where we saw lots of damage. All the bridges across the Seine had been blown up. After that we loaded in Swansea for Antwerp and then back to Swansea.

Jacinth (3) of 1937, J.A. Simpson's first Robertson ship. *[J. and M. Clarkson]*

Robertsons had been given the management of a captured German ship called the *Klio*, built by A.G. Weser in 1925, and renamed *Empire Conclyde*. They gave me the master's job and I joined her in Grangemouth on 16th October 1945. I found her a smart little oil-burning steamer. She was allocated to the London and Edinburgh Shipping Company and put on the run between Leith and London.

This was one of the best times I had in my sea career. Five days in Leith, five days discharging and loading at Carron Wharf, London and 40 hours at sea on passage between Leith and London. I had my wife and family in lodgings in Edinburgh so saw them every time we came north.

Unfortunately, it only lasted until February 1946 when she was handed over to the Russians and we left her in Surrey Commercial Docks, London. Her Russian name was *Shota Rustaveli*.

When I took her over in Grangemouth the German crew were still on board. I had heard stories about the wonderful binoculars, sextants, and so on that were to be had on these captured German ships. I don't know whether someone had been there before us but we had no such luck. All I found were some Christmas tree decorations under the settee in the saloon. I have them still and they go on the tree at Christmas time.

After leaving the *Empire Conclyde* I was sent back as mate of the little *Cairngorm* (3), one of the smaller ships in Robertson's fleet. I think she carried about 800 tons. William Robertson owned quarries in North Wales at Llanddulas, and a lot of their trade was in limestone from these quarries to steel works. The Superintendent's idea was that I should get some experience at taking the jetties at these quarries before being made permanent master in the company. I was in the *Cairngorm* from March 1946 until May 1946 but during that time we mostly ran to Dublin with coal and never made a voyage to the quarries.

On 23rd May 1946 I was appointed master of the *Fluor* (2). She was coal-burning steamer built in 1925 - a fine steam coaster with good accommodation for the master. Our main runs were with limestone from North Wales to Ford's works at Dagenham and then cement back to Glasgow, Liverpool or Belfast. I had to learn the hard way to take the jetties at Llanddulas without any previous experience. However, I managed all right.

A master in Robertsons was expected to do his own pilotage in the London River. You got paid for that. I can't remember exactly how much but I think it was £1 in and out and 10s for each shift of berth. It was also a condition in the company that, before becoming master, you had to take a Clyde pilot's licence. I got a fortnight's paid leave to do this after leaving the *Cairngorm*.

There were some unwritten rules attached, apart from learning all the courses, buoyage and depths. You had to enrol at Glasgow Technical College and it did not matter whether you attended or not as long as you paid your fee. In return they gave you some typewritten sheets with the type of question you were likely to be asked. I was also told that I must go to the Pilot Office and buy a Clyde Pilot's Handbook as, no matter how well you knew your stuff, you would not get the licence without doing so.

After complying with these rules I went home and, with the help of my father firing questions at me, soon had it all off pat. Captain Chalmers was the pilot master and examined me. I was successful and was granted a licence.

I was master in *Fluor* from 23rd May 1946 until October 1946. Besides the stone and cement cargoes, we carried coal and steel rails. During the summer of 1946 I had my wife and son with me, but unfortunately we had the most appalling weather. They joined me in Ayr and we made two voyages to Barrow-in-Furness. One of the pilots there was very kind and took us for a car run to the Lake District.

From Barrow-in-Furness we went to Penmaenmawr in North Wales to load stone for Ipswich. The weather was so bad we had to lie in the Menai Straits for shelter for a while. From Ipswich we went up to Blyth and loaded coal for Dublin, then sailed north about and had the only good weather of the whole trip, coming down through the Sounds of Islay and Mull. From Dublin we came across to Manchester and my wife went home from there.

On one voyage we loaded steel rails at Workington for Southampton consigned to the Southern Railway. On completing loading a chap handed me a parcel containing magnets for adjusting the compass. How we got to Southampton I'll never know for the compass went completely haywire. The *Fluor* had her bridge amidships and, of course, these long rails ran right underneath. I was so glad to see the Needles Lighthouse I took a pilot up to Southampton. I loaded these rails several times later in a motor ship with the bridge aft and never had the same problem with the compass.

I was discharging stone at Ipswich when VJ-Day was declared. This time we did not complete discharge and got the two days' holiday. I went home to Scotland.

The company gave me command of *Jade* (1) in October 1946. She was a fine motor ship built in Holland in 1939. She was fast too and could pass most of the other coasters around at that time. She was considered to be Robertson's 'crack' ship at that time and I was very proud to get her.

Shortly after I left the *Fluor* in Southampton to join the *Jade*, the *Fluor* was run into by a P&O liner and sank at her berth. All hands scrambled ashore, however, but they lost all their gear. She was later salvaged, converted to oil burning and sailed on for a while.

I was in the *Jade* from October 1946 until December 1948 and during that time was all around the UK coast but again mainly carrying stone from North Wales to London and cement back again to west coast ports.

During the summer of 1947 my wife and son were with me again. This time we had glorious weather all the time they were on board. They joined the ship in London on August Bank Holiday. We were lying at buoys at Erith waiting to go up to Ford's jetty at Dagenham to discharge stone. The ship was dressed overall as it was a big regatta day. They were racing for Dogget's Coat and Badge.

After discharge we loaded cement for Liverpool. We had a slow discharge and had several trips to Chester where we hired a boat on the River Dee. After that we went up to Silloth and loaded coal for Cork. Again we were a long time discharging and were able to enjoy our spell in Cork.

I remember the agent was a very fine elderly gentleman. His daughter took us for a run in her car to the Blarney Stone and various other beauty spots. The agent's office was like something out of Charles Dickens, with cobwebs everywhere and the dust of ages over all. After Cork we went over to Llanddulas and loaded stone for London. The family went home from there.

The steamer *Fluor* (2), built for Robertsons in 1925. *[Ships in Focus]*

On one voyage we went to Workington and loaded steel rails, 60 feet long, for Southampton. Previously most of these rail cargoes had been discharged at Angerstein Wharf on the Thames. It was decided that the foreman from Workington would go down to Southampton and show the dockers there how to handle these long rails. Like dockers everywhere, the Southampton men took umbrage and sent him packing. Nobody could show them how to handle rails!

For some reason the ship was berthed at the Ocean Terminal where the liners berthed. Within a couple of days there was hardly a window left in the terminal building as slings of rails crashed into them. The harbour master got us shifted to another berth and eventually we got discharged. Instead of being discharged in a couple of days we took about 10 days, which was all right for the ship's people.

One November afternoon when sailing from Rothesay Dock, Glasgow I was unfortunate in getting a rope around the propeller. We re-moored the ship and I decided to dive down to see if I could clear it. We passed a heaving line underneath the ship with a heavy shackle to weight it down, lowered the jolly boat and I dived in and pulled myself down on the heaving line. It was a crazy thing to do in the month of November. The water was desperately cold and the visibility underwater was nil. I managed to stay under long enough, after a second attempt, to feel that the wire was only looped over the boss of the propeller and there was an end dangling down. I came on board, had a good rub down and got dressed; then from the jolly boat we were able to fish up the dangling end of wire. We took it to the capstan aft and hove away and out it came. I was lucky as it might have meant a dry docking.

While in London on one voyage I was interviewed by the London Pilotage Authority for a job as a sea pilot. I was placed fifth on turn. However, as soon as I became 35 years old my name was taken off the list, the age limit for becoming a pilot there being 35.

In December 1948 I was asked to appear before the Forth Pilot Authority for an interview, there being vacancies for two pilots at Grangemouth and one at Bo'ness. The *Jade* was going to be in Belfast at the time so I 'phoned the Superintendent and told him I would fly from Belfast to Renfrew, attend the interview and, if I was not appointed, I could fly back and no one would be any the wiser. This I did and was successful in being appointed as a Grangemouth pilot. I informed the Superintendent and he asked me to call at the Head Office in Glasgow on my way to the airport. On arriving at the office the super asked me if I would take the *Cairngorm* from Ayr to Douglas, Isle of Man, as the captain had fallen and hurt his leg. Naturally, I wasn't all that keen as all my gear was on the *Jade* and I was dressed in my best 'go ashore' clothes. However, Robertsons had treated me very well so I agreed to go on condition that I would be relieved at the first port after Douglas. In Douglas we were berthed at an outside berth where the ship took the ground at low water. There was a very heavy swell running in the harbour and when she took the ground she bumped very heavily before finally grounding. When she floated on the next tide I informed the harbour master that it was not a safe berth and we were shifted into the inner harbour. After Douglas we were ordered to Llanddulas to load stone for London. No relief appeared and I was still in my one and only suit of clothes. Luckily for me the *Jade* arrived from Belfast to load with the mate as master and I had time to go on board and collect a few things. We left Llanddulas on 23rd December for London. A few hours out the chief engineer informed me there was a leak in the engine room. I asked him to keep the pumps going and pump it out. Some time later he came back to the bridge and said the pumps could not hold the water. I went with him to the engine room and saw that there was a lot of water and the flywheel on the engine was throwing it up in the air like a fountain.

The nearest port was Milford Haven and I decided to make for it. I informed Land's End Radio and told them the position and that we were in no immediate danger. I had scarcely made the call when the salvage tug *Bustler* came on the air and informed me he was coming to my assistance. I told him I did not require assistance and would make Milford Haven on my own. When we arrived at Milford Haven the pilot came on board and said we were to moor to a buoy. The harbour master said we could sink at the buoy but not in his harbour! I went ashore with the pilot and he ran me in his car to the agent's house. It was Christmas night and he had a party going. I managed to get through on the 'phone to the owners in Glasgow and told them the position and that, as far as I knew, the ship was in no danger.

Afterwards the agent suggested I had some Christmas cheer and offered me a large drink of whisky. The pilot had stayed to run me back to the boat and on the way we called at his house and had some more Christmas cheer. On the way back to the ship, the mood I was in, I didn't care much whether she sank or not! On arriving back on board the chief engineer informed me that the engine room was dry. Lying in the quiet water in the harbour the pumps were able to cope. The next day, Boxing Day, the super arrived from Glasgow. It was decided to take her round to the Bristol Channel and put her in dry dock. We dry docked at Cardiff and found she had two rivets knocked out below the engine. This must have happened when she was bumping the bottom at Douglas. She had no double bottom in the engine room. I told the super I was going no further and wanted to be relieved. He agreed and I took the train to London and went down to Ford's Jetty at Dagenham where the *Jade* was discharging. I collected my gear, made for King's Cross Station and took the night train home on 30th December 1948. I was home for New Year and started my piloting career on 10th January 1949. I was a pilot on the Forth, first at Grangemouth and then at Methil, for 30 years and retired in February 1979. Before concluding these reminiscences, a few lines about William Robertson, the Gem Line as it became known later. I was happy during my time with them. They were a fine coasting company, founded by William Robertson. During my time the company was run by two grandsons of William Robertson, Mr. James and Mr. Frank Robertson. They were good people to work for and took a personal interest in their men. Captain Mitchell was Marine Superintendent. I think his father had been in the company before him; he and I got on very well. Mr. Yates was Engineer Superintendent. He joined the company while I was with them and I believe he became a director later.

I enjoyed most of my time at sea, but was happy to become a pilot and have one foot on shore. I was able to see my family growing up, which I would not if I had continued going to sea.

Appendix 1: Robertson ships by builder

Includes only powered ships delivered directly to the fleet. *Denotes ships not ordered by Robertson, but taken over at the builder's.

J. and R. Swan, Maryhill
- *Jasper* (1) 1865
- *Diamond* (1) 1867
- *Amethyst* (1) 1870

T.B. Seath, Rutherglen
- *Agate* (1) 1878
- *Jasper* (2) 1880
- *Topaz* (2) 1883

John Fullerton and Co., Paisley
- *Sapphire* (2) 1881
- *Amethyst* (2) 1883
- *Pearl* (3) 1885
- *Gem* (3) 1887
- *Jacinth* (2) 1888
- *Emerald* (1) 1889
- *Peridot* 1890

Scott and Co./Scott and Sons, Bowling
- *Diamond* (2) 1886
- *Ruby* (2) 1888
- *Nugget* (2) 1889
- *Garnet* (2) 1889
- *Sard* (1) 1890
- *Cornelian* (1) 1890
- *Olivine* (1) 1890
- *Pebble* (1) 1890
- *Pyrope* (1) 1890
- *Asteria* (1) 1891
- *Topaz* (3) 1891
- *Onyx* (2) 1891
- *Topaz* (4) 1892
- *Amber* (1) 1892
- *Iolite* 1893
- *Spinel* (1) 1893
- *Beryl* (1) 1893
- *Jargoon* (1) 1893
- *Opal* (1) 1894
- *Citrine* (1) 1894
- *Malachite* (1) 1894
- *Zircon* 1895
- *Girasol* (1) 1895
- *Sphene* (1) 1895
- *Nephrite* (1) 1896
- *Topaz* (5) 1896
- *Kyanite* (1) 1897
- *Fluor* (1) 1898
- *Corundum* (1) 1899
- *Brilliant* (1) 1901
- *Hematite* 1903
- *Onyx* (3) 1903
- *Ruby* (3) 1904
- *Essonite* (1) 1904
- *Amethyst* (3) 1910
- *Onyx* (4) 1910
- *Agate* (2) 1917
- *Gem* (4) 1924
- *Pyrope* (2) 1936

John Shearer and Son, Kelvinhaugh
- *Coral* (1) 1892
- *Turquoise* (1) 1893
- *Morion* (1) 1894
- *Pearl* (4) 1896
- *Tourmaline* (1) 1898
- *Achroite 1898*
- *Olivine* (2) 1902
- *Malachite* (2) 1902
- *Cairngorm* (2) 1904
- *Kyanite* (2) 1904
- *Sagenite* 1904

A. Rodger and Co., Port Glasgow
- *Obsidian* (1) 1898
- *Axinite* (1) 1899
- *Citrine* (2) 1899
- *Obsidian* (2) 1902
- *Sphene* (2) 1902
- *Emerald* (2) 1904
- *Felspar* (7) 1908

Carmichael, McLean and Co., Greenock
- *Prase* (1) 1899
- *Plasma* 1899

Ailsa Shipbuilding Co. Ltd., Ayr and Troon
- *Sard* (2) 1909
- *Beryl* (2) 1924
- *Turquoise* (2) 1924
- *Fluor* (2) 1925
- *Sapphire* (3) mv 1935
- *Olivine* (5) mv 1952
- *Gem* (5) mv 1952
- *Pearl* (5) mv 1953
- *Amber* (2) mv 1956
- *Amethyst* (4) mv 1958
- *Topaz* (7) mv 1962
- *Tourmaline* (3) mv 1962
- *Sapphire* (5) mv 1966

Scheepsbouwwerft v/h T. Nederlof, Sliedrecht
- *Malachite* (3)* 1920

Yarrow and Co. Ltd., Scotstoun
- *Essonite* (2)* 1921
- *Kyanite* (3)* 1923

Burntisland Shipbuilding Co. Ltd., Burntisland
- *Diamond* (3) 1927

A. and J. Inglis Ltd., Glasgow
- *Cameo* (3) mv 1937

Henry Robb Ltd., Leith
- *Spinel* (2) mv 1937
- *Jacinth* (3) mv 1937

A. Vuijk en Zonen, Capelle
- *Prase* (2) mv 1938
- *Jade* (2) mv 1938
- *Cairngorm* (3) mv 1938

N.V. Scheepswerf 'De Merwede' v/h Van Vliet and Co., Hardinxveld
- *Citrine* (4) mv 1939

Grangemouth Dockyard Co. Ltd., Grangemouth
- *Sapphire* (4) mv 1949
- *Emerald* (3) mv 1952

Scheepswerf 'Gideon' v/h J. Koster Hzn., Groningen
- *Brilliant* (2) 1958

Nieuwe Noord Nederlandsche Scheepswerven N.V., Groningen
- *Gem* (6) mv 1969

Martin Jansen, Leer
- *Cairngorm* (4) mv 1973

The most prolific builder for Robertson was Scott and Sons, Bowling. Their *Spinel* (1) of 1893 sails smokily from Preston (above). Broken up after 40 years of service, her successor was built by Henry Robb Ltd., Leith, and was almost as long lived (right). *[Harry Stewart/J. and M. Clarkson; Robertson archives]*

Appendix 2: losses of Robertson ships

Major casualties from all causes of owned and managed ships are listed in chronological order. Further details will be found in the fleet lists. Details of insurance payments are from company records.

Date	Name	Cause
28.5.1868	*Garnet (1)*	Stranded at Langness Point, Isle of Man.
8.11.1879	*Chrysolite*	Wrecked on Tory Island, off County Donegal.
19.8.1880	*Jasper* (2)	Wrecked on the Island of Whithorn.
23.1.1889	*Pennon*	Stranded on Ailsa Craig
21.11.1889	*Strathesk*	Wrecked off Haulbowline Light near Carlingford.
2.4.1890	*Garnet* (2)	Wrecked off Mull of Galloway Light Vessel.
22.8.1890	*Latharna*	Stranded near Yarmouth, Nova Scotia.
5.1.1895	*Pearl* (3)	Sank off Dungeness in collision with *Primera.*
23.5.1895	*Zircon*	Sank off the Goodwins in collision with *Ahdeek.*
5.12.1895	*Topaz* (4)	Foundered off Start Point.
5.1.1897	*Larry Bane*	Stranded at Selkar Rock, St. Bee's Head.
22.12.1897	*Ensign*	Stranded at Cleats, Arran. Repaired and sold.
3.11.1898	*Onyx* (3)	Foundered off the South Arklow Light Vessel.
1.1.1903	*Cairngorm* (1)	Wrecked at the entrance to Harrington harbour.
4.8.1903	*Emerald* (1)	Sank off The Smalls in collision with *Kilmore.*
17.10.1903	*Kyanite* (1)	Sank off Dover collision with *Buccleugh.*
26.11.1905	*Peridot*	Wrecked at Skernaghan Point, Islandmagee.
22.3.1906	*Sard* (1)	Wrecked two miles west of Portrush.
4.10.1908	*Amethyst* (2)	Sank off Wicklow Head in collision with *Daisy.*
4.12.1908	*Iolite*	Stranded on Grand Lejon Rocks near St. Brieuc.
26.4.1910	*Dalriada*	Wrecked on Russell Rocks, north of The Maidens.
18.2.1911	*Agate* (1)	Wrecked on Rowancarry Rock, Kenmare River.
17.10.1914	*Corundum* (1)	Collision with *Kyleness* in the English Channel.
23.11.1914	*Malachite* (2)	Gunfire from *U 21* in the English Channel. Reputedly uninsured.
25.12.1914	*Gem* (3)	Mined off Scarborough. War insurance payment £4,400.
4.4.1915	*Olivine* (2)	Torpedoed by *U 31* in the English Channel. War insurance payment £11,000.
31.7.1915	*Turquoise* (1) *Nugget* (2)	Gunfire from *U 28* south west of the Scilly Isles on passage to the Dardanelles as fleet messengers. War insurance payments £7,500 and £8,800 respectively.
3.8.1916	*Sphene* (1)	Blown up by *UB 18* in the English Channel. War insurance payment £22,200.
18.12.1916	*Opal* (1)	Mined off the Chicken Rock, Isle of Man. War insurance payment £16,000.
1.2.1917	*Essonite* (1)	Torpedoed by *U 55* off Trevose Head. War insurance payment £17,000.
15.2.1917	*Kyanite* (2)	Blown up by *UC 65* in the Irish Sea. War insurance payment £17,000.
12.3.1917	*Topaz* (5)	Torpedoed by *UB 18* in the English Channel. War insurance payment £23,000.
2.5.1917	*Morion* (1)	Blown up by *UC 65* in Ballyhalbert Bay, County Down. War insurance payment £8,000.
20.11.1917	*Jargoon* (1)	Sank off Belfast Lough in collision with *Tunisian.* Insurance payment £29,000.
12.3.1918	*Fluor* (1)	Taken in prize at Riga or scuttled at Leningrad. Raised and broken up. War insurance payment £31,000.
10.4.1918	*Obsidian* (2)	Scuttled off Helsinki. War insurance payment £33,000.
13.4.1918	*Diamond* (2)	Collision with *Lily* off Rathlin Island. Insurance payment £10,350.
6.6.1918	*Huntsland*	Torpedoed by *UC 77* in the English Channel.
8.6.1918	*Hunsgrove*	Torpedoed by *U 82* off Trevose Head.
2.7.1927	*Nephrite* (1)	Wrecked on Umfin Island, County Donegal.
23.12.1927	*Pyrope* (1)	Stranded north of Kettleness Point.
7.12.1928	*Jacinth* (2)	Stranded near Londonderry. Refloated and broken up.
24.3.1929	*Olivine* (3)	Stranded at Woodcombe Point, near Prawle Point. Refloated, repaired and sold.
17.3.1931	*Citrine* (3)	Wrecked near Port Erin, Isle of Man.
4.9.1931	*Opal* (2)	Foundered south west of the Longships.
30.12.1936	*Diamond* (3)	Sank off Greenhithe in the River Thames in collision with *Heranger.*
13.2.1937	*Hematite* (2)	Foundered between the North and South Bishop, Pembrokeshire.
12.4.1939	*Sapphire* (4)	Sank off the South Bishop Lighthouse in collision with *Clan Cameron.*

24.4.1940	*Girasol* (2)	Sank off the North Foreland in collision with *Contractor*.
25.5.1940	*Spinel* (2)	Bombed and abandoned at Dunkirk. Repaired by Germans. Recovered in 1945.
30.12.1940	*Agate* (2)	Wrecked north of Oversay Lighthouse, Islay.
c27.3.1941	*Olivine* (4)	Disappeared in the Irish Sea.
9.6.1941	*Dagmar*	Bombed and sunk near Anvil Point Lighthouse off Bournemouth.
31.1.1944	*Emerald* (2)	Torpedoed by an E-boat south east of Beachy Head.
20.8.1944	*Coral* (2)	Torpedoed by *U 764* in the English Channel.
6.2.1946	*Sphene* (3)	Wrecked between Tintagel and Boscastle.
10.10.1946	*Fluor* (2)	Sank at Southampton in collision with *Strathnaver*. Refloated and repaired.
5.1.1950	*Turquoise* (2)	Stranded near Maryport. Refloated, repaired and sold. Insurance payment £16,500.
26.5.1950	*Felspar*	Beached near Deal following collision with *Cabo Espartel*. Refloated, repaired and sold. Insurance payment £7,000.
10.9.1950	*Cameo* (3)	Wrecked on Arklow Bank. Insurance payment £79,200.
6.5.1951	*Pyrope* (2)	Stranded off Rhum. Refloated and repaired.
7.7.1951	*Jargoon* (2)	Sank in the English Channel in collision with *Tormes*. Insurance payment £25,300.
4.3.1954	*Asteria* (2)	Stranded on Drogheda Bar. Refloated but constructive total loss. Insurance payment £22,650. Sold to breakers for £4,165.
2.1.1956	*Citrine* (4)	Foundered off the Lizard.

On 20th January 1969, whilst outward bound from Gothenburg, her 14-man crew abandoned *Amethyst* (4) about six miles west of Vinga Lighthouse when her cargo of paper pulp began to shift. The accommodation and engine room were flooded, but she remained afloat, albeit with a severe list (above). Swedish tugs and salvage vessels were soon on the scene, and towed *Amethyst* into the shelter of the island of Hono. The crew (who had been picked up from a lifeboat and a life raft) helped to jettison at least 250 tons of deck cargo, dramatically reducing the list (left and below). *Amethyst* was towed into Gothenburg on 22nd January, and resumed her voyage to St Louis Rhone on 2nd February. It was considered that her cargo of pulp had not been stowed sufficiently tightly, and that it shifted when the vessel listed on encountering heavy seas. See also page 109. *[Robertson archives (4)]*

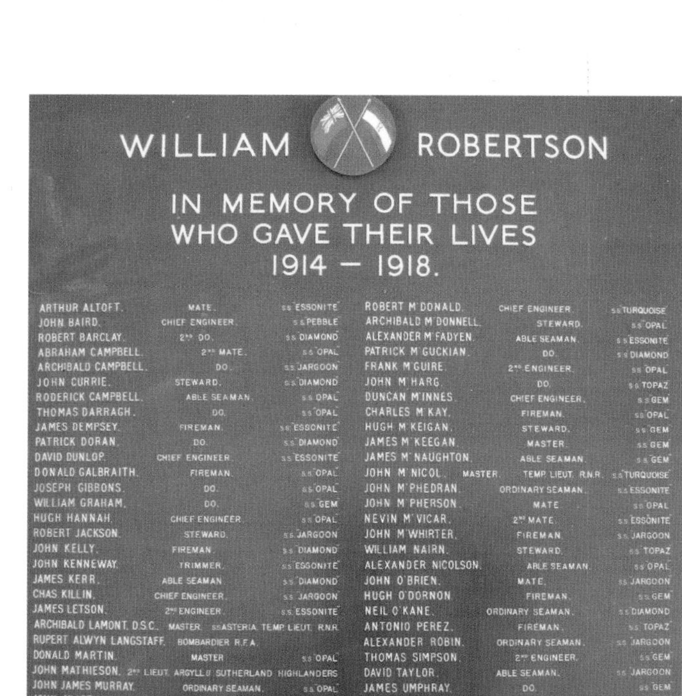

WILLIAM ROBERTSON

IN MEMORY OF THOSE
WHO GAVE THEIR LIVES
1939 - 1945

ROSS BARBOUR	BOSUN	S.S. OLIVINE	JAMES Mc GUIRE	CHIEF ENGINEER	S.S. EMERALD
J. BRYSON	A.B.	S.S. EMERALD	DONALD Mc LOUGHLIN	A.B.	S.S. OLIVINE
ROBERT CAHOON	FIREMAN	S.S. CORAL	JOHN Mc NEILLAGE	FIREMAN	S.S. OLIVINE
PATRICK CAMPBELL	O.S.	M.V. CAIRNGORM	CHARLES Mc SHANE	SECOND ENGINEER	S.S. EMERALD
LEONARD CORNISH	A.B.	S.S. OLIVINE	THOMAS MILLIGAN	BOSUN	S.S. CORAL
ALEX. DALZIEL	FIREMAN	S.S. OLIVINE	WILLIAM MOORE	COOK	S.S. OLIVINE
T. E. DAWSON	FIREMAN	S.S. EMERALD	NORMAN NICHOLSON	A.B.	S.S. CORAL
JAMES HOLDEN	MATE	S.S. EMERALD	WILLIAM PEARSON	COOK	S.S. EMERALD
JOHN KENNEDY	MASTER	S.S. EMERALD	JOHN ROOKE	FIREMAN	S.S. EMERALD
JOHN R. KENNEDY	FIREMAN	S.S. CORAL	THOMAS ROSS	MASTER	S.S. OLIVINE
DONALD Mc AULEY	O.S.	S.S. OLIVINE	FRANK THOMAS	BOSUN	S.S. EMERALD
JOHN Mc AULEY	CHIEF ENGINEER	S.S. OLIVINE	MATTHEW WHELAN	O.S.	S.S. EMERALD
JOHN J. Mc AULEY	FIREMAN	S.S. OLIVINE	GEORGE A. WILLOCK M.C.	CAPTAIN	SEAFORTH HIGHLANDERS
DONALD Mc COLL	SERGEANT	R.A.F.	FRANK WOOD	FIREMAN	S.S. EMERALD
NEIL Mc GUGAN	MATE	S.S. OLIVINE	VICTOR WOODHEAD	A.B.	S.S. EMERALD

GEORGE YENDALL SECOND ENGINEER S.S. OLIVINE

VESSELS LOST BY ENEMY ACTION AND WAR RISK

S.S. OLIVINE	ON PASSAGE FROM GLASGOW TO SHARPNESS	29TH MARCH 1941
S.S. EMERALD	E-BOAT TORPEDO OFF BEACHY HEAD	31ST JANUARY 1944
S.S. CORAL	UNDER WATER EXPLOSION OFF ISLE OF WIGHT	20TH AUGUST 1944

These two plaques (left and above) record the names of Robertson employees who lost their lives in the two world wars and a list of ships lost. *Olivine* (4) is treated as a war loss. The plaque below at Carnlough records one of Robertson's worst peacetime disasters, the loss of *Peridot*. *[Robertson archives; Tom Wilson]*

S.S. PERIDOT MEMORIAL PLAQUE

ON THE NIGHT OF NOVEMBER 26TH 1905
A COASTAL STEAMER THE PERIDOT
HAVING BEEN ANCHORED OFF CARNLOUGH AWAITING THE TIDE
SOUGHT SHELTER IN LARNE LOUGH FROM A STORM
BUT NEVER REACHED SAFETY
STRANDING IN A HEAVY SEA AND BREAKING UP
AT SKERNACHAN POINT ISLANDMAGEE.
THIS PLAQUE IS ERECTED BY
LARNE & DISTRICT HISTORICAL CENTRE COMMITTEE
TO COMMEMORATE THE SEAFARING MEN WHO LOST THEIR LIVES
IN THE PERIDOT DISASTER
MOST OF WHOM WERE FROM THE VILLAGE OF CARNLOUGH
HUGH O'KANE CAPTAIN, PATRICK BLACK MATE,
JOHN McMAHON CHIEF ENGINEER, JOHN DARRAGH SEAMAN,
JAMES McKINTY FIREMAN, JAMES STEWART FIREMAN,
ALEXANDER McNEILL COOK,
AND ALEXANDER FERGUSON SECOND ENGINEER,
ROBERT McKELLER SEAMAN, OF SCOTLAND.

Watch ye therefore for in such an hour as ye think not your Lord cometh
MCMXCVIII

Other minor incidents are recalled in these photographs. The gash in the bows of *Citrine* (4) resulted from a close encounter with the *Hendonhall* (5,244/1944) owned by the West Hatlepool Steam Navigation Co. Ltd. in the Manchester Ship Canal on 16th May 1950 (above).

The *Prase* (2) stranded in the entrance to Campbeltown Loch when she dragged her anchors whilst sheltering from a gale on 20th January 1957 whilst on a voyage from Glasgow to Northern Ireland. The Campbeltown Llifeboat, seen standing by (right), helped to pull her off later that day. *[Robertson archives (2)]*

Appendix 3: profitability 1891-1949

Caution needs to be exercised when reviewing Robertson's surviving accounts. Until 1949 operations were conducted either in William Robertson's name or as a partnership involving his family. With these arrangements there was no requirement to present accounts in a formal manner to the Registrar of Companies, as would be required with a limited company, and the surviving accounts appear to have been drawn up largely to give those involved an indication of how the business was doing. No explanation has survived as to how the accounts were drawn up, but it is clear that accounting methods were not consistent over time. In some cases two sets of figures are recorded, sometimes on the same document.

Year	Value of fleet[1]	Profit/loss[2]	Profit %[3]	Dividend[4]
1891	-	-	-	16%
1892	-	-	-	13¾%
1893	-	-	-	14½%
1894	-	-	-	11½%
1895	-	-	-	7¾%
1896	-	-	-	10½%
1897	-	-	-	16½%
1898	-	-	-	17%
1899	-	-	-	16%
1900	-	-	-	21%
1901	£237,167	+£40,213	17%	16¼%
1902	£270,948	+£22,738	8½%	8¾%
1903	£265,440	+£23,254	8¾%	8¼%
1904	£302,029	+£27,305	9%	9¾%
1905	£296,576	+£22,063	7.5%	6¾%
1906	£322,172	+£35,593	11%	9¾%
1907	£305,035	+£48,626	16%	13¼%
1908	£300,902	+£32,613	10¾%	8¾%
1909	£351,220	+£52,217	15%	9%
1910	£356,720	+£52,102	14½%	9%
1911	£356,720	+£31,031	8¾%	7½%
	£242,060[5]	+£31,031	12¾%	
1912	£328,000	+£49,220	15%	13%
	£212,314[5]	+£49,220	23%	
1913	£242,060	+£58,219	24%	-
	£199,850[5]	+£58,219	29%	-
1914	£198,850	+£30,716	15½%	-
	£175,882[5]	+£30,716	17½%	-
1915	£141,314	+£69,361	49%	-
1916	£110,353	-	-	-
	£126,998[5]	-	-	-
1917	£114,941	+£176,244	153%	-

Year	Value of fleet[1]	Profit/loss[2]	Profit %[3]	Dividend[4]
1918	£104,860	+£186,354	178%	-
1919	£118,397	+£154,752	131%	-
1920	£145,752	+£43,201	30%	-
1921	£204,376	-£5,741	-3%	-
1922	£229,362	+£6,623	3%	-
1923	£230,184	-£12,094	-5¼%	-
1924	£263,974	-£16,689	-6¼%	-
1925	£317,555	-£33,381	-10½%	-
1926	£295,503	-£21,433	-7¼%	-
1927	£299,479	-£21,845	-7¼%	-
1928	£299,479	-£20,125	-6¾%	-
1929	£305,328	-£21,396	-7%	-
1930	£331,032	-£4,890	-1½%	-
1931	£291,157	-£4,253	-1½%	-
1932	£276,154	-£27,054	-6¾%	-
1933	£257,867	-£13,594	-5¼%	-
1934	£242,497	-£5,801	-2½%	-
1935	-	+£30,694	-	-
1936	-	+£18,607	-	-
1937	£240,918	+£27,948	11½%	-
1938	-	+£5,191	-	-
1939	£331,400	+£137,753[6]	-	-
1940	£397,986	+£128,830	32%	-
1941	£258,099	+£140,229	54%	-
1942	£210,260	+£88,670	42%	-
1943	£186,710	+£83,119	44½%	-
1944	£166,326	+£62,627	37½%	-
1945	£144,925	+£78,842	54%	-
1946	£133,038	+£90,933	68%	-
1947	£141,121	-		-
1948	£133,096	-		-
1949	£251,229	-		-

Notes on the table

1. This is the insured value, from 1901 until at least to 1911. It has some merit in indicating the likely replacement cost of the ships, and their approximate market value, but is unlikely to have been revised frequently, especially during wartime.
2. Given in the accounts as 'steamer dividend' until 1918 and thereafter simply as 'profit'. It takes no account of the need to put money in reserves for replacement vessels, and there are indications that it may include receipts from sales of ships and even war loss insurance payments.
3. The crude percentage profit figure has been calculated simply by dividing the value of the fleet by the figure referred to in the accounts as 'steamer dividend' or 'profit'.
4. The dividend figure is taken from the accounts, and reflects earnings beyond those from the Robertson fleet, largely investment income. In 1900, for instance, William Robertson held shares in several Scottish-based shipping companies, including Clan, City, and Craig Lines, the Scottish-Australian McIlwraith McEacharn; in the North British and Great Central Railways; and a small number of shares in three sail and two steam ships. Investment income increased in the prosperous years leading up to the First World War, and by 1918 the massive sum of £335,000 was invested in War Loans, although a substantial part of this would result from war loss insurance payments, as lost ships were not generally replaced during wartime.
5. Two partial sets of figures for the years from 1911 to 1916 survive. The first figures for the value of the fleet quoted for each year appear to have been calculated on the same basis as the pre-war figures. A different basis was then used to calculate the figures, with the insured value of the fleet revised downwards, increasing the percentage profit. The 'revised' figures are given in the second line (indicated by the superscript 5), with percentage profits recalculated alongside.
6. The apparently high profits for 1939 reflect a change in the accounting period.

Given the caveats and reservations expressed above, are the figures useful? The way that the figures for percentage profits closely follow the declared dividends for the years before the First World War suggest they are indeed meaningful, as the dividend would indicate how well those involved in the business felt they were doing. The profits also follow the expected trends. They rise to enormous heights during the great shortages of tonnage, and hence high freight rates, during and just after the First World War, then quickly fall so that for the first time ever the company is trading at a loss in 1921. From 1923 losses continue for 11 successive years, being most severe in 1928 and 1932, but quickly recover after 1935. Profits during the Second World War and afterwards are surprisingly high, given the extent of government regulation of shipping.

Particularly impressive are the remarkably good figures for dividends and/or profits for the period from the first surviving accounts in 1891 until the First World War: 16% or just over in four years. Dividends are consistently high in the 1890s, except for 1895, and in the 1900s remain mostly at 8% or above despite this being a notoriously difficult decade for shipping. The figures help confirm that William Robertson's company was well run, both during the founder's time and when managed by his sons and grandsons.

1969-1973

Figures for turnover and profit before tax (below) have survived for the four years from 1969 to 1973 (the Powell Duffryn take over came in 1970). Comparison of the fluctuation of the profits from operating ships compared with the much steadier returns from quarrying (at least for 1971 to 1973) says much about the shipping business, and why Robertsons no longer wished to remain independent. The figures to 31st March 1971 refer to 15 months.

	William Robertson Shipowners Ltd./Gem Line Ltd.			**Kneeshaw, Lupton and Co. Ltd.**	
Year	Turnover	Profit	Dividend	Turnover	Profit
1969	£1,970,265	£111,985	-	£566,648	£33,425
to 31.3.71	£2,585,900	£268,905	£180,840	£698,864	£93,991
to 31.3.72	£2,167,160	£138,190	£80,000	£622,404	£94,606
to 31.3.73	£2,341,190	£257,223	£150,000	£683,883	£98,549

The ships in 1974-75

A league table of the profitability of each ship in the fleet for the year to 31st March 1975 shows a fairly close correlation between the newness of the ship and her profitability (below). Notable exceptions are *Amber*, 19-years-old but third in the league table, and *Jade*, the third newest ship, but ninth out of 12 in the league table. Not unexpectedly, the number of days lost also relates approximately to the age of the ship. The older the ship, the more time it would spend under repair, and the older, less profitable ships would tend to be the first to be laid up. There is no explanation as to how profitability was calculated; presumably it was a simple calculation of earnings minus crewing, running and repair costs and probably did not take into account depreciation, which would have been heaviest for the most recently built vessels. The way '49 + 28' is quoted for *Emerald's* days lost suggest one figure is for repairs, the other for lay up.

Name	**Profit**	**Years old**	**Dwt**	**Days lost**
Cairngorm (4)	£159,094	2	3,440	-
Gem (6)	£135,159	6	2,921	14
Amber (2)	£127,151	19	2,410	34
Sapphire (5)	£106,094	9	1,660	23
Topaz (7)	£101,196	15	2,430	1
Olivine (5)	£77,174	23	1,828	36
Tourmaline (3)	£89,758	13	2,430	22
Amethyst (4)	£60,423	17	2,319	25
Jade (2)	£51,580	8	2,780	36
Brilliant (2)	£50,737	17	1,442	21
Cameo (4)	£47,153	23	2,132	34
Emerald (3)	£19,683	23	1,830	49 + 28

Not surprisingly, Robertson's newest ship *Cairngorm* (4) was its most profitable in 1974-75 (top left). Less predictably, the 19-year-old *Amber* (2) came third in the league table despite losing 34 days through repairs and surveys (top right, at Preston 26th March 1963). Because of her lengthy time out of service, *Emerald* (3) was the least profitable (bottom). *[World Ship Society Ltd.; Harry Stewart/J. and M. Clarkson; Robertson archives]*

Appendix 4: naming scheme

The title 'Gem Line' was derived from William Robertson's practice of naming his ships. However, by no means all names are of precious stones, and 'gems or minerals' would be more appropriate, but even then the names of *Pebble* and *Cameo* barely fit this definition. In fact, a purist might also baulk at the word 'Line' in the title of what was basically a tramping operation and which, apart from the short-lived service between Preston and the Baltic, could hardly qualify as a 'line of steamers'.

The use of gem names was by no means confined to William Robertson, although the company's use of mineral names was more unusual. Amongst contemporaries also using this nomenclature and sometimes duplicating names adopted by Robertson were James MacArthur of Glasgow, the Dundee Gem Line and - most confusingly - A. and C. Robertson and John C. Robertson of Grangemouth (there is no evidence of any close relationship with these Robertsons). However, Robertsons' persistence in using these names and the size and longevity of their fleet ensured that the names became a trade mark, certainly in northern European shipping.

It is interesting to note that, despite the fleet's heavy involvement with the carriage of coal and limestone, the only Robertson name connected with these minerals is Coral, perhaps because of possibilities of confusion, although flint would have been a candidate. Quartz is also notable for its absence, and would have gone some way to complete the alphabetical sequence of names.

Minerology encompasses chemistry, crystallography and geology, with each contributing its own arcane vocabulary. The following descriptions are as non-technical as possible.

Achroite	A colourless variety of tourmaline.
Agate	Agate consists of very fine crystals of silicon dioxide (also known as silica or quartz, and the basis of a number of gems) containing stripes or bands of almost any colour. Agates form as nodules in volcanic rocks when cavities fill with silica in solution, which crystallizes on the wall of the cavity and slowly fills it. The name agate comes from the river Achates in Sicily, where agates were found about 3,000 years ago when the island was a Greek colony.
Amber	Fossilised resin from pine trees.
Amethyst	A form of silica or quartz, violet or purple in colour due to impurities of iron and aluminium. The Greeks and Romans believed it protected from drunkenness, and used it make goblets or pendants.
Asteria	Any ornamental stone which, when cut in a particular way, reflects or transmits light in the shape of a star. Asterias are usually rubies or sapphires.
Axinite	A complex mineral consisting of aluminium, boron, calcium, magnesium, manganese, iron and silicon, so called because it forms axe-like crystals.
Beryl	A gem containing aluminium, beryllium and silicate which when pure is colourless, but may be tinted with almost any colour. The name comes from the Greek for the blue-green colour of the sea: blue beryls are known as aquamarines. Emeralds are green beryls.
Brilliant	A name given to the finest type of diamond.
Bronzite	A variety of the mineral magnesium silicate which is bronze-coloured from small amounts of iron oxide.
Cairn-gorm	A yellow or wine-coloured form of quartz, taking its name from a Scottish mountain.
Cameo	Two layers of precious stone of different colours, having a figure carved in relief in the upper, whilst the lower serves as a ground.
Chryso-lite	A silicate of magnesium and iron, chrysolite means 'gold stone', and is typically brown or yellow. Olivine and peridot are varieties. Chrysolite is an ingredient of meteorites.
Citrine	A naturally-occurring yellow variety of quartz sometimes known as 'burnt amethyst', because when heated amethysts often turn this colour.
Coral	The underwater accumulation of the skeletons of tiny animals. Reefs of coral are the basis of limestone.
Cornelian	Also known as chalcedony, cornelian is a semi-transparent form of quartz to which iron impurities impart a red colour.
Corun-dum	A particularly hard mineral consisting of aluminium oxide and which is used an abrasive. Red corundums are known as rubies, others as sapphires.
Diamond	Crystals of pure carbon formed at extreme temperatures and pressures; the hardest known substance.
Emerald	A bright-green variety of beryl.
Essonite	A type of garnet consisting of calcium aluminium silicate, less hard than other varieties of garnet and getting its name from the Greek hesson, 'inferior'.
Felspar	A mineral forming part of many igneous rocks, felspar consists of silica, potassium and aluminium and is the basis of china clay.
Fluor	The mineral calcium fluoride is known as fluor or fluorspar. Many forms emit light when exposed to ultra violet radiation, and the mineral gave its name to this fluorescence. Blue John found in Derbyshire is a form of fluorspar.
Garnet	Small crystals of metal silicates which are often a deep red in colour, the more transparent ones being considered semi-precious stones.
Gem	Any kind of precious stone, especially one that has been cut or polished.
Girasol	A reddish opal, also known as fire opal.
Hematite	The richest form of iron ore, characterised by its dark red colour, named from the Greek word for blood.
Iolite	Transparent blue or violet crystals consisting of silicon, aluminium, magnesium and iron.
Jacinth	A reddish-orange variety of zircon.
Jade	A translucent mineral containing calcium, magnesium and iron and which is green, blue or white. The name means 'loin stone', from its supposed ability to treat disorders of the loins or kidneys. Remarkably, the gullible still believe that inert minerals produce 'energy' which positively influences bodily functions.
Jargoon	A translucent variety of zircon from Sri Lanka.
Jasper	A dark red, opaque form of quartz.
Kyanite	A blue mineral consisting of aluminium silicate. Although considered a gemstone, it is mainly used in ceramic products and as electrical insulation.
Malachite	A green mineral consisting of copper carbonate.
Morion	Black, smoky quartz.
Nephrite	A name given to jade for its supposed efficacy in treating kidney complaints.
Nugget	A native lump of rock, especially applied to gold.
Obsidian	A dark-coloured glass formed when volcanic lava cools. Because it is non-crystalline, obsidian can be worked to give an incredibly fine edge, much sharper than steel. It was used to make arrowheads and swords, and is now used to produce surgical scalpels.
Olivine	A pale-green form of chrysolite.
Onyx	A form of quartz with layers coloured white, brown or black.
Opal	A form of quartz valued because of its delicate red colour, and found mainly in Australia.
Pearl	Pearls form inside the shell of an oyster or certain other shellfish, usually around grains of sand.

Pebble	Any small stone worn smooth and rounded by the action of water.
Peridot	A gem-quality olivine.
Plasma	In mineralogy, a translucent, green quartz.
Prase	A variety of quartz in which the dark green colour is due to traces of nickel.
Pyrope	Any fiery, red-coloured gem.
Ruby	A variety of corundum which varies in colour from purple to red.
Sagenite	A variety of agate in which slender, needle-like crystals of iron or magnesium oxide have grown, often giving the effect of a fan or sunburst. Sagenite was popular as a gem stone in the 18th century.
Sapphire	The name given to gem quality corundum when it is blue or any colour other than red (see ruby).
Sard	A yellow or orange cornelian.
Sphene	Wedge-shaped crystals containing titanium, calcium and silicon which are often deep yellowish-green.
Spinel	Crystals of magnesium aluminium oxide which are usually red or orange. The name spinel is also given to a class of minerals with a similar three-dimensional crystal structure.
Topaz	A silicate of aluminium and iron. The pure crystals are colourless but topaz can be yellow, white, blue, or green depending on the impurities present.
Tourmaline	A brittle semi-precious stone consisting of a complex silicate of aluminium, iron, magnesium, sodium, lithium and potassium, found in a variety of colours.
Turquoise	Opaque, sky-blue to apple-green crystals of copper and aluminium phosphates. So named because it was believed to originate in Turkey, although in fact it was mined further east and merely traded through Turkey.
Zircon	A mineral consisting of crystals of zirconium silicate which is used as a refractory material (for example, lining nuclear reactors).

Names were used up to seven times during the Robertson ownership of the fleet, the record being held by the name Topaz. This is the fifth *Sapphire*, built 1966, photographed in ballast on 30th August 1970. Note the trademark short white line on the hull and grey masts. *[Les Ring/World Ship Society Ltd. 63791]*

Appendix 5: colour scheme

Although colours of hull, funnels and house flags are usually well recorded, intimate details of colour schemes are rarely available. The following is based on details published by the late P.N. Thomas in an article about modelling the steamer *Sard* (2), which was in the fleet from 1909 to 1943. Differences which can be discerned from photographs of the motor ships are noted. Inevitably there were variations, and anyone modelling a particular ship should ensure they have a photograph.

Hull: black with red boot topping, and a white line beneath the bridge. The line was an enduring distinguishing feature of Robertson ships and it has been suggested that, when Robertson was operating a mixed fleet, one of his steamers which came upon a sailing ship from the fleet would be expected to offer to tow the latter. The white line helped identify a ship from the fleet.

Funnel: plain black.

Steel decks: red oxide.

Inside bulwarks: mid brown.

Superstructure: originally mid-brown, then mid-brown to half the height of the lowest deck house and white above, and all white in motor ships from about 1950. Mid-brown for the fore end of the boiler casing in steamers and the forward side of the raised quarter deck in motor ships.

Ventilators: black with red inside the cowls.

Lifeboats: originally black with light-grey canvas covers; later white.

Davits: black.

Masts and derricks: where wooden these were varnished with black fittings and where metal were painted grey. The grey masts were another distinctive feature, shared with another well-known Glasgow company, The Clan Line Steamers Ltd. In some photographs masts appear black or brown.

Windlass and winches: black.

Bridge front: teak cladding or white.

Hatches: black sides with light grey canvas tarpaulins; the metal hatches on the later motor ships were brown or red.

Engine room skylight: mid-brown.

Water tanks: mid-brown.

House flag: blue/white/blue bands with a red R on the white.

Appendix 6: Stephenson Clarke ships with Gem names

The fourth *Emerald*. *[Fotoflite]*

1. EMERALD (4) 1978-1999
O.N. 377571 1,584g 1,002n
299.5 x 47.8 x 17.9 feet
Oil engine 4SCSA 6-cyl. by Mirrlees, Blackstone Ltd., Stockport.
10.1.1978: Launched by Clelands Shipbuilding Co. Ltd., Wallsend-on-Tyne (Yard No.339).
4.1978: Completed for Stephenson Clarke Shipping Ltd., London as EMERALD.
10.1999: Sold to Wind Shipping ApS, Koge, Denmark and renamed EMERALDA under the St. Vincent and Grenadines flag.
7.2004: Sold to Irbe Redereja S.A. (Baltic Shipmanagement Ltd., managers), Riga, Latvia.
9.2004: Renamed EMERALD.
6.2005: Transferred to the Cambodian flag.
7.2005: Sold to Foster Venture Korp (Glynde Ventures), Nakhodka, Russia and renamed ELEONORA.
2.2006: Renamed STINGRAY.
2.2007: Sold to Jessy Shipping Co. Ltd. (Whitley Management Corporation), Nakhodka, Russia and renamed TESSA.
6.2007: Sold to Inter-Trans Co. Ltd., Nakhodka.
1.9.2009: Still in service.

2. PEARL (6) 1979-1983
O.N. 308579 1,598g 1221n
301.8 x 43.9 x 17.0 feet
Oil engine 4SCSA 8-cyl. by Mirrlees National Ltd., Stockport; 1,800 BHP, 11.5 knots.
27.2.1967: Launched by the Goole Shipbuilding and Repairing Co. Ltd., Goole (Yard No. 555).
5.1967: Completed for the Klondyke Shipping Co. Ltd., Hull as SOMERSBYDYKE.
1978: Acquired by Stephenson Clarke Shipping Ltd., London.
1979: Renamed PEARL.
1983: Sold to Bremar Shipping Ltd., Cayman Islands (Lindsay Terminals and Trading Co. Ltd., Leith) and renamed ROSEMOUNT.
1984: Sold to Iona Shipping Ltd., Cayman Islands (Spenlow Trading Ltd., London, managers) and renamed MULL.
1987: Sold by the Admiralty Marshall to Ocean Carriers Ltd., Colombo, Sri Lanka and renamed GIANNIS.
1991: Sold to Viento del Sur S.A., Panama (J. Mourtos Brothers (Shipping) Co. Ltd., Piraeus, Greece) and renamed ANNA II.
1993: Transferred to Everest Maritime Ltd., Kingston, St. Vincent and the Grenadines (Viento del Sur S.A. (S. and G. Mourtos), Piraeus).
1994: Sold to Dannah Shipping Lines S.A., Panama City (Senyar Maritime Establishment, Dubai) and renamed DANAH I under the Belize flag.
30.9.1998: Breaking up began by Khanbai Yusufbhai and Co., Kolkata, India.

3. GEM (7) 1992-1996
O.N. 722396 7,482g 4,365n 11,848d
135.7 x 19.3 x 8.26 metres
Werkspoor-type oil engine 9-cyl. 4SCSA by Fabrica de San Carlos S.A., San Fernando,

Pearl (6) in Stephenson Clarke livery. *[Fotoflite]*

Gem (7), registered at Newcastle. *[Roy Fenton collection]*

Spain; 6,000 IHP, 12.5 knots.
8.2.1974: Launched by S.A. Juliana Constructora Gijonesa, Gijon, Spain (Yard No. 238) for Auxiliar de Transportes Maritimos S.A., Gijon as GUARDO.
8.1974: Completed for Ership S.A., Madrid, Spain
11.1992: Acquired by Stephenson Clarke Shipping Ltd., Newcastle-upon-Tyne.
12.1992: Renamed GEM.
9.1996: Sold to Arendal Bulk K/S, Arendal, Norway.
12.1997: Managers became Orient Ship Management Norway A/S, Arendal.
3.1998: Renamed ARENDAL BAY.
5.1998: Sold to OSM Maritime Services Ltd., Hong Kong (Orient Ship Management Norway AS, Arendal).
7.2000: Sold to Al Whadania General Trading Co., United Arab Emirates and renamed KHUULA under the Cambodian flag.
19.12.2000: Arrived at Chittagong to be broken up.

4. AMETHYST (5) 1992-1997
O.N. 722397 8,254g 3,824n
142.9 x 20.1 x 7.2 metres
M.A.N.-type oil engine 7-cyl. 4SCSA by Empreza Nacional 'Bazan' de C.N.M. S.A., Cartagena, Spain; 5,248 IHP, 12.25 knots.
11.6.1987: Launched by S.A. Juliana Constructora Gijonesa, Gijon, Spain (Yard No. 310) for Auxiliar de Transportes Maritimos S.A., Gijon as CARDONA.
21.12.1987: Completed for Ership S.A., Madrid, Spain.
11.1992: Acquired by Stephenson Clarke Shipping Ltd., Newcastle-upon-Tyne.
1.1993: Renamed AMETHYST.
1997: Renamed SEA AMETHYST under the Isle of Man flag.
4.2009: Sold to Amadore Maritime Ltd. (Transyus Shipping Co., managers), Nikolayev, Ukraine and renamed AMADORE.
27.8.2009: Still in service.

Amethyst (5), the largest ship to trade under a Robertson name. *[Roy Fenton collection]*

Two other Stephenson Clarke ships were intended to have Robertson names. Ordered in 1995 from P.T. Pal Indonesie at Surubaya, *Topaz* and *Tourmaline* would have been, respectively, the eighth and fourth ships of these names. This may have been partly due to the influence of Technical Superintendent Bob McLean, who had worked for Robertsons. Within a few months, however, ownership of Stephenson Clarke passed to the International Maritime Group, and the Indonesian orders were cancelled. *Topaz* may well have carried her name when launched in October 1996, and there are reports that she was completed as *Rio Topaz*. The shipyard offered the ships for sale, and they were acquired by the German Egon Oldendorff group, and renamed *Wilhelmine Oldendorff* and *Theodor Oldendorff*, respectively. Both were subsequently sold.

Gems in colour

A selection of colour illustrations begins with a painting by George Nelson (1822-1905) of the *Sard* (1) sailing from Whitehaven about 1891 (top). The pierhead painter George Laidman of Kings Lynn depicted a grey-painted *Brilliant* (1) during her long spell under requisition during the First World War: note the gun on her poop. Her correct number is shown, HMT 1162, but the flag hoist, URKX, is not the TDMQ listed in the 'Mercantile Navy List' (middle).
Sold in 1958 the 33-year-old steamer *Fluor* (2) survived for another 15 years under the Panama flag as *Inca* (bottom, at Istanbul). *[Philip Robertson collection; British Mercantile Marine Memorial Collection; World Ship Society Ltd. 20289]*

A light *Olivine* (5) approaches Eastham Locks and departs down the Mersey on a beautiful 10th May 1972: note the gorse in flower on the embankment in the upper photograph. Whilst not immaculate, she is still in good condition for a 20-year-old ship in the rough and tumble of the coastal trade. *[Paul Boot (2)]*

Emerald (3) discharges ballast water as she heads up the Nieuwe Waterweg for Rotterdam on 30th May 1974 (top). She is seen again leaving Preston on 29th August 1964 (middle). In both photographs her boats retain Robertsons' traditional black; not, one would have thought, the best colour to be seen on a wintry sea. As other photographs show, white gradually replaced black. As the *Hanadi* she was photographed at Eleusis, Greece on 1st August 1982 (bottom). Lebanese-owners Sea and Land Transport Co. 'Marina' S.a.r.L., have painted their initials on the casing below the funnel. She was to have one further owner and another name before being broken up in Greece four years later. *[Paul Boot; Jim McFaul/ World Ship Society Ltd. 42870 and 15102]*

An immaculate *Cameo* (4) displays her elongated hull as she passes a Mersey landmark on 15th July 1971 (above). In contrast, 13 years later she looks distinctly run down at anchor in Piraeus Roads on 30th September 1984 (below). Her new name *Mania* is an interesting choice: she still carried it when demolished at Eleusis two years later. *[Paul Boot; Nigel Jones]*

In unusual lighting conditions, *Amber* (2) approaches Cardiff on 28th May 1974. *[Nigel Jones]*

Pearl (5) on a grey River Thames, 16th May 1971 (top left), her last year in Robertson colours. She was sold to British owners to become *Pauline H*, as which she first retained a black hull (upper right, on the Nieuwe Waterweg 11th June 1972), but later lost her cargo gear and was repainted blue, a scheme which needed more attention than her owners and crew seemed able to give (lower left, again on the Waterweg, 12th May 1975).

Still in Robertson colours, although now in Stephenson Clarke ownership, *Amethyst* (4) passes Seacombe on 17th February 1980, just weeks before her sale (bottom right). *[George Garwood/World Ship Society Ltd. 10707 and 16181; Nigel Jones; Paul Boot]*

The third *Tourmaline* was photographed on the Thames on 19th June 1970 (top left) and in Stephenson Clarke colours at Lerwick on 31st July 1981 (top right). She is seen again in September 1990 at Brest when in Maltese ownership as *Sorocco*, with her mainmast replaced with a crane (bottom left). In the bottom right photograph, *Sapphire* (5) discharges roadstone from a North Wales quarry in Carriers Dock, Liverpool on 21st July 1973.

[George Garwood/World Ship Society Ltd. 8196; Jim McFaul/World Ship Society Ltd. 18643 and 33716; Roy Fenton]

Gem (6) was the last ship in which Robertsons had any design input. She is seen first approaching Eastham in wonderful lighting conditions on 8th February 1976, and again creeping into a Llanddulas jetty on 18th June 1983 in Stephenson Clarke colours. The penultimate ship acquired by Robertsons was *Jade* (2), seen discharging on 28th July 1978 (bottom). *[Paul Boot (2); Les Ring/World Ship Society Ltd. 43974]*

INDEX OF SHIPS

All ships mentioned are indexed. Names in capitals are those carried whilst in Robertson ownership or management. For owned ships, the page numbers in bold type are those of fleet list entries. To help locate a particular Robertson ship, their dates of build are noted along with the number indicating the order of the name in the fleet.

Sapphire (4) in later colour scheme (see also page 101). *[Fotoflite incorporating Skyfotos]*

M.S. „CITRINE."

GENERAL ARRANGEMENT.

SCALE 1/8" = 1'.

(Of Original)

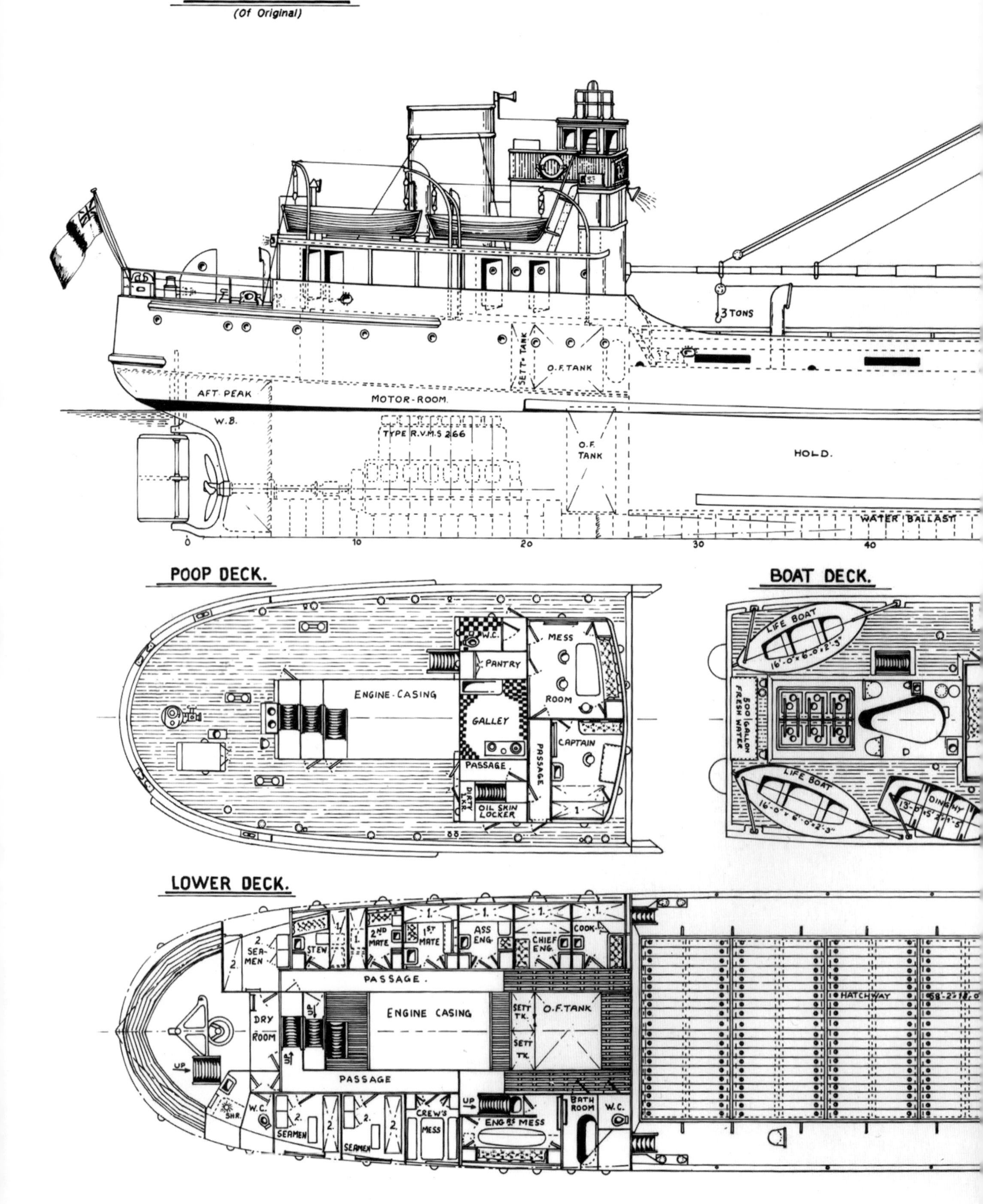